Talking on
the Water

Conversations

about Nature

and Creativity

~-~-~-~-~-~-~-~-~-~

Jonathan White

TRINITY UNIVERSITY PRESS
SAN ANTONIO

Published by Trinity University Press
San Antonio, Texas 78212

This book is dedicated to my mother, Jai White, and to the memory of my father, William White. I love you.

Cover design by Sarah Cooper
Cover illustration: istock / Dmitri Maruta
Book design by Amy Evans

The author gratefully acknowledges permission to reprint from the following: *The Selected Poetry of Rainer Maria Rilke*, edited and translated by Stephen Mitchell. Copyright © 1982 by Stephen Mitchell. Reprinted by permission of Random House, Inc. "The Women Speaking," by Linda Hogan, from *That's What She Said: Contemporary Poetry and Fiction by Native American Women*, edited by Rayna Green. Reprinted by permission of Linda Hogan.

ISBN-13 978-1-59534-786-2 paper
ISBN-13 978-1-59534-787-9 ebook

Trinity University Press strives to produce its books using methods and materials in an environmentally sensitive manner. We favor working with manufacturers that practice sustainable management of all natural resources, produce paper using recycled stock, and manage forests with the best possible practices for people, biodiversity, and sustainability. The press is a member of the Green Press Initiative, a nonprofit program dedicated to supporting publishers in their efforts to reduce their impacts on endangered forests, climate change, and forest-dependent communities.

The paper used in this publication meets the minimum requirements of the American National Standard for Information Sciences—Permanence of Paper for Printed Library Materials, ANSI 39.48–1992.

CIP data on file at the Library of Congress

20 19 18 17 16 | 5 4 3 2 1

Contents

Acknowledgments

The voices and efforts that have influenced this book are many. I wish to thank Linda Gunnarson for her professional assistance in the beginning stages of the work; Donna Sandstrom for her thoughtful co-editing of the early editions of "Animal Presence" and "Voices from the Sea"; Nita Couchman for her help with transcriptions and editing; Ted Braun, Alice Braun, and my family for abiding assurance; and Lindsay Aiken for suggesting the title, *Talking on the Water*.

I am grateful to Susan Ristow, Amy Evans, Erik Migdail, Kim Nishida, and other staff of Sierra Club Books for their careful attention to design, marketing, and production details, and to my editor, Jim Cohee, for his invaluable guidance and criticism. Throughout the writing process, Richard Nelson gave me support and friendship, and took time away from his own work to help me with mine; Gary Snyder offered wise counsel and encouragement; Donna Laslo stayed up late to discuss sections that troubled me. Holly Hughes and Thomas Coleman read through each chapter in process, raised critical questions, and gave me many hours on the phone or in coffee shops to discuss everything from editorial details to chapter order. Thomas Coleman gave me far more support than any friend could ever ask.

Talking on the Water would not have been possible without the generosity of the people whose interviews comprise these chapters. In each case, they dedicated time before, during, and after the interview. I am deeply grateful. I also wish to thank the board of directors and staff of Resource Institute, especially Anna Manildi and Lela Hilton, for many years of companionship and laughter, and for believing in me and the mischievous possibilities of sailing around the Northwest coast on an old wooden schooner. To the schooner itself, the people who joined her, and the places we visited, I thank you for the unforgettable magic.

Preface

I recorded these interviews over twenty years ago. Much has changed since then. The Resource Institute closed its doors, the schooner *Crusader* was sold to a young family in Seattle, and some of the interviewees have passed away. Yet the reflections on nature, humanity, and spirituality found in these pages are as relevant and poignant as ever. So much so, in fact, that in reprinting the collection we chose not to change a word.

The pressing environmental issues of the 1990s—overpopulation, deforestation, depleted fisheries, burning fossil fuels and the consequent global warming—are still pressing. The first Earth Summit, in Rio de Janeiro in 1992, brought together over a hundred world leaders to address the global threat of atmospheric pollution. It was an encouraging event. At that time carbon dioxide (CO_2), a by-product of fossil fuel burning and an indicator of global warming, hovered in the atmosphere at 350 parts per million. The goal was to keep it at that level or less.

The years ahead saw four more world conferences on the environment. They also saw rising CO_2 levels. By the 1997 Kyoto conference, atmospheric CO_2 had reached 375 ppm. By the 2012 Earth Summit (also known as Rio+20), CO_2 was close to 400 ppm. A year later it passed 400 for the first time in recorded history. When 196 world leaders convened at the Paris Talks in 2015, ocean acidification and sea level rise—both by-products of global warming—had been added to the discussion. CO_2 levels had topped 405 ppm. The last decade, in fact, has seen the largest increase per year in CO_2 than any of the previous four decades.

But there are also signs of hope. When *Talking on the Water* was published in 1994, scientists had discovered that chlorofluoro-carbons used for refrigerants had created a hole the size of Russia in the ozone. Through a series of international agreements, global production of chlorofluorocarbons was reduced and finally halted in 2010. The ozone began to repair itself, and although the size of the hole changes from year to year, some scientists believe it will be healed by midcentury.

The natural world is remarkably resilient. I witnessed this firsthand when I was helping to remove derelict fishing nets in Washington's Salish Sea. Thousands of nets have been lost over the last half-century, drifting with the tides and settling on the bottom, often suffocating reefs that were once crowded with life. Yet within weeks of the nets' removal, signs of life reappeared, and within months many of these reefs were again thriving.

I'm also heartened by the power of people—individuals and groups—who quietly and effectively change the world. On Orcas Island, where I live, I was a trustee of the local land trust in 2005 when Turtleback Mountain came up for sale. The 1,600-acre mountain, an island centerpiece, had a price tag of $17 million, over fifty times the value of our largest acquisition.

The board was split; half felt that the project was too big for our small island community (population 4,000). The purchase was fiscally irresponsible and could mean the end of the trust, they argued. The other half believed that saving Turtleback from devel-opment was the most important work we could do. We had to try, even if it meant failing.

The debate went on for weeks and at times grew heated (mind you, these were all dedicated conservationists!). In the end we took on the project and in eight months raised the $17 million to buy Turtleback. What surprised us most was how far-reaching the ef-fort was. Checks, some of them six figures, came in from Seattle, Vancouver, New York, Alaska, and California. The mountain has been open to hiking since 2006 but is otherwise protected in perpetuity by a conservation easement. These stories give me hope and energy. They remind me of my love for the natural world, and they remind me of what I love about humanity. I felt this same hope while rereading *Talking on the Water.* Almost every interview touches on the value of direct experiences with the natural world. These experiences, whether climbing a mountain, hanging out with animals, or sailing an old wooden schooner, remind us of who we are. They remind us that we are not separate from the world, *this* world. They remind us that we are part of the brilliance of the universe. As Dolores LaChapelle says, "When you've had these experiences, you know who you are and you can't be pushed around."

Talking on the Water

The adventures that led to *Talking on the Water* had their beginnings in 1983. In the spring of that year, I returned to the Northwest from the West Indies. After nearly two years living aboard a small sailboat, I was ready to join the company of others, to learn more about the water, nature, people, and boats. I looked around for a graduate program that could satisfy these needs, but soon realized I wasn't going to find what I was looking for at a university. What classroom experience could ever match the lessons taught by the ocean?

At a waterfront shop, less than a week after my return, I came across a faded picture of an old wooden boat. The caption read, "FOR SALE: Sixty-five-foot schooner, *Crusader*. Needs work, make offer." The next day I packed my Volkswagen bug and drove down the coast to Tillamook, Oregon. I met the owners at the head of the bay, followed them over *Crusader*'s deck and down her forward companionway. For several hours, we sat below and drank tea in the warmth of the woodstove, our noses filled with the smell of moist canvas, cedar, and punky fir. Even though *Crusader* was painted all orange and leaked over 100 gallons a day, I didn't care. In spite of everything, or maybe because of it, she had magic, and I had already fallen in love.

On my way home I penciled out a vision of a big wooden boat, good teachings, interesting people, and the wilderness waters of the Northwest Coast. It might work, I thought, and that was enough. I wrote letters to twenty writers, artists, and visionaries asking if they would be interested in teaching aboard *Crusader*. Five wrote back with enthusiasm: Gary Snyder, Annie Dillard, Peter Matthiessen, Barry Lopez, and Jerzy Grotowski. Again, it was enough.

The next week, I started Resource Institute, a nonprofit organization, and then spent the following ten years working with others to create a program of floating seminars. With *Crusader* as a base, we did trips with topics ranging from natural history, anthropology, mythology, and woodcarving to photography, singing, Sumi brush painting, and poetry writing. We even produced a play on board *Crusader*. We sailed in the San Juan and Gulf Islands, Desolation Sound, around Vancouver Island, up to the Queen Charlotte Islands, and throughout southeast Alaska. We caught fish, wrote essays, danced, and laughed. We made movies and wrote books, did research, drifted near calving glaciers. We kayaked with whales and hung out with salmon, bear, fir, and spruce. No matter what we did, it was always the wilderness, both on and off the water, that served as our primary guide. And looking back now, it feels like we did *everything;* yet each trip brought experiences beyond what any of us could have imagined.

Talking on the Water grew out of these experiences. We asked questions like: How do we think and talk about nature? Who are our real teachers? What is possible to learn? With small groups of thoughtful people, I learned that wherever we are, the place itself becomes a teacher, just as we teach each other through the laughter and conversation around the galley table in a quiet anchorage. Following the inspiration of good examples is as important as anything we can do, and the natural world is full of them—animals and trees and people.

In working on this book, it wasn't so much that I wanted answers to the questions we were asking, but I wanted to learn more about how to approach the questions themselves. The interview form seemed best for this, because it offered a lot of room for personal and spontaneous interaction. It also allowed for a dialogue in which the people I interviewed could respond to one another as well as to me and to our audience.

I think of the conversations in *Talking on the Water* as the roots of an integrated community. While at first these roots may not appear to be linked, a closer look reveals that they are sustained in common ground. A poet, a biologist, a science fiction writer, and an ex-Dominican priest all share a deep and long-standing concern for their relationship to nature. How they think and talk about this is as full of surprising similarities as it is of obvious differences. These chapters reveal connections we hadn't noticed before.

Among the more important issues raised in *Talking on the Water* are hunting, killing, eating, and death. If we follow these topics through several talks, we find deeper questions that are related. In "Life-Ways of the Hunter," Richard Nelson explains how most of his sense of connection to the natural world comes from being a hunter. "I am passionately in love with deer but I also kill them," he says. "I appreciate the fact that I am made out of the animal I love. Somewhere, both literally and physically, a deer looks out through my eyes; and some day my body will feed deer, too." In "The Unreturning Arrow," Paul Shepard says experiences such as hunting can serve a valuable purpose without having to be an ongoing part of one's life. "The humane treatment of wild animals and the practice of hunting are not separable," he says. "Kindness toward animals demands a true sense of kinship, which does not mean we should treat them like our babies. Instead, it means realizing the many connections and transformations—us into them, them into us, and them into each other from the beginning of time."

In "Coming Back from the Silence," Ursula Le Guin says if we deny the fact that we eat each other in order to live then we deny wilderness itself. In response to Paul and Richard's comments, however, she says we should be able to feel our connection to nature without killing animals. The trouble with hunting, she says, "is that it relates to what Hemingway said: 'You can't be a man until you've killed another one.' I say bullshit! Why don't you try it without the gun?" In "Animal Presence," James Hillman suggests if we had rituals that more directly addressed the killing necessary for daily eating, we might be less crazed in those other killings—the murders on television, Vietnam, Iraq, and so on. "Practically," he says, "I don't see how we can even begin to kill, each of us, the food we need to eat daily. But we can stop for a moment when buying food, preparing food, and eating food to thank the Lord. But the Lord is not an abstraction in Heaven; the Lord we need to thank is the animal itself . . ."

Another important question is, What lessons can we learn from indigenous people? The response varies. Richard Nelson, who lived with Alaskan Indians, suggests we follow their example of recognizing spirit in the world around us. Dolores LaChapelle and Matthew Fox say native people can teach us, among other things, the value of ritual. "Real ritual puts everything together," says Dolores LaChapelle, "the old things and the new things, nature and animals." David Brower reminds us that the Constitution of the United States was inspired by the Great Binding Law of the Iroquois, where rules were not written down and decisions were made with the welfare of the next seven generations in mind. Paul Shepard uses hunter-gatherers as a model, suggesting that modern humans have not evolved beyond our ancestors into a separate way of being. While it may not be practical to "go back," it may be possible to realize we never left. Integrating our own society with desirable characteristics of so-called primitive people may be just what we need.

On the other hand, there are comments throughout the book about the danger of romanticizing native people. Janet McCloud, a Tulalip Indian, refused to give interviews for years because of her distaste for Indian wannabes. "When you put Indians on a pedestal, you're bound to be disappointed—and so are we. . . . Native Americans don't have the anwer," she says, "but we can offer one piece of the puzzle." Peter Matthiessen believes most traditional people don't feel the separation from nature that we feel in Western culture. The land is who they *are*. "We can learn something from this," he says, "but as Westerners I'm not sure we can fully experience it. . . . The Indian's love of the earth has nothing to do with environmentalism. We can't consciously adopt Indian attitudes toward nature because they don't *have* any attitudes toward nature."

My own inclination is to·believe we *can* find the experience of being a part of the world, and for Western culture this work is more urgent than any other single effort. What we may be able to learn from indigenous cultures is the confidence that it can be done. "Look at this beautiful, spiritual land," says Janet McCloud. "It's just waiting for you to recognize it." And how are we going to recognize the land? How are we going to fully recognize ourselves as part of it? If there is any single well that feeds the roots of all these conversations, it is the issue of separation. In our society, the autonomy of the individual is sacred. We believe that anything that threatens our right to think for ourselves, to make our own decisions, or to live the way we want to live is morally wrong. In *The Practice of the Wild,* Gary Snyder says that American society "operates under the delusion that we are each a kind of 'solitary knower'—that we exist as rootless intelligences without layers of localized contexts." The term solitary knower, he says, is "a way of talking about the myth of the individual ego that has no parents, no community, and no other connections. The self is forever set apart with no real association to the rest of the world."

Lynn Margulis comes at this issue from another angle. In "Living by Gaia," she remarks that, with the exception of bacteria, individuals with single genetic systems don't exist. "All other living organisms . . . are complex communities of multiple, tightly organized beings. What we think of as an individual animal, such as a cow, is really a collection of entities. . . . It's not the individual, but the community of life that evolves by cooperation, interaction, and mutual dependence."

I have always been puzzled by the fact that Western society produces the world's greatest leaders in conservation and yet we are also the most consumptive and ecologically destructive society on earth. James Hillman says this apparent contradiction stems from the same psychological ground: neither the people who want to save nature nor those most involved in destroying it feel they *are* nature. The first group are essentially moralists, "and moralists are always above what they are judging. The second group are the conquerors, Promethean and Herculean in their ability to overcome nature."

So what can we do? There is no single answer, but many encouraging suggestions. For example, Gary Snyder, Richard Nelson, and Gretel Ehrlich speak in favor of staying in one place. It makes no difference whether you live in the city or in the country, says Gary Snyder; getting to know the ecology of your locale is what makes life become real. When Ursula Le Guin discusses her book *Always Coming Home,* we hear about similar concerns. But she also brings up other issues, such as the way we use language to create "a false and irresponsible separation." By changing our use of language, she suggests we can open doors to new behavior.

Dolores LaChapelle is convinced we won't find integrated living through more ideas and planning, but through direct experiences in which we know we are part of nature, with no questions asked. "When you've had these experiences," she says, "you know what you want and you can't be pushed around." Matthew Fox expresses a similar view when he says, "Thinking about God is no substitute for an experience of God." He goes on to say that the environmental revolution can't happen without spirituality. "It's not a left-wing, secular, ideological battle. It's something much deeper, and it involves all of us."

James Hillman would argue that it's not necessarily a virtue to be integrated and centered. Allowing ourselves to get into quandaries engages us with the real world and gives us access to deeper issues.

I hope *Talking on the Water* reads like a Hillman quandary. Instead of offering answers to any of these questions, I hope it gives access to a deeper appreciation for the complexity of the topic. I learned early on, in fact, that the images that come into mind about nature are not just of bugs and trees that live "out there," but also of the natural world "in here." We can't wake up in the morning, take the next breath, or think the next thought without demonstrating that we *are* nature. As long as we insist on thinking of ourselves as separate from—either better than or inferior to—the rest of nature, we will always be hungry for something "out there." We will consume the world out of a sense of desperation, and never get the nourishment we most need. There is ultimately no place—no canyon, no city, no church, no school, and no culture—that we can afford *not* to include in our "geography of hope."

A Call from One Kingdom to Another

G RETEL EHRLICH has many talents. Not only is she an accomplished writer of fiction and nonfiction prose, she also has extensive experience in theater, dance, and film.

During her teenage years, Gretel made many visits to New York City from her home in Santa Barbara, California. In New York she saw modern dance and ballet, European films, photographs, and paintings, and experienced music at the hands of masters, reading voraciously all the while. It was through this exposure, which fueled an abiding interest in the arts, that Gretel chose to pursue further studies in these fields.

From 1963 to 1976, Gretel moved between the East and West Coasts to study theater and dance (in New York City and at Bennington College in Vermont) and film (at UCLA). In 1967 she took a position with NET Television in New York as editor in the cultural affairs department. A year later she returned to Los Angeles and, with the encouragement of Francis Ford Coppola and Tamara Asseyev, began writing screenplays and directing documentary films.

Although these years were intensely urban in focus, Gretel always had a love for animals and the natural world. Her family raised horses during her childhood in Santa Barbara. "I used to sleepwalk when I was little," she says, "and go out to the barn to sleep with the horses or to another part of the house to sleep with the dogs. It was where I felt most comfortable." Even while working on films in the sixties and seventies, she took up winter mountaineering and climbed many of the peaks in the eastern Sierra.

Gretel Ehrlich's books include *Islands, the Universe, Home* (1991), *Drinking Dry Clouds* (1991), *Heart Mountain* (1988), *The Solace of Open Spaces* (1986), and three books of poetry. In 1986 she was honored by the American Academy and Institute of Arts and Letters with a Harold V. Purcell Award for prose. She has also been the recipient of an NEA Fellowship (1981), the Whiting Award (1987), and a Guggenheim Fellowship (1988). Her work has been published in *Harper's, Atlantic Monthly, Time, Antaeus,* and numerous other magazines.

This interview took place aboard the schooner *Crusader* in Sitka, Alaska. Gretel's warm humor and generous nature made for an easy, flowing conversation, interrupted only occasionally by coffee refills.

~·~·~

JONATHAN WHITE: Your first four books were written in Wyoming, yet that's not where you're from. How did you end up there?

GRETEL EHRLICH: I had been interested in filmmaking for a long time. In 1969 I made a portrait film of the first woman jockey to race at the big tracks. Then I became interested in making films about people who were living obscure lives in obscure parts of the country and did a film about a sawyer in Colorado.

In 1976 I received a grant from the Corporation for Public Broadcasting to make a film about sheepherders in Wyoming. It was part of an idea for American ethnographic films I had been interested in for years. In preparing for the sheepherding film, I met a young filmmaker named David Hancock. I needed a partner, and so we talked over the phone, wrote letters, and exchanged films. I never actually met him until the spring before we started shooting in Wyoming. We had already formed a strong friendship, and when I stepped off the plane, we fell in love almost instantly. But by then, at age twenty-nine, he was diagnosed with cancer and went into chemotherapy. He worked on the film for a few weeks, then had to stop—he was too ill to continue.

As it turned out, we spent six months together before he died. At that point I quit filmmaking. It was too painful to go on.

J W: But you stayed in Wyoming. Why?

G E: I had a sense that the best place for me to grieve for David was with animals and out on the land. There were many things at play: when you're sick, the instinct is to go to bed. When you're grieving, the same instinct makes you want to find a place that is uncomplicated, accepting, and tolerant. I wanted to hook up with whatever it is that makes things live and die, and I wanted to be with people who weren't going to talk it into the ground.

Anyone who lives and works in the natural world has a tacit understanding of death. If you know about death and about how things come into life—about the joys and sorrows associated with these things—without psychologizing it to death, there's nothing more that needs to be said.

J W: It's like being face to face with destiny, and nothing but.

G E: Face to face with death! When I was twelve, a painter told me, "You have to mix death into everything. Then you have to mix life into that; otherwise the painting won't be human." His words made me wince. I wanted to be a painter, and at that age all I knew about death was it was something in a paint tube to be squeezed out when you wanted to add meaning.

I wanted desperately to come to some understanding of what death was about, so I followed my instincts and stayed on the ranch where we had filmed the lives of the sheepherders. It was a huge place; they had over fifteen thousand head of sheep, and during lambing there were two or three shifts going twenty-four hours a day. It was like working in the emergency room of a large city hospital. At the end of the night shift, there was always a pile of dead lambs as high as the roof. They were just thrown out the back door—a pile twelve feet tall or more. During your shift, you took care of what was living and you didn't worry about the rest. You just did the best you could. I wanted to see that; I wanted animals to die in my arms; I wanted to see them dead and I wanted it to be unsentimental and unceremonious. Not just death, but birth and growth, too. In the spring, with the coming of songbirds and new grass, we took the ewes and young lambs onto grazing land in the valley. It's an enormous basin—a hundred miles across—and you can see the mountains in the distance where we took the sheep in July. After the summer in the mountains, we'd return to the valley again.

I was also living in a community of ranchers with large families who worked together every day, all day long. It's a real community, with old people and young children, lots of weddings and funerals. When old hired hands died, we'd sit around at the funeral and tell stories about them. We'd watch the children of these families grow up and take over their parents' ranches.

The intense grieving process over David's death lasted for a couple years. I tried to normalize it as much as possible, not seclude myself or go off and cry in my soup. Tears would come up, but people just kept doing what they were doing. They knew I was going through something. And of course there's a lot of good humor that comes with seeing so much life and death over the years. A friend of mine, Bobby Jo, called up once. "Come on over and cry in my kitchen," she said. "Okay, okay," I finally answered, both of us laughing.

J W: Were you writing during this time?

G E: Writing has always been my strongest interest. When I was six, my grandmother asked me what I wanted to be when I grew up and I said, "I want to write novels and I want to have a ranch with a lot of handsome men working around me." Well, I wrote the novel and got the ranch, but I'm not sure about the rest!

Writing was so important to me that I didn't dare try to publish anything until I was ready. Although I read voraciously, I didn't major in English or go to graduate school or study with established writers, so I was pretty intimidated at the thought of writing a book. But when I moved to Wyoming, I decided it was time to start writing seriously. I had nothing to lose, and so I gave myself a year to find out whether I could make it as a writer. I started rereading everything: Faulkner, Lawrence, Tolstoy, Chekhov, and Japanese writers such as Kawabata, Soseke, Ariyoshi, and Dazai. I read essayists too, because a producer once said to me, after seeing one of my earlier films, "Do you know what you've done? You've written an essay, only in film form."

In 1978 I moved off the ranch and rented a one-room log cabin on a river that flows out of Yellowstone Park. I thought it would be a good place to write. I had almost no money at all, but enough to get through the winter—what turned out to be the third worst winter in Wyoming's history. It started snowing on the sixth of November and never stopped. It was thirty to sixty below every night for months and months. I was alone, completely snowed in, with no skis or snowshoes, and not even enough wood for heat. That winter was probably the coldest and loneliest time of my life. But I did write a small book of poetry called *To Touch the Water,* which was published by a university press.

When spring came, I heard about a cabin for rent across the basin in a little town called Shell. I met a friend's aunt who had cowboyed all her life and told her that I'd been herding sheep and was interested in learning to cowboy. Everyone laughed (cowboys always laugh at sheepherders). She called back that night and said if you want to learn to cowboy, be ready at five o'clock in the morning. Her name was Mary Francis—"Mike"—and that morning began an apprenticeship that continued until she died in 1989. She was a tall, elegant woman who was well known in Wyoming. She had cowboyed with men all her life and was very good at everything she did. People loved to have her come and help out at their places. We worked together as a team. She taught me how to rope, how to work with cattle out on the range or in a corral, and how to sort them for shipping. We had a wonderful time together, and I felt immediately at home in Shell. It was that year that I started to work on the essays that became *The Solace of Open Spaces*.

J W: The Wyoming lifestyle is radically different from the one you lived in New York City and Los Angeles. Did the challenges ever seem overwhelming?

G E: Cowboying on some of these big ranches is difficult work. You get up hours before daylight, and a lot is expected of you before you go to bed at night. But there is also excitement in the challenge. For example, on a very cold, frosty morning you might get bucked off your horse first thing, get back on, then trot hard and fast for an hour before daylight. You might ride thirty to fifty miles a day, and your horses get tired. But you are also part of their body, and their needs and yours are completely dependent on one another. Maybe it's an easy day—warm and beautiful and everything goes well. But serious storms, flash-floods, or blizzards come up suddenly. That's when you give your horse everything you have because you know your survival depends on it. There's a real understanding there: you know you need him and he knows he needs you. If you're lucky, together you'll make it.

I don't think there's any other way to get to that understanding than to put yourself at risk and to allow yourself to feel small in the face of the natural world. The power of storms—or of stupid mistakes we make in the wild—throws you into the urgent task of saving your life or the lives of others, both human and animal. That attention and awakeness doesn't come just anywhere.

J W: When I first started sailing offshore, I was terrified by high winds and heavy seas. Yet the inevitability of bad weather is partly what lured me offshore to begin with. When I sailed into a near hurricane in the mid Atlantic, I felt strangely grateful for the chance to finally meet my fear. I remember being thrown around in the cabin, stuffing raw hotdogs down my throat, and praying into the dark for my survival. It was the first time I realized how absurd my prayers were—survival was *my idea* of a good ending! There are larger hands at work, and I came out of that storm confident that, although the ocean may love me, it doesn't care if I live or die. There aren't many experiences that could offer me that lesson so powerfully.

G E: Isn't it funny how we're always eating the most stupid food at the most serious times? I mean, hotdogs? I'm sure people find a way of encountering these experiences in other places or in other ways, too. As Meng Chiao wrote, "The danger of the road is not in the distance; ten yards is far enough to break a wheel." I think Robert Wilson approaches this in theater, and Stravinsky and many others have found a way to work this way in the arts. It's just that some of us need very big hands to teach us our lessons. I had to get struck by lightning—not once, but twice—to wake up!

J W: You're still recovering from the last incident. Will you tell the story?

G E: The first incident was in 1987, but that was ground lightning, which travels laterally and then up. I remember a white flash and then a queer feeling like sequins trickling down my legs. My feet arched and burned, and I felt a thump at the base of my skull, as if someone hit me over the head from behind.

In the recent incident, there's no way of knowing exactly what happened because when you're hit directly you remember nothing. I was unconscious for an hour. When I regained consciousness, I thought I had been shot in the back. I woke in a pool of blood and I couldn't move at all. I couldn't swallow and I couldn't move my right arm or either of my legs. I thought, "If I don't die, I'm going to be in a wheelchair for the rest of my life!"

I lay there awhile expecting to die. When that didn't happen, I tried to drag myself across the ground by the elbows, the way soldiers do. But that wasn't very efficient. As the feeling began to return to my legs, I got myself up and made slow progress to the house, where I called 911. It took an hour for the ambulance to come, and the hospital I was taken to didn't do much for me. At that point I knew if I was going to survive through the night, I was going to have to do it on my own.

For the next week I was taken to a series of hospitals, but the care was not adequate to say the least. Finally I called my parents. They came for me in a plane and flew me home. I arrived at the doctor's office in Santa Barbara unconscious. They had to pull me out of the car and resuscitate me right there on the street. It was good, because they could see without question what was wrong. As soon as I was put on the cardiac unit in the hospital and could see the lights on the heart monitor flashing, I felt a great sense of relief.

I wasn't able to do very much for a long time. I could walk a little, but mostly I watched the ocean and the fall storms come and go. It was a very different interaction with the world than I was used to.

J W: Was the slowing down to recover and the gesture of calling for help part of the teaching given by these "big hands"?

G E: Yes. I was raised to value independence and self-reliance, to get back on the horse that bucks you off. While a lot of that training is absolutely wonderful, the other side of it is to know when to ask for help. Asking for help is not an admission of failure, but an admission of being human and of having an interest in being part of life, which includes the willingness to help and be helped by other people. There have been many times when I would have been much better off if I had been able to ask for help. On the day I called my parents from Wyoming, I had reached a point where I knew I was facing life or death. If my parents hadn't been home, I would have called someone else.

The big lesson is about impermanence. We tend to think we have an identity that is tied to the place we live or the things we do or what we think of ourselves. Yet all these things can be taken from us instantly. It's hard to explain, but the lightning accident reminded me that my expectations are not tied to anything. When I was still very sick, I was visited by a Japanese monk who said to me, "You know a lot about being strong, but you don't know very much about being weak. This is your chance to learn that. Unless you know both sides, you cannot behave compassionately." My Japanese friend helped me to understand that slowing down isn't just a matter of marking time until I can get back to real life, it *is* real life.

JW: You're writing a book about the lightning experience, aren't you? Will you talk about how you approach a project like that?

GE: I'm doing a lot of research on lightning and how it's regarded historically, culturally, and medically around the world. I'm thinking about the interconnections between the heart—the organ most affected in people struck by lightning—and fire, passion, destruction, and creation. The connection between lightning and healing is extremely interesting. When I told Leslie Marmon Silko what had happened to me, her eyes opened wide. "In the Laguna Pueblo culture where I'm from," she said, "people struck by lightning are immediately initiated into a medicine society and become healers. Everything in their life changes—who they are, what they do, who they're married to, everything. It's not that it's dictated; it just happens." "That's great, but what happens to people in my culture?" I asked. "I don't know," she answered, "but I bet you'll find out!" I haven't become a healer, but everything else Leslie said has been true in my experience. In my research for the new book, I've found that this equation of shamanism and lightning is very common among indigenous people around the world.

I'm also interested in what actually happens when a person is struck by lightning. I mean, from the point of view of both physics and metaphysics, what happens to the brain when a million volts of electricity courses through your body? What kind of injuries do people suffer? Why? How are their lives affected spiritually? I'm learning that very little is known about all this.

JW: It sounds like the writing process brings you closer to an understanding of these experiences. Does writing also serve as a tool to bring you closer to nature?

GE: I wouldn't say my writing brings me closer to nature—maybe it brings the people who read what I write closer to nature. It's tough to bring yourself to the truths that result from experience. I take all my cues about writing from the images around me. In writing, you work to find a language that actually embodies the life of what you are writing about. Wallace Stevens calls this "the palm at the end of the mind." I'm not saying I have succeeded, but as with any form of expression, whether it's writing, painting, or dance, you try to go directly from the gut.

The Navajo talk about the land as if it were parts of the body and soul. I sometimes think of landscape that way. It's a matter of transposing identities and seeing how that makes you feel and think. You can easily spend a day noticing the human aspects of a tree or the treeness inside you. I don't mean to trivialize it; allowing the life of other beings to enter yours is an important and valuable skill for a writer and for all humans. When you surrender like that, you can't write from the ego, which is so dominant in our culture. I like the word *inter-living,* because in order to express something well you need to have observed the details of it so closely that the boundary between its life and yours becomes blurred. Thus you have books like Octavio Paz's *The Tree Within.* And it's not the acquisition of knowledge that's important but a kind of seeing through into the primary processes of being that will, in turn, tell you the basic nature of the entire world.

When our cows were pregnant in the spring, they would lie down in the snow and groan in the late afternoon sun. I'd go out and sit with them for hours—just hang out with them. I learned a lot from doing that. The more I gave myself over to being with them, the more equality I felt between us. They have a kingdom of their own consciousness, and you can enter into as much of that as you want. I think that's what writers have to do. When you write fiction, you give yourself over to the characters; when you write nonfiction, it's the same. Emerson said, "You must treat the days respectfully, you must be a day yourself. And not interrogate life like a college professor. Everything in the universe goes by indirection. There are no straight lines."

J W: You have a lot of talents to draw on—dance, theater, writing, cowboying, painting. Do you see all these skills playing a role in what you're doing today?

G E: When you're out cowboying, you're just trying to figure out what's going on and what's needed in order to accomplish the task at hand. People who work in that world become incredible observers— you learn to see so many clues to what's going on or what took place an hour before, or a day before, or what's about to come. It really stretches you to see more deeply than if you were just going for a stroll.

If there is something I keep coming back to as a reference point, it's Buddhist meditation practice. It's like a compass needle that keeps turning me, making me understand what the act of seeing is about. I might be following a bunch of cows on the trail or painting in my living room, but the attention to detail and the nourishment it brings is the same.

I can't separate any of this from the knowledge that comes from living in the same place for a long time. When you walk out the door, you already know *so* much, because of what the place has taught you. And the scene gets deeper each day. When you have that experience of intimacy, you can apply it in any direction, whether it's in relationship to a group of people on another continent, a theater production, or an animal that has just shown up on your doorstep. That's why it doesn't matter, at bottom, what you do. If you go deeply enough into any one process, you'll understand something about all the processes around you.

It seems odd that someone who loves to cowboy also goes to Paris and writes an opera. But to me it makes perfect sense. All these things are, after all, just forms. So it doesn't matter what you dip into as long as you dip into something, and dip deep.

Meditation teaches you that there is no nationalism and no identity, that it's all really a process of seeing down into the well. Paradoxically, the more specific and intimate your experience is, the more it tends to transcend itself. I can use the connection I have with Wyoming, for instance, to understand your relationship with this boat and the waters of the Northwest coast, although I may never know that particular intimacy. I may not choose to know it, but I understand the process and therefore in my writing I can imagine other people's lives.

J W: When did you start Zen practice?

G E: When I moved back to Los Angeles from New York in 1968. Buddhism had been a lifelong attraction, but I didn't really understand how to get started. When I was in boarding school, I read D. T. Suzuki. I put his books inside my hymnal during chapel because I disliked the go-to-church Christian regime. I didn't believe I was a sinner and I didn't understand original sin or a revengeful God; none of it made any sense to me. When I learned that Gary Snyder studied and practiced in Japan and then in the States, I realized I might be able to find serious and respectable teachers here. One day I called the L.A. Zen Center where Maizumi-roshi teaches and went down there. A monk gave me meditation instruction and I started sitting. Later, I studied with [Chögyam] Trungpa but it was really the practice itself that made the difference. I've always had the need to experience things in my body. As I practiced more, the despair I felt about being in a complicated, contradictory world started to go away.

I learned to see living and dying as a process, as a natural continuum, rather than a series of psychological ups and downs. Euro-American cultures have a way of emphasizing the ups and downs, the comedy and the tragedy of life, beginnings and endings. Everything is a lurid drama. Zen practice and my life in Wyoming helped me to see life differently. In sitting practice you learn to recognize, but not cling to, the interior monologues of the mind. You actually experience your thoughts rising, going through the mind, and then exiting again. Your body stays put while the next wave of thought passes through. You learn that you don't have to hold on; you don't have to keep reestablishing your identity or your pain or your hope or your fear. Life keeps coming in and going out. I was dumbfounded when I found this out. I still have as much to give and receive as ever, but I know I don't have to keep driving off a cliff and then struggle to get back up again. This teaching has allowed me to be in a place truly and let it come into me instead of spreading myself over it in some futile gesture of domination.

J W: How has your practice changed the way you work with animals?

G E: I met two or three very fine teachers in Wyoming. One of them is a man named Ray Hunt, who works with young horses in a Taoist way, although he may not know what a Taoist is. He's an old cowboy from Idaho who figured out that you can work with the mind and energy of an animal and get better results than if you break them with domination and fear. He never ties up young horses or hobbles them; he tries to teach them while he's riding, sending messages with his legs and body and voice instead of scaring them into doing things before they're ready. I started taking my young horses to him—it was like finding another Suzuki-roshi; I mean, he was practicing Dharma while working with horses right there in Wyoming!

Another wonderful teacher is a man named Bud Williamson, who shows people how to corral and work wild or domestic animals quietly and calmly, without intimidation. We were always working our cows from behind, hitting them and using cattle prods to funnel them into chutes so we could vaccinate them. It seemed so aggressive to me—not that I was above doing it—and I longed for a more gentle way. So along came Bud, who said to us, "Just imagine you're a cow and think of what would scare you. As you're getting forced down the alley way, at what point do you become so paranoid that you've just got to get out of there? Well, that's precisely where you should build a side gate, a narrow alley, and a squeeze chute." We rebuilt our sorting corrals, and it worked. The cows loved it. Before they knew it, they had been given their shot and released again. We didn't have to hit them or yell at them at all. Bud showed us we don't have to be the dominant being in the scenario, that we can take a more cooperative posture.

We did the same thing with our land. In 1987 I met Allen Savory, who's been working with ranchers and farmers all over the world to help stop the deterioration of natural resources. As a result of going through his courses, we started looking at our place as a whole ecosystem. Instead of looking at it from the point of view of what *we* wanted to produce, we started looking at the whole ecosystem and asking what *it* needed. What did the nesting birds need? The elk and deer? The grasses? We worked out a management plan that allowed for all of these needs, and it's brought extraordinary results. We learned how to do high-intensity, short-duration grazing, which is a process of putting all the animals together on a relatively small piece of land for a very short time, then moving them to another "pasture," then to another, letting the other grass rest. This process is modeled on the way buffalo moved through these same areas not long ago. As a result, we restored five species of native grasses that haven't been seen on a ranch in twenty years, developed artesian springs, and were able to leave grass for elk and deer, too. We worked hard on a management plan that allowed for maximum species diversity, not just production, and we found that our stock was getting healthier from all the changes.

All this proved to me that you can use domestic animals as a tool to restore a natural resource. The argument that grazing should be done away with because it abuses the land doesn't address the root problem. When you learn about this land historically as a whole ecosystem, you learn that the grass *needs* to be grazed. Ungulates and grass coevolved. Bunchgrass that isn't grazed dies in about eight years. It chokes itself to death, and you end up with barren soil.

In addition, we stopped selling our calves in the fall, and completely stopped using feed lots. Cattle don't need anything but grass! You could do away with many agricultural and health problems if you did away with supplemental feeding of cattle and sheep.

J W: Was it difficult to kill and eat the animals you raised yourself? How does that fit into this larger, interconnected scheme?

G E: I was excited the first time we brought our calves to the sale barn. I had always heard it was a day to celebrate. It was the day you got paid and went out to eat and drink with everyone. Well, when my calves came into the sale ring, my heart hurt. By that time I thought of myself as a hardened ranch person. I had experienced a lot, but when you raise and nurture a group of animals, then have to watch them being sold off, it's painful.

Eventually we started keeping the animals over until they were eighteen months old. They ate nothing but native grasses and native hay. I felt good about providing the world with lean and organic beef, but at the same time it's always a terrible reality to take a life.

Before raising cattle, we used to hunt deer and elk for food in the winter. I remember the first elk that my husband, Press, shot. I was asleep and dreamed of a person with burst lungs, choking to death on their own blood. I was startled awake, and when Press came in a half-hour later, he said he had just shot an elk through the lungs. I went with him and helped gut and dress out the animal. Any death at all—an animal or a human—is a powerful thing. You never get over it. I always tried to give the animals the best life I could while they were alive, and I tried to treat the ones we raised for food and the ones we used for work as equals. That was the best I could do.

J w: There doesn't seem to be any way around the taking of life to sustain life. Perhaps that's one of the great lessons animals can teach us. You've talked about how several people's teachings have changed the way you work with animals and the land, but what about animals themselves as teachers?

G E: Animals teach you every chance they get! On a ranch, you work intimately with horses and dogs. The highly complex and sensitive nature of horses hasn't been bred out of them. Working horses and dogs are eager to please, but they'll never give up their dignity.

If I decide at breakfast which horse I want to ride, that horse seems to know before I even walk out the door! And when I'm riding, a horse mirrors my mood in subtle and often hilarious ways. If I'm distracted or distant or a little pissed off, he'll give it right back. If I'm fearful, he may buck me off. It's self-defense, really, because he's just trying to get away from what's scaring him.

When you ride alone, often you're not aware of your mood until the horse does something to wake you up. A horse holds you in the present—to who you are at the time, not who you've been or who you want to be.

It breaks my heart when people say sheep are stupid. They've been bred for docility, but that's not their fault. The sheep we used to take from the valley up to the mountains are smart enough to know which day it is. If you don't show up by dawn, they'll break the gate down and start off by themselves.

Dogs are another story. When I first moved to Wyoming, I met a wonderful three-legged Kelpie named Rusty. Kelpies are an Australian herding breed that look like big foxes. They're smart and very responsive to humans. When Rusty sired puppies, I took the first little brown one that came out and named him Sam, after his grandfather.

I was always impressed with how aware Rusty was. Our ranch sat right in the middle of the migration route of deer and elk. In the fall, deer would come down to the hay meadows to eat and bed down for the night, returning to higher country at first light. You couldn't see this upper hay meadow from our house, but Rusty always knew what was going on up there. Once, while we were eating dinner, he suddenly started whining and scratching our arms. We followed him outside to the top of the hill, where he just sat down and looked out over a meadow filled with elk. He wanted to share the pleasure of the sight with us.

During calving season, what we called "ranch ESP" is heightened, and often I am awakened in the night with a feeling that something is wrong. I don't know what it is, but I get dressed and go out. I don't even know where I'm going, but instinct leads me to the right place. Rusty is tuned into all this, too. One snowy spring day my cow named Spot wandered off to calve alone. We hadn't noticed she was missing. As we walked back toward the house, Rusty sat down on a mound of manure in the corral and wouldn't move. From the window we could see this little outline of a dog staring out toward the field. I called and called, but he wouldn't come. Finally, Press went out and followed him down to the lower field. It was foggy, and he couldn't see well, but he came upon Spot at the fence line. Her calf had been born half under the barbed wire fence and a coyote was eating its legs off. Press took off his socks and put them on the calf's hind legs, rolled him up in his jacket, and carried him to the barn.

Spot herself was no ordinary cow. She was given to me by Mike, the woman who taught me to rope and handle cattle, when I helped calve out a bunch of her heifers. This cow's unusual intelligence saved our herd a few times. Once, just after a bad May storm when three feet of snow fell unexpectedly, she led the herd off the mountain—where the calves would have suffocated from the snow or else frozen to death—over a steep embankment and back to the barn. She was waiting at the barn when we arrived on snowshoes.

We live in the embrace of this intelligence all the time, anywhere we are. And the moment we turn our backs on it, the consequences are large and sometimes fatal. It's a lesson in mindfulness that comes from an animal rather than a book or a roshi. It's not just one human trying to teach another, but larger than that: it's a call from one kingdom to another.

Voices from the Sea

UNTIL THE 1960s, most knowledge about whales was compiled from autopsies of stranded or harpooned carcasses. Roger Payne changed all that. Following his instinct, and against the better judgment of his colleagues, Roger insisted on studying live whales in their natural environment. Although there is still a lot to learn about whales, Roger's studies of whale behavior, vocalizations, identification, and migratory patterns have made enormous contributions to the field, and his benign techniques are now used all over the world. Roger's special interest in underwater acoustics led him and a colleague, Scott McVay, to discover that humpback whales sing, a discovery that has profoundly affected scientific thinking and public awareness of whales.

Roger spent the first eighteen years of his life in New York City, where he nurtured a love for music. An accomplished cellist, he claims that his passion for music led him to all his other interests. As an undergraduate at Harvard University in 1956, Roger researched the directional sensitivity of the ears of bats. He went on to study the ability of owls to locate prey in total darkness and received his Ph.D. in animal behavior and neurophysiology from Cornell University in 1962. Roger's postdoctoral studies at Tufts University focused on the ears of noctuid moths, and particularly on how moths use their acute sense of hearing to avoid bats.

A recipient of numerous honorary memberships and awards, including a MacArthur Fellowship in 1984, Roger is now director of

The Whale Conservation Institute in Massachusetts. Among its numerous projects in conservation, education, and research, the Institute has been involved in the study of right whales in Argentina since 1970. It is the longest continuous study of individually identified whales in the world.

The following interview took place over the course of two summers in southeast Alaska. On both occasions, Roger was on board the schooner *Crusader* for humpback whale research in the waters of Frederick Sound. On an August evening we happened on a large pod of whales at the entrance to Seymour Canal. Roger was as excited as a five-year-old at Christmas. We shut down the engine and drifted all night, sharing watches and listening to the whales through hydrophones. As far as I know, Roger never slept. He was either lying on deck, headphones in his ears, watching the star-filled sky, or tinkering with the mess of sound equipment and wire that tumbled out of the pilot house and into the sea. The last image I remember was of Roger leaning over the starboard rail. In the red light of the instrument panel I could see him looking into the water, shaking his head and smiling.

~·~·~

JONATHAN WHITE: We've been observing humpback whales here in Frederick Sound during their summer feeding season. How is their behavior different here than when they're in Hawaii or off the coast of Mexico in the winter?

ROGER PAYNE: Well, here they're feeding and sleeping. As soon as they've filled their bellies utterly, they go into sort of a torpor and sleep for a while. Hours later they awaken, hungry again, ready for the next meal.

Hawaii and Mexico are the breeding grounds of this particular population. In Hawaii, they're feeding little, if at all. They're very active socially with each other. The males are competing for females, and some of the females are busy taking care of newborn calves.

The other obvious thing is that the males sing virtually all the time in Hawaii. They also sing in Alaska, but it's very rare. You might hear a song every week or every two weeks, and then not even a whole song, but just a song fragment.

j w: Why do you think that is?

r p: I suspect that singing is connected with breeding, for songs are most often heard on breeding grounds. I'm surprised they sing in Alaska at all. They may be practicing the song or retaining it in their memories, or keeping versions that have come from other areas in front of the ears of whales that are visiting from other regions. But we don't know, and so I can't really say for sure why it is that whales sing.

j w: When we put the hydrophones down and drifted with the whales the other night, I was astounded by the loudness and variety of their vocalizations. In contrast to the absolute silence of Frederick Sound, it sounded like an underwater party of old men, burping, laughing, falling off their chairs, magnified a hundred times. For me, it added another dimension to their world.

r p: I was totally blown away by what we heard the other night, too. We've always called those vocalizations social sounds, but we're not sure what they mean. I only call them social sounds to distinguish them from songs. Most of them appear to be a different vocabulary. I've never in my life heard so many different sounds as we heard the other night. Marvelous, riotous sounds. They changed my whole perception of how much noise humpbacks make up here. I must say these sounds take you in a compelling fashion into the concept that, my lord, maybe these animals are having some sort of conversation with each other. There were a lot of them around when we were listening—maybe twenty or thirty—so there were plenty of chances to hear comments from other whales.

j w: I couldn't listen without getting giddy—like that noise we heard just before a whale breached.

R P: Yeah, you mean the one that goes "dee-bomp, dee-bomp . . . bom . . . bom . . . bom . . . bom whee whee whee whee wheewhee-whee!!!" [Roger imitates the pre-breaching sounds like a jazz scat singer: first the notes descend rhythmically, growing lower and slower; then they rapidly ascend, growing shorter and higher until they're more like a squeal.] And then finally we saw a breach. Yeah, that was fabulous.

J W: What is your current thinking about why humpback whales sing?

R P: I think songs are sung by a male in hopes of a female, in hopes of being more attractive than other males. And I suspect that the form of the song is shaped and selected by females; in other words, males learn to sing what attracts females. That's my guess. There are all kinds of things the song could be. A good song might give a male a momentary advantage over other males, giving him more opportunities to mate with the female.

Another possibility is that songs are a means by which a female can get some idea of the general fitness of a male, by noting how long he is able to hold his breath. If the female is listening from shallow water, the male will be unable to hide the fact that he is returning to the surface for a breath of air. Owing to the acoustics of the sea, the sound will become faint as he approaches the surface. So, if she hears the song get faint, she knows he's going to the surface for a breath. She could, for example, tell how often a given male needs to breathe. This suggestion was first made by Jim Darling, a man who's been studying these humpbacks for a long time. I think he may be right.

Another theory about why whales sing suggests that males are competing with each other, that their songs are actually threats hurled at each other. The idea here is that they recognize each other's voices and know whether it's worth it to pick up the gauntlet, so to speak, and go through with a fight. It would save time during the breeding season if males didn't have to settle their differences. They'd recognize the sounds of other males, and think, "Oh, my God, that's Fred, there's no way in the world I can beat him, I think I'll just retire from the field."

A lot of other explanations have been proposed for songs. Whales might use them the way the Aborigines of Australia claim to use songs as a means of memorizing the details of a long journey. But that doesn't make sense for humpbacks, because whales that share the same winter breeding grounds return to several different feeding grounds in the summer. If the song was something a whale memorized to find its way to a particular point, it should vary according to the whale's particular destination. But that's not what happens. Instead, all the whales on the same wintering ground—no matter where they spend the summer—sing the same song.

There are other theories. One is that songs might contain a saga, the story of the humpback's existence. If that's the case, I would expect the conditions on which they were commenting to repeat after a while. But even though we have samples of songs that go back forty years, we still haven't heard any repetition.

J W: Their songs are sweet and sad. The psychologist James Hillman says the feeling we get around an animal may be evoked by the animal itself. When we see an eagle, for example, we feel respect or awe, but we don't feel warmth—at least not the same kind of warmth we feel around a whale. When I see a whale and hear its song, I feel a certain sadness. Hillman says that maybe this has something to do with what the whale is feeling, something that it is communicating.

R P: It's a fascinating idea, but I have no personal evidence for it. However, if whales don't have a language like ours, what are they doing with their enormous and fancy brains? I have wondered whether one of the things they are doing is communicating emotion directly. When humans communicate with words, it's usually an attempt to elicit an emotional response. If I were speaking to a woman with whom I had fallen in love, I would try to use my language to bring her to the same emotion. Poets speak affectively of love. This is the way humans use language, but I can imagine a different approach. Maybe whales have developed a way where they can simply evoke the emotion itself in another whale. Of course, that's only speculation. No one knows what whales use their large brains for.

Since they live in an acoustic world where they need sound as a means of "seeing" what's around them, whales might have especially sophisticated acoustic processing techniques. It has never been clearly demonstrated that large whales can echolocate, which is a means of learning about their surroundings by making sounds and listening for the echoes. But we do know that porpoises echolocate with exquisite precision, and porpoises and whales are members of the same order, Cetacea. If you or I snapped our fingers, we might get some idea of the dimensions of this room, but we wouldn't be able to detect the two brass pipes supporting this table, these benches, and so forth, at least not without a sophisticated analysis. That kind of analysis may be what porpoises do with their fancy brains.

But bats do pretty much the same thing with a brain the size of the tip of your smallest finger, while the brain of these dolphins is the size of a human brain. I think we're going to discover that whales and dolphins use their brains for something entirely different than humans do. That's why I'm intrigued by the thought of them using their intelligence to communicate emotions directly.

One of the theories put forward some years ago for how whales name things was tested with an experiment that was unfortunately flawed. The theory stated that the way a porpoise names a fish is simply by imitating the sound it receives when it hits the fish with an echolocation pulse. As I mentioned before, the porpoise detects the fish by making a sound and getting an echo off it. The characteristics of the echo form an acoustic image, not a visual one as we are accustomed to. The theory is that maybe this acoustic image is what the porpoise uses as the name of the fish, by imitating it later when it wishes to "say" the fish's name to another porpoise.

Humans are more visual than acoustic. If we wish to refer to an object like a car to someone whose language we don't speak, we might find a photograph and point to it. We communicate by creating visual images. Porpoises may do this same thing, only with sound.

J w: Marine mammals are sometimes very curious about people and their boats. For example, a pod of orcas approached our boat a few months ago off the coast of British Columbia while we were sailing.

They came right up to us—just a matter of a few feet away—and then dove under the boat, surfacing again immediately off our bow. We were in a wide open channel and they could have gone anywhere. Just how interested do you think these animals are in us?

RP: I've watched a lot of right whales in the waters off Argentina, and I often get the impression that they're bored stiff. When anything new or different comes into the area, they eventually start messing around with it. In Argentina, you can't moor a boat in the area where right whales congregate without them messing with the anchor line and dragging it away.

We used to install tide gauges, which are sticks driven into the beach face, in order to measure the tidal differences. The whales would come and mess them up. There was a female who seemed to derive particular pleasure in breaking the gauges. She would come along with her calf, ease up to one of the stakes, and slowly lean on it, putting her head against it. You could see her start to apply pressure by moving her tail up and down broadly. The stick would lean more and more until it broke. She'd swim off as it fell to the bottom. Finally, we had to design our stakes with breakable joints so they could be repaired easily. That's what it took. Sometimes the whales would break as many as three or four stakes a day.

We used to use small boats to hold our *sonobuoys*, devices that broadcast the sounds picked up by hydrophones under the boat. We used to moor the boats holding the sonobuoys in different places around the bay. But we always had the same problem. Whales kept messing up their moorings, getting tangled up in the anchors and moving them away. We slowly realized it was deliberate. They were doing it intentionally, fooling around with the boats until something let go.

There's an interesting thing happening in the coastal waters of Baja California. It's called the "friendly gray whale phenomenon," where gray whales come so close to whale-watching boats that the tourists can reach out and pat them. If I remember right, the first time this happened was in 1978, when someone reached out with a broom and scratched a gray whale that was hanging around a tourist boat. The whale seemed to like it and leaned into the broom, presenting its other side to be scratched, and so on. The following year there were two or three whales behaving this way, and something like six or eight the year after, until the news apparently spread among the whales that boats were safe and even offered pleasant contact. The whales proceeded to seek out boats filled with tourists, until there were hundreds of whales doing it. Now there are more whales seeking contact with boats than there are boatloads of people to pat them, and so the whales compete with each other for the attention of boats. In Baja, it's boatloads of tourists, not whales, that are the scarce resource.

The whale biologist Jim Darling, who lives on Vancouver Island, was once called by a policeman who said, "There's a crazy gray whale out there. We're going to have to destroy it." Jim asked, "What did it do?" And the policeman said, "It rammed my boat." "Did it roll over onto its back right after it rammed your boat?" Jim asked. "Well, yes," the policeman answered, "as a matter of fact it did." And Jim said, "Well, scratch its belly, that's what it wants."

These are the same gray whales whose species were originally named "devil fish" by the men who discovered their breeding grounds in Scammon's Lagoon. Even though Captain Scammon and his men made a rich haul of oil and blubber while hunting these whales in the late nineteenth century, the men thought they were very dangerous animals. When they tried to kill the whales, the whales fought back!

So I think that whales' reactions to boats and to people are those of great curiosity, and for a long time that curiosity proved to be painful or fatal, particularly in the case of large whales that were harpooned. One of the wonderful things that has happened in recent years is that more people are accepting the possibility that these animals are approaching us in a peaceful way. Maybe it's safe to be around them. People have swum up to them and actually touched them in some cases, though that is illegal in U.S. waters. Whenever that's been done intelligently, the results have been positive.

There's a good example of this in Dingle, a small fishing port in Ireland. The so-called Dingle dolphin swims up to humans and allows them to pat or touch him. He doesn't accept food at all. People have tried, but he won't accept. He fishes for himself. One of the people who trained him first is a young woman named Sheila Stokes. She was a legal assistant with no special knowledge of dolphins. She went around to fishing villages asking the fishermen if there was a dolphin in their area. Finally, in Dingle, a fisherman said "Oh yes, there's one. He lives by those rocks over there. We see him every day." So she and her boyfriend got a tiny boat—about eight feet long—and they went out and swam with that dolphin on forty-two separate days until on the forty-second day the dolphin finally allowed her to touch him. Everybody has hailed this dolphin as being a wonderful, very tame, exceptional animal. Having visited it, it's my suspicion that he may be particularly hard to tame and unexceptional. What *is* exceptional is Sheila Stokes. She had the patience to swim for forty-two days near the dolphin without success. I mean, how did she feel swimming out there on the thirty-eighth day of failure? How about the thirty-ninth and the fortieth, and then the forty-first? I suspect this dolphin is basically a scaredy-cat. But by having had somebody persistent enough to bring him into contact with humans, he now accepts us and spends most of his energy messing about with us. He obviously likes people—now.

J W: Do you think it's exploitive when people make a business out of this behavior?

R P: There is, of course, a major business in people interacting with dolphins or seeing them in captivity. Dolphinariums are an example. I feel that some of the tricks that people get dolphins to do are degrading and should be stopped. I don't believe in them. But other tricks that show the natural abilities of dolphins—jumping for example—can be inspiring for those who have not seen dolphins in the wild. And until somebody can demonstrate that television has replaced reality—real first-hand experience—then my feeling is that those few dolphins in captivity are playing an important role as ambassadors. They are training humanity to have a different attitude toward not just dolphins but all wildlife. I believe that if you could explain to the dolphins what role they were playing, they might go along with it. If I were living in a world controlled by another species whose opinion of me was that I would make good fertilizer, good oil, and good meat for dogs and cats,

I think I would willingly give part of my life to being an ambassador to change the opinion of their children toward me. Maybe I'm somewhat crazy, but that's how I would feel.

There has been a huge struggle over the question of California condors, as to whether they should be caught and raised in captivity until we can change our ways enough to guarantee them a space in the wild. Those who are opposed to the idea believe a condor sitting in a cage with its wings folded and unable to soar on the thermals of its native California coast is not really a condor. My feeling is people aren't thinking of it from the point of view of the condors. Let us suppose for a moment that our fears for how badly they suffer in captivity are wrong and, in fact, their suffering is a thousand times worse. And let us suppose that that suffering continues for not just five or ten generations, but for a hundred generations. At the end of that time, let's assume we are standing with a condor that is about to be released. We say to him, "Well, was it worth it, all those hideous years your ancestors suffered in captivity?" I'm guessing his reaction would be, "I'm sure my ancestors didn't enjoy it, but I'm out of here. I've got my eye on blue sky."

My feeling is *anything* beats extinction. *Anything!* When people damn zoos and aquariums, they forget that most people don't live in the country but in cities where they see rats, pigeons, cockroaches, mice, dogs, cats, and nothing more. I have never felt deeply inspired by these species—have you? Maybe cats, but not truly, deeply inspired, not the way I felt when I first walked into the New York aquarium and saw the indescribable grace of a snow-white beluga whale. I had never seen anything more beautiful. The power of that image—standing face to face with whoever is on the other side of the aquarium window—is unique.

Some firsthand experiences are incomparably valuable. Until somebody demonstrates that this is not the case with captive dolphins, I will worry that getting rid of zoos and aquariums is more negative than positive. The function of zoos and aquariums is important to the future of the species that inhabit them. For example, if the rivers containing dolphins become so polluted that the dolphins can no longer survive, their only hope will be a long period in captivity. During that time, we will have a chance to rehabilitate the rivers, eventually transplanting the dolphins back into healthy systems. But if we have shut down all the aquariums and cease all efforts to improve techniques for keeping dolphins safely in captivity, then all we will do is stand back and wring our hands as we watch the last river dolphins die.

You asked about the business of whale watching. It doesn't make any difference what I or anyone else says, nothing will ever mean as much to a person as seeing a whale close-at-hand in the wild. That is something you never forget. Seeing whales at close quarters is a very important experience for people to have in terms of positioning their attitudes in favor of the wild world.

Whale watching is attacked vehemently by some people. They say, "Stay away from whales, don't bother them, it's their world, it's not our world," and so on. It's a wonderful position philosophically, but it doesn't do much for the protection of whales and it doesn't do much for winning friends for whales in high places or for building lobbies. Effective lobbies are populated by people who have had firsthand experience with their subject. Even if you feel sure that whale watching is bad for whales, you have to realize there is no evidence that it has had a significant negative effect, and you have to explain why year after year the same whales return to the same areas and feed in the same ways.

In Hawaii, humpback whales are giving birth to calves as quickly as biologically possible. If humpbacks are suffering in Hawaiian waters, why are they coming back? The facts are simply inconsonant with the great destruction a lot of people think whale watching is doing. I think whale watching is performing an extremely valuable function in terms of attracting people's interest and attention to whales. That's a brutal fact. For example, there are more calves born to humpback whales in whale watch areas than are known to be born to these whales anywhere else.

J W: Whale watching is a rapidly growing business. I've watched it grow tremendously here in Alaska over the last five years. First, is the history of whale watching long enough to really know its effect on whale populations? Second, as the business increases, so does the potential for harassment. What about the long-term effects on the quality of life for whales?

R P: Those are wonderful points, Jonathan, and I hear you loud and clear. I too worry about the subtle long-term effects. Whale watching has been going on long enough in some places, like eastern Massachusetts, to detect its effect. The populations of whales in that area are increasing. The same individuals are coming back every year. The rate at which they're giving birth is as high as it can be. Those are important considerations.

You also mentioned quality of life. What is the diminution of the quality of life of a chickadee that lives in your backyard, eats artificial foods from your feeder, and is now, in fact, totally dependent on them? If you removed the bird feeders throughout New England, you'd probably halve the populations of chickadees, nuthatches, downy woodpeckers, titmice, and other species that come with them. My feeling is that all of us are experiencing a diminution in quality of life. There's no way of pretending that the great undiscovered, unexploited herds of game that once existed in North America are still here. My God, they're totally gone, absolutely destroyed by our distant ancestors who seem to have brought final destruction to a number of other species as well, including wooly mammoths and wooly rhinos.

There's no question that there is a certain diminution of the lives of whales. But how bad is it? Look at the alternative. The alternative is an active whaling industry, unopposed, as was the case under the Golden Gate Bridge in San Francisco until the mid 1960s. The Del Monte whaling station, just a little farther inland, was killing whales until 1971!

So it's all a trade-off. There's no way we can completely turn our backs on whales now. If we do, the thing that will get them in the end will be lack of caring—things like accidental entanglement in fishing gear and accumulation of toxins in the oceans. The other considerations are minor. If we build a group of people who love whales, who have learned to love them through close encounters in an aquarium or sitting in a whale watch boat, they will no longer shrug their shoulders and say, "Aah, that's too bad" when they hear that a hundred thousand dolphins die accidentally every year in fishing nets. Instead, they'll get mad, and maybe one in every ten thousand will be vociferous enough to lean on their representatives to the point where something actually happens to alleviate the situation. In that sense, I think whales are better off than they've ever been, even though some of them are probably having their lives diminished in areas where there is too much contact with humans. But those areas are small compared to the vast herds of whales swimming in seas most of us will never see.

JW: What is it that so attracts people to dolphins and whales? I was out with them just the other day and thinking, "What is it in me that wants to get so close to these whales? Would I be making the same effort to get close to them if they were the size of salmon?"

RP: That's a wonderful question. Why would you make a greater effort to see a redwood than a dogwood? Dogwoods have flowers, redwoods don't. Whales and redwoods both make us feel small and I think that's an important experience for humans to have at the hands of nature. We need to recognize that we are not the stars of the show. We're just another pretty face, just one species among millions more. The star of the show is nature, and we just may be the most unsuccessful species that's ever appeared on Earth, threatening our own existence in fewer generations than any other species ever has. Our fancy brain, which is a lot of fun to own, is very dangerous. I can't think of anything we've discovered in nature that is as dangerous. Cobra venom, hell, that's nothing to worry about. Just stay out of reach of the cobra. But you can't stay out of reach of human beings. The snowfields here in Alaska are polluted with outfall from factories located thousands of miles away. The flesh-eating mammals up here have accumulated these deadly compounds in their system. We can't get away from it any longer. As Pogo says, "We have met the enemy and he is us."

But when you encounter a large species like a redwood or a whale, it introduces awe into your life. And awe is a very rare but very important experience. It's what started the major religions. Experiencing awe in the hands of the wild can cause you to feel the same essential ecstasy. It's an experience you can't find by watching television.

J W: Why is awe so important for people to experience?

R P: I think awe is like a sign saying, "You have captured my attention." Awe awakens attention and respect. When you find something that takes hold of human beings and causes them to change their ways—I mean, what is that worth? A trillion dollars? A hundred trillion? All the money that exists? More than that?

I was talking with a politician in Maine, a woman for whom I have great respect, and I said to her that I was frustrated by [then] President Bush and his lack of interest in the environment. I asked her, "How would you get his attention? How would you get the president to focus on the environment?" Without a moment's hesitation she said, "Through his grandchildren. They're probably the only people he really trusts. They're the only people he speaks to who don't have another agenda." So what would it be worth to have one of the president's grandchildren go up to him and say, "Grandad, why is it you allow forests to be ruined for lumber that's shipped off to Japan? Why is the Tongass National Forest going overseas in freighters? Why do you do that?" What would that be worth? How many hours of how many conservationists' time would it count for if the president heard that question from somebody he didn't fear?

We cannot speak with nature, but our sense of awe in it allows it to speak to us. The few things that happen to people in their lives that really affect how they live and what they respect and how they go about the business of their day-to-day lives, those experiences probably occupy a total of, what, a half a minute? One minute of a lifetime? Yet they're what really matter. All the rest is just the packing material in which your life gets shipped.

But let me come back to the question you asked about why whales affect us the way they do. I think part of it is because they're mammals, and we have a natural sympathy for creatures that approach life in a similar way that we do. People seem to sense in whales a different presence than they do in other large animals like, for example, a whale shark. Even though they're as big as a whale, whale sharks are cold-blooded, and we sense that they may not be very smart, and . . . well, they're just not the same as a whale.

I can't imagine a whale shark embracing its young the way we see mother right whales do. In that sense, whales are more like sea otters. Why are sea otters so unbelievably attractive to people? I suspect it's partly because they're so tactile, that they hold and cuddle and embrace their young. It's a very basic instinct. For instance, the thing that was so important to Sheila Stokes, the woman who trained the Dingle dolphin, was to embrace it. And she did. There's a large difference between just watching an animal and being able to embrace it—a huge difference.

People laugh and call conservationists tree-huggers. They laugh at someone who wants to hug a whale. But it's only their own embarrassment that causes them to laugh, and their laughter betrays their discomfort with people who are courageous enough to embrace what they love.

J W: What has been your closest encounter with a whale?

R P: One night just before leaving Argentina, my thirteen-year-old son and I took a long walk on the beach. As we did, we passed close to the water's edge where there was a mother whale and her calf. As she rolled, causing a great slow disturbance in the water, she raised her flipper into the air so it towered over us. It had the sense of a benediction. I mean, no pope could have waved in such a way as to give me a more complete sense of blessing. And what were we being blessed by? By life, I suppose. The feeling it gave me was unforgettable.

I've never had an experience with a whale that really scared me. I've felt scared in retrospect, but never at the time. I don't have any gee-whiz whale stories where it's me against them—you know, the standard macho nonsense. I've had whales nearly breach on my boat. The most recent incident of this was last year off the coast of Colombia. I had to swerve the boat to prevent the whale from landing on it. There's a woman who works in my laboratory who had a whale breach directly on top of her boat. Not a glancing blow, but a direct hit across the bow. The boat was totaled, but I haven't had that sort of experience.

j w: One of the reasons I'm so drawn to these animals is that they have qualities I respect. When I go to a party and I see someone laughing or being playful or listening carefully to someone else, I am drawn to them. I want to be close to them and I want them to like me as a friend. In some ways it's the same kind of thing that draws me to the whales. I want them to like me the way I want a friend to like me.

r p: That's wonderful. I share those feelings. One of the great disappointments in my life with whales happened in Argentina with a whale named Troff. Since we've been there, Troff's had five calves. She's a wonderfully successful, excellent mother. I've spent a lot of my life watching her because she's often right off our camp. On three occasions I've been on the water next to her, only to discover that she's terrified of my boat. She gets away from me as fast as she can. As far as I can tell, I cause her maximum panic whenever I get anywhere near her. That's been a great disappointment.

There's another Argentine right whale I feel close to, but it's the same with her. I remember the first time I saw her after she had been away a couple years. I'd been watching a whale off in the middle of the bay all afternoon and it was inching its way toward the coast. It seemed to take forever to come in close. And as I watched it I slowly realized, My God, it's Y-Spot. And tears came to my eyes. It was a very emotional thing. I thought she had died. It was this encounter that first taught us that the whales only come back to Argentina every three years. When I saw Y-Spot again, it was just incredible, like thinking a friend had been lost in a war, then encountering them again. But as far as I can tell, neither Y-Spot or Troff thinks of me as a friend. It's deeply disappointing because I've spent a lot of time watching them, and I love them both.

j w: There's another level at which this desire to get close doesn't seem exclusively personal—I mean, when it's not just you and a particular animal, but both of you together as part of nature.

R P: I've never met anyone who spends time getting close to animals who isn't more of a person because of it. Just as the modern whaling industry brings out the worst in people, having the courage to love an animal brings out the very best in people. That's what courage is—the willingness to admit, even in the face of adversity or nonacceptance, that you love something. Blowing everything away that threatens you like Rambo isn't courage, it's cowardice. Admitting you love something, that's courage.

J W: I met a man in eastern Oregon who loves birds and spends a lot of time around them. We called him the birdman. At one point in our conversation he raised his hand and whistled and within four or five seconds a chickadee flew in and perched on his finger. He brought the bird up close to his face and fed it a seed from his palm. It was such a tender, honorable contact between them, a huge man and a tiny bird. It seems that many of us are seeking a personal connection—a sense of belonging or acceptance—through our encounters in the field.

R P: Everybody could gain something from having more contact with the natural world. It brings rewards unequaled by anything else they could find in the human world. A friend of mine, Bill Eddy, says, "When you live in a world that is created entirely by people, like a city, eventually you begin to confuse the creator with human beings. And the bible of that world, in which the virtues of the creator are extolled on every page, is the Sears Roebuck catalog."

If people are willing to give themselves the gift of some improvement in their life, there is nothing that can beat having a deep and prolonged contact with nature. There's nothing I know of that's likely to be more rewarding. I once had a chickadee perch on my finger and take a seed from my hand. I'll never forget it. Never. Any situation where you allow an animal to trust you, and you trust it, builds a faith in your ability and the truth of what that represents. I think nothing could be a greater gift.

The Archdruid Himself

DAVID BROWER is persuasive, extraordinarily accomplished as an outdoors person, and relentless in his efforts on behalf of the planet. Whether you call him "the Archdruid of the Conservation Movement" or "John Muir reincarnate" or simply a gifted and determined leader, there is no denying that without him, the conservation movement would not be what it is today.

Born in Berkeley, California, in 1912, David developed his ecological interests by collecting and breeding butterflies—in fact, he discovered a variety that was named after him. His mother lost her sight in 1920, and he often acted as her eyes at home and on walks in the Berkeley hills. He spent the summers of 1930 to 1932 as guide and secretary at the Berkeley Echo Lake Camp. In 1934 he and a friend bartered firewood for food for a seven-week Sierra knapsack trip, his first extended wilderness experience. It led him to the mountains again and again, where he guided thousands of people on Sierra Club summer and winter trips, eventually making sixty-nine first ascents in the High Sierra and Yosemite Valley. David met his wife, Anne Hus, in 1941, while he was editor at the University of California Press. They married in May of 1943 and now have four children and three grandchildren.

David became the first executive director of the Sierra Club in 1952. Under his leadership, the Sierra Club grew exponentially in membership and effectiveness. As Stephen Fox writes in *The American Conservation Movement,* "It was Brower, preeminently Brower, who transformed the Sierra Club into (as the *New York Times* said) 'the gangbusters of the conservation movement.' To a rare degree he had the quality which he valued most highly in Muir: the ability to transcend his powers as an observer and to become in addition a keen advocate. He stands with Muir and Marshall in the line of great mountaineer-conservationists."

After a conflict with the club's board of directors, David was forced to resign in May of 1969. A month later he was directing the John Muir Institute for Environmental Studies. In July of 1969, he founded Friends of the Earth and the League of Conservation Voters, adding Friends of the Earth International in 1970. David founded Earth Island Institute in San Francisco in 1982 and is now its chairman.

I met up with David and Anne in southeast Alaska while they were traveling home from a conference in Russia to help protect "The Blue Gem of Siberia," Lake Baikal. We spent a week aboard the *Crusader,* sailing in Frederick Sound, Stephens Passage, and Endecott Arm. The following interview took place one early morning at anchor in Gambier Bay.

~·~·~

JONATHAN WHITE: The extent to which the earth is jeopardized by current trends is unfathomable to many of us. How do we get a grasp of just how urgent our situation is?

DAVID BROWER: It's important to realize how recently our species arrived on the planet and how rapidly we have changed things. An effective way to get an image of this is to squeeze the four and a half billion years of the earth into six days of creation.

Thus the earth was created on Sunday night at midnight. There was no life until Tuesday at noon. In the course of the next four days, millions upon millions of species come and go. Saturday morning about seven o'clock there has been enough chlorophyll and green plants that fossil fuels begin to form. At about four o'clock in the afternoon, the great reptiles come on stage, but they're all gone by nine o'clock that night. The whales go back to sea at ten, the seals go back by eleven. There's nothing remotely resembling us until three minutes before midnight. Homo sapiens don't arrive until a half-minute before midnight, and we continue as hunter-gatherers until agriculture is invented, one and a half seconds before midnight. Buddha comes on the scene a third of a second before midnight, Christ a fourth of a second. The Industrial Revolution begins at a fortieth of a second, and at one two-hundredth of a second before midnight we discover how to split the atom. Now it's midnight, and some of us are asking how much longer we can continue on this trend.

Some of these figures are subject to contention. At the turn of the century, for example, scientists thought the age of the earth was around five million years. They now estimate it at four and a half billion years. The estimates for the age of life vary, too, particularly the age of Homo sapiens. But even considering this, the effect of the timeline isn't significantly distorted.

The point of the story is that we can't continue to destroy the earth's life support system indefinitely. It just doesn't compute. Global warming, acid rain, holes in the ozone layer, the loss of genetic diversity and desertification are just a few of the problems that have surfaced in my lifetime. By one estimate, we're extinguishing a plant or animal species every minute, and extinction is forever.

j w: What about the loss of wilderness?

d b: It's hard to get across how little wilderness is left. We've encroached on all of it in one way or another. It wasn't too long ago that my oldest son and two friends took a trip across the Brooks Range in Alaska, for example, and their trip was essentially the last that knew that area as wilderness. Very shortly after that, oil was discovered, the pipeline went in, the haul road, the massive development at Prudoe, and a wilderness the size of Massachusetts was gone. In my lifetime we've lost 95 percent of the redwoods and all but three hundred of the six thousand miles of salmon streams in California alone.

When François Leydet translated Eliot Porter's book, *In Wildness Is the Preservation of the World,* he got stuck on the word *wildness.* You can't translate it into French. It just doesn't work. One of the reasons for this might be because there's no wilderness left in France.

Wilderness is important for a whole lot of reasons, and whether you get there or not, it should be part of what Wallace Stegner calls for, a geography of hope. As he says, "We simply need that wild country available to us, even if we never do more than drive to its edge and look in. It can be a means of reassuring ourselves of our sanity as creatures, a part of the geography of hope."

j w: You like to quote Nancy Newhall's statement, "The wilderness holds answers to questions we have not yet learned how to ask." What does that mean to you?

d b: From the simplest things to the most complex, we have so little knowledge of how nature works. The genetic information it takes to create a human being, for example, fits into a sphere a sixth of an inch in diameter. It's a miracle that so much information can be compressed into such a tiny space. Our species is the result of three and a half billion years of passing on this information—the miracle, the magic, or whatever you want to call it—of life. And what's the source of that information? *Wildness*. As the six-day creation story shows, there wasn't anything but wildness for almost all the time life was on Earth. Unwildness is a very recent addition. It's wildness, the trial and error, the symbiosis, the successes, the failures, throughout all these years that has shaped everything there is. Robinson Jeffers wrote, "What but the wolf's tooth whittled so fine / The fleet limbs of the antelope? / What but fear winged the birds, and hunger / Jewelled with such eyes the great Goshawk's head?" The seagulls didn't learn a thing from our technology about how to fly. The forest didn't learn anything from forestry school. The knowledge is coded in the DNA and passed on and on. It is one of the most remarkable things, and it has all been informed by wilderness.

Photosynthesis is another good example of a remarkable yet elemental process in nature. It supports all life on Earth, and scientists still don't know how it's done. The slow, smokeless fire of decay at the other end of the process is equally mysterious.

Forest biologist Chris Maser figures it takes hundreds of years from the time a big tree falls until it's recycled into soil. How does that happen? What converts it into soil? We know so little but we do know there are many organisms that play a role in it, from bacteria, protozoans, beetles, mites, and ants to millipedes, termites, spiders, and small mammals. A fallen tree supports a biological community that may be essential to the existence of the forest itself. The recent studies on mycorrhizal fungi, for example, show that conifers in Northwest forests require the fungi to get water, phosphorus, and nitrogen from the soil. The roots of most of these trees have to be inoculated by the fungi within a year in order to survive. Chris Maser says the fungi can't disperse their spores by themselves but depend on animals to eat them and poop their spores out all over the forest. The chemistry of the wild is extraordinary stuff. It's part of the miracle that everything is connected to everything else, not just in forests but everywhere we go.

My feeling is we need to save wilderness for its own sake, for the mysterious and complex knowledge it has within it. Thoreau was right when he said, "In wildness is the preservation of the world." We can't reconstruct it. We can only restore its ability to perpetuate itself. I'd like to approach the argument to save wilderness from that point of view rather than how good it is for your health to be out in it, or how beautiful it is, or how good it is for your soul.

J W: What are the best strategies for implementing a change in our attitude and use of the environment?

D B: I guess there is no best way but the way that seems to work at the time. You can try everything—that's what I've done. Initially it was articles in magazines, then books, film, video, interviews, speeches, and conferences. I guess the most important elements are boldness and tirelessness. We just have to keep plugging away. Something will work for a while, then people get used to it and they don't hear it anymore.

I suppose I like what books have done best. They're the basis for a lot of the other things that can happen, like full-page advertisements, interviews on television, reviews in the press and in magazines, and so on. Books are retrievable, too. You know where they are on the shelf and you know roughly what pages the information is on. Everything seems to stem from the book.

J W: Are books about conservation issues commercially viable?

D B: Books about conservation issues are sometimes a little hard to sell. But even if they aren't commercially viable, they should be published and lean on those that are. When I came on duty at the Sierra Club in 1933, the average yearly sale of books was about $1,500. By the time I left, the yearly sale was up to $1.3 million. A lot of people joined the club because of the books, too. In 1933, the Sierra Club had fewer than 2,000 members. The last count I heard was 650,000 members, and this kind of trend has been true for a good many other organizations, too. The new challenge this presents, of course, is not to get so consumed in the growth that you forget what you're about.

J W: Will you give some examples of how these tools—books, films, videos, advertisements, and so on—have worked?

D B: In the late 1930s, the Sierra Club was fighting to establish Kings Canyon National Park in the Sierra Nevada. I was twenty-six at the time, and it was really my first battle. I found two things that worked well: articles in the *Sierra Club Bulletin* and a film. I made most of the film myself. It was just a silent color film, but it showed what the potential of Kings Canyon was, what the country was like, how it was enjoyed by Sierra Club trips, and what would happen if it wasn't saved. I toured the state and the country showing that film to as many audiences as possible. Ansel Adams put together a beautiful, large format book too, called *Sierra Nevada: The John Muir Trail*. The book had quite an effect, particularly on Franklin Roosevelt, Secretary [of the Interior] Harold Ickes, and some others. Ansel brought the potential park to the people. And we won the battle; we got the Kings Canyon National Park. I think it was that success that convinced me of the effectiveness of books and photographs.

I've recently shifted from film to video. A good example of what can be done with a camcorder and a lot of guts is what Sam LaBudde did. Sam is a biologist who wanted to get aboard a tuna boat to witness how the fleet was killing dolphins. He was thirty-two at the time and he finally got a job as a cook, though he had never cooked before. Through a series of accidents, we got him a camcorder the day before he got on board. He told the fishermen it was a toy he'd received from his father and he just wanted to see how it worked. If they had known what he was intending, he might have been thrown overboard.

Sam came back with devastating footage. One tape showed a catch that killed over a hundred dolphins and got three tuna—that was the kind of slaughter that was going on. His footage became the basis of news stories around the world, including a segment on *60 Minutes* in Australia. It was very moving material.

Sam and Earth Island Institute made a film on tuna fishing and the dolphin issue that won some awards. We used it as the basis of advertising campaigns in newspapers and mailers. In the course of this effort, Earth Island's membership went from five thousand to thirty-five thousand members. In 1991, Sam was invited to receive the Goldman Award for environmental action. They awarded him $60,000, which was pretty nice. At the reception Sam walked out on California Governor Pete Wilson when he was making a speech about the noble work of our men in the Gulf War. He just got up and walked out. It's that kind of boldness that made it possible for him to win the Goldman Award in the first place. Of the $60,000, Sam gave $50,000 to a cause that would enable other people to get camcorders and go out and do what he did, and the other $10,000 he used to retire his student debt.

J W: What about strategies that work within the system? Like legislative strategies, for example?

D B: As far as I'm concerned, the most effective strategies are going to have to relate to getting legislation enacted and seeing that it's enforced. We can't turn our backs on the fact that many of the most important decisions are made by politicians in the legislative arena. This arena controls our civilization by coercion, and I don't know any way to short-circuit that.

Corporations are bound by law to their shareholders. Because of this, corporations can be sued by their shareholders if they're negligent in the pursuit of profit. I would like to see legislation drafted that would change this. Corporate CEOs and officers should be allowed to bypass a profit-making opportunity for social or environmental reasons without the threat of being sued by the shareholders. As it is now, there is no moral or legal incentive for corporations to use their conscience.

When a corporation goes to potential investors, it's required to reveal information about its spending habits, its CEOs, and so on. But it doesn't have to reveal any information on the effects its operation has on the environment. I would like to see these corporations bound by law to let their investors know how their money will affect the earth. Environmental impact analyses should be required and made available for potential shareholders and also for corporate takeovers.

One of our principal problems is we don't have enough legislative activity in the environmental organizations. We had a lot until the mid-fifties, but then a Supreme Court decision made it illegal for nonprofit organizations to engage in legislative activity without jeopardizing their status. That decision was a devastating blow to the environmental movement. So, right now, one of the most important pieces of legislation to fight for is the reformation of the Internal Revenue Code to permit public nonprofit organizations to do their political duty without being penalized.

Big corporations know how to affect legislation. They make massive expenditures affecting public opinion—which is in effect grassroots lobbying. They do it every day in their advertisements, their commercials on television, ads in magazines, in the papers, and on the radio. It's a cost that's built into making their profit. The nonprofits are handicapped because they can't do anything approaching what the corporations do. The corporations have the corporate interest at heart. As I mentioned earlier, they are bound to their shareholders by law. The nonprofits have the public interest at heart. It's high time we stopped penalizing the nonprofit organizations that have the public interest at heart.

J w: Didn't the Sierra Club lose its tax status because of legislative activities? Would you tell the story?

D B: Yes, it did. The Sierra Club has been legislatively active since its inception in 1892. It remained so until the Supreme Court decision in the fifties. That decision forced us to make resolutions that made us appear less legislatively active than we were. We did this to protect our tax-deductible status, but the resolutions still inhibited us from doing a lot of work that needed to be done.

In 1960, I created the Sierra Club Foundation, which was tax-deductible and would be in position to take over if the Sierra Club ever lost its tax-deductible status. And it did, as you say, just a few years later, when we were running full-page ads to save the Grand Canyon. At the instigation of Mo Udall [U.S. representative from Utah], the IRS determined the ads were not lawful under our status. But it didn't matter; the foundation was ready for that. When we lost our tax status, although we could not get tax-deductible money directly into the Sierra Club, we got it in through the Sierra Club Foundation. Ironically, our membership grew because of public outrage at what the IRS had done. Mo Udall, who denied having anything to do with it at the time, later told me in privacy that it was the worst mistake he'd ever made.

J w: The Sierra Club is among the more conservative groups. What about other environmental organizations and their strategies, such as the Nature Conservancy's approach of buying up land or Earth-First!'s monkey-wrenching?

D B: As far as I'm concerned, the diversity of the attack is essential. Although a lot of people will disagree, I think EarthFirst! is important to the Nature Conservancy. I have two sound bytes on EarthFirst!: One is, they're giving CPR to the rest of the environmental movement, which badly needs it. And the other is that I wish EarthFirst! was unnecessary, but the deterioration of the earth is going on so rapidly right now that its kind of action to get public attention is essential.

When it gets down to it, the damage to property at the hands of EarthFirst! is insignificant compared to the damage to property by people with chainsaws. The cases where trees are spiked to discourage logging are usually where the administrative, legal, and traditional remedies have been exhausted.

When I was executive director of the Sierra Club, Russell Train, who is an outstanding Republican conservationist, said, "Thank God for David Brower because he makes it so easy for the rest of us to be reasonable." So then I founded Friends of the Earth to make the Sierra Club look reasonable, and Dave Forman formed EarthFirst! to make Friends of the Earth look reasonable. And now we need an organization that makes Forman look reasonable. It's amazing how many audiences cheer that thought.

The assault on the earth is funded by the Fortune 500s and their friends and their customers. Other organizations are too slow in waking up the public to this. It's a case of corporate greed and greed on the part of the corporate customer, too. My wife, Anne Brower, sums it all up in one word: *greedlock*. I hope the other organizations will follow the Sierra Club pattern of being an educational foundation, a litigation group, a politically active group, and a nondeductible legislative group. The Sierra Club should be in the land-acquiring business, too. I would like to see all the organizations take advice from the Nature Conservancy, Conservation International, Trusts for Public Lands, and from the hundreds of land trusts that get into this business. When the government is as irresponsible as ours has been, preserving land will have to be the work of private hands.

Most environmental organizations don't concern themselves enough with nuclear war. They don't see it as an environmental threat, but it is. If we had an exchange of nuclear weapons between the [former] Soviets and the United States where we used just ten percent of our inventory, there would be hundreds of millions of people killed right away. But on the day of that exchange, a deterioration of the ozone barrier would begin and a year later no crops would grow. That just about finishes off any last hope we'd have of surviving.

J W: What do you believe are the most important changes that must be made if we are to have hope of reversing the current destructive trend?

D B: First, we must set the goal of building a sustainable society. We don't have one. The industrial nations are not on a sustainable route by any means. On the cover of the book *Building a Sustainable Society*, by Lester Brown, is the quote, "We do not inherit the earth from our fathers, we are borrowing it from our children." Lester says he got that quote from me, though I don't remember having said it. Nevertheless, I was being too conservative. We are not borrowing from our children, we are stealing from them. It's supposed to be illegal to steal from children, but we steal from them in our misapprehension of what we're doing to the earth because somehow we have seen it as limitless. The Renaissance was devoted to exploring and exploiting the limits of the earth and it's now time for a new renaissance where we recognize the limits and live within them.

Industrial nations recycle next to nothing. The challenge of technology, science, and our own behavior as individuals is to follow the example of nature—waste less and recycle more. Clearly, the cheapest way to find energy is not to waste it.

We continue to act as if there's no limit to the fossil fuel resource. Past administrations, and that includes Mr. Carter, Mr. Reagan, and Mr. Bush, have all operated on the theory that the faster you use up energy resources the better off you are. That's the theory of strength through exhaustion. The faster you exhaust your resources the stronger you'll be. It can't possibly be true, but it's still being practiced by all the industrial nations of the world. We have yet to see what kind of conservation the present administration will practice.

The present human population of the earth is 5.3 billion, far too many for a sustainable future. It's still anybody's guess what the sustainable number is. At the Renewing the Earth Conference last year, I heard that Professor E. O. Wilson, an outstanding biologist from Harvard, estimated the carrying capacity of the earth to be two hundred million if we continue with the appetites we now have for resources. I'd never heard a figure that low, so I called him to verify. On the phone he said, "No, I didn't say that, but it sounds reasonable." That was good enough for me. If we use that figure, we're over-populated by five billion people!

According to the most recent statistics from World Watch Institute, the world's population is growing by 95 million people per year. That's a net increase—births over deaths—equal to the population of Mexico *every year*. At this rate, the world's population will double by 2050.

J W: Are there models we can use for building a sustainable future?

D B: I think we need to look hard at some of the earlier societies that were indeed sustainable. In his book *In the Absence of the Sacred,* Jerry Mander goes back to review what the Indians could have taught us, tried to teach us, and may in fact still teach us.

The Great Binding Law of the Iroquois Confederacy, which has been in existence for thousands of years, served as a model for the United States Constitution. There is good evidence that the Iroquois Confederacy also influenced the work of Friedrich Engels and Karl Marx, and possibly others in Europe as well. Thomas Jefferson, James Madison, and Benjamin Franklin all consulted the Iroquois when coming up with the principles of the new confederation. They just didn't listen long enough.

The laws weren't written down by the Indians but passed on orally from one generation to the next. They believe that once you write the rules down, you end up dealing with the rules instead of what's fair from case to case. They also make their decisions with a commitment to the seventh generation of unborn children.

In our present situation, we're just trying to get a stay of execution so our *first* generation of unborn children will have a fighting chance.

J W: The issues are complex, but at bottom it seems we need to change our attitude and our ideas about standard of living.

D B: A friend of mine says, "To hell with the standard of living, I want a better life," and I suppose a good test for that is to look closely at what we call a high standard of living. What do all our possessions do for us that we are so afraid to lose them? We seldom think about what they cost the earth or other generations. What do my camcorders cost the earth?

You hear all about the benefits of growth, but you never hear about the costs. If global warming continues, what is the best estimate of the cost of repairs to the coastal areas that will be damaged by flooding? What will it cost Holland to prevent itself from being inundated by a rising ocean? I recently learned that Siberia has 26 percent of the world's remaining forests. It occurred to me that because these forests absorb carbon dioxide and keep it locked up, the rest of the world should pay the Soviet Union not to harvest those trees.

It's quite possible to get by with a lot less use of resources. We just happen to have gotten into a civilization where consumerism is a great god—the more you consume the better. The faster and earlier you throw something away and replace it, the better. Our attitude toward growth, too, is a form of insanity. Anne and I were in Japan in 1976, where I was giving some lectures. In the course of my talk I'd say, "You're now very proud of your 8 percent GNP rate, which means roughly that when a Japanese child born today is old enough to vote, you'll need thirty times the resource base you have now. And by the time that same child retires, you'll need two hundred times your present resource base. If all the world's forests aren't enough for Japan's needs now, what are you going to do?" They would smile sweetly— they're always polite—and say they didn't intend for the 8 percent growth rate to continue. And I'd answer, "Why don't you stop growing while Japan is still beautiful and livable?"

The message is getting through, but awfully slowly. There's nothing like asking a large audience, "How many of you haven't changed your mind on anything in the last year?" After a minute a few hands go up. The truth is, I haven't changed my own mind on anything in a long time. It's time I did. We've got to make a U-turn, and we've got to do it pretty fast; the bridge is out ahead.

J W: The idea of saving the planet seems abstract, unreal and, on some level, even arrogant. Wendell Berry says, "We are not smart enough or conscious enough, or alert enough to work responsibly on a gigantic scale." Don't we need to focus on smaller, less abstract things, like communities, neighborhoods, households, our own soul for that matter?

D B: No, we don't. That's exactly what we're doing, that's the cause of the trouble. We've been concentrating on ourselves—contemplating our own navels—too long. It's this whole business of being so concerned about what happens to you that you forget what's happening to everything else. As a result—I'm sorry about Wendell Berry; he's right about everything else, but he's absolutely wrong on this—the life support system has degenerated. And my feeling is, if we caused it, then we can be the cause of its reversal. But we damn well better get at it and not say it's too abstract or something or other. It's exactly what we've got to get our minds on and that doesn't mean you forget the kids at home. You've got to do both. I like the expression, "It's not either/or, it's both/and."

J W: It sounds like you want our species to survive.

D B: I think it's a good idea. The survival of the race is built into our very being. All species have that drive. When you watch salmon swim up the streams to spawn and die, you can feel the sacrifice they make. They have one chance at reproduction—that's it. We're luckier to have more chances at it.

We also need to realize that a healthy earth is not only necessary for our own survival, but for the survival of other species as well. Kenneth Brower said, "A living earth is a rare thing, perhaps the rarest in the universe and a very tenuous experiment at best. We need all the company we can get on our unlikely journey." I like to look around and see the company of all these trees. We're related and I'm glad they're making a stand.

As the mountaineer Geoffrey Winthrop Young said, "We're not proud enough of being alive." Once in a while, it's a good exercise to take inventory of ourselves. Think of your skin, for example. It's an extraordinarily important organ because it separates the wildness outside from the wildness within us. And it's not totally impermeable, either. It can perspire or absorb, but it also keeps us dry in the rain and pretty much held together. We take inventory of the wildness outside us, but the wildness within is something we rarely think about. Look at the extraordinary organization of our ears, eyes, digestion, and circulation system, or the reproductive processes.

The other night I was meditating about how many senses we have. Our five senses are just the beginning. In addition to seeing, hearing, tasting, smelling, and touching, we have a sense of ethics, of right and wrong, a sense of place and of time, a sense of mass and energy. We have a sense of love and hate, power and despair, hope and hopelessness. Right now I think a good many people are short on their sense of power and hope and very long on the sense of hopelessness.

J W: What are some of the signs that give you optimism for the future? What are your personal sources for optimism?

D B: The chief cause of my optimism now is the response I get from audiences when I give my speech about restoring the earth—for putting the natural and human life support systems back in order. After giving my pitch for healing the earth and promoting programs like the International Green Circle, I usually ask how many people would be willing to commit a year of their lives out of the next ten to work on this. I'm encouraged when two-thirds of the people put their hands up. And, as an environmentalist, I'm glad to be talking about something that has some promise to it, rather than just more bad news.

Noel Brown said, "It's healing time on Earth." People love to know that. It turns them around. They stop feeling hopeless when they know there's a chance to heal things.

J W: Will you tell me more about the International Green Circle? Was it your idea?

D B: Actually, no. It was John Berger who did most of the good work on that with his book *Restoring the Earth*. I picked up on what he did and found out there have been some good examples of restoration in the past and some extraordinary opportunities ahead of us. I see it as the only likely route to peace.

It all started with the need for an international group that would take up where the Peace Corps left off. We wanted to call it the Earth Corps, but that name was improved upon by Gorbachev in January of 1991 when he called for an International Green Cross. The idea is that the Red Cross helps people in structures hurt by the earth and the Green Cross protects the earth hurt by people in structures. But we ran into problems with using the symbol of the cross. The Jewish people don't like the cross and the Muslims like the crescent instead. Finally we came up with the name International Green Circle. It's pretty hard to find people who object to a circle, especially because we live on a spherical planet.

There is so much public support for restoration and the International Green Circle that the real challenge now is in organizing it. We're bringing people from different countries, with different colors and creeds, economic situations, ages, and sexes, to work together in teams around the world. Lake Baikal is a good example where people from the United States, Canada, and the former Soviet Union are working together to figure out how to save the lake—the Gem of Siberia, as it is called. If the Russians continue using the lake as a sewer, according to their own figures it will be dead in sixty years, and it would take six hundred years to restore it. So we're trying to avoid killing it in the first place.

In its own way, our Park Service has been very good about restoration. They've cleaned up a lot of areas and removed all evidence that structures were ever there. They've done that in Yosemite and in other places.

We have the capability to protect, preserve, and celebrate nature. Restoration is one of the most exciting and important jobs we have. It will require new ways of working together, new technology, new teaching, and new curricula.

J W: You've described the Judeo-Christian ethic of multiplying, sub-duing, and replenishing the earth as an environmental disaster. You've also said technology is outstripping our respect for other species and the earth. Can we reverse these trends within the present context or do we need to make radical changes in the foundational models of how we think and live on Earth?

D B: I think our scientists have got to figure out how to undo the dam-age they've done. They've got a jump start on that because they know the processes they went through to cause the damage in the first place. For example, they have got to reverse what the CFCs are doing to the ozone layer. PCBs and CFCs were supposed to be the magical answer with no environmental problems. We now know they both cause huge environmental problems. Science gets blindsided by itself again and again. I think it's because there's far too much hubris among scientists. I think I'm arrogant enough, but they outdo me. They think they've got the answer. Well, I think I've got the answer: scientists shouldn't take anything apart unless they can put it back together; and they shouldn't put anything together unless they can take it apart.

J W: Why do you have faith in the same people and processes that have gotten us into this mess?

D B: It's the same kind of faith I have in people traveling the moun-tains. The rule is when you're lost you retrace your steps to the last rec-ognizable landmark. Then start out on the right track. It's only the scientists and the high-tech people who know how to undo the dam-age they've done. I wouldn't know where to start.

J W: Are scientists, loggers, miners, corporate executives really any more blameworthy than the rest of us? Isn't our addiction to a certain standard of living and our consequent silence about the risks of ex-ploitation a kind of collusion with all the processes that wreck the world?

D B: I would still rather point my finger at these people who sold us on consumerism and early obsolescence, and who essentially usurp the media that could otherwise help us correct our course. I just heard, for example, that the computer chips and raw materials that go into a computer are not designed to last more than ten years. When they build equipment for the army, on the other hand, they build to last. The engine in a 747 jet airplane goes and goes and goes. When they build a car, it goes for a while and that's all. Again and again, they're not offering us what we need, but what will make them money. And they're not interested in what the limits of the earth are in producing the materials that go into their products.

Big businesses don't produce lamps that are energy efficient. There are a few lamps on the market that use one-fourth the energy and last ten times as long as commercial brands, but they're not what you find at Safeway. And in Detroit, they don't produce the car that will get fifty miles per gallon. Instead of doing it themselves, they blame Japan for having done it. This is all part of recalling the acts of the Misfortune 500. The only way you can save yourself from this trend is not to watch television, read the papers, or listen to the radio, because they're all filled with a constant appeal to consume more.

J W: What do you think about the theories of Lovelock, Margulis, Gould, and others who suggest that ozone depletion, global warming, and other trends may be smaller cycles within a larger cycle over which we have less influence than we think?

D B: I think we *are* influencing these cycles. I am concerned about Mr. Lovelock. He doesn't seem to care if the earth goes on living with or without us. I'm rather prejudiced, because I'd like it to continue with us. I like his idea that life is an interrelated mechanism that lives on in one form or another, but I'd rather have the shorter view and do something that keeps human beings in some balance on the earth.

J W: How do you see our romance with the idea of space travel fitting in with our future on Earth?

DB: The problem with space travelers is they want to escape from the responsibility of having to do right by the earth. Freeman Dyson has imagined a nuclear-powered spaceship that can travel ten times as fast as the Apollo and he wants to get one of those going and visit other parts of the universe. But he had to stop the experiment when they prohibited further testing of nuclear material in the atmosphere. Meanwhile, his son George Dyson wanted to build seagoing canoes and visit other beaches. Freeman hasn't gotten off the planet yet, but George has seen a lot of beaches. George's goal is quite beautiful, I think: to find freedom without taking it from someone else. And, you could add, to find power without taking it from someone else, or, to find freedom and power by sharing them.

JW: On the one hand, it's easy to rationalize why Sam LaBudde needed to be surreptitious with his camcorder or why EarthFirst! activists thought of spiking trees to wake people up. But on the other hand, some of these methods seem to have at their roots a mentality similar to the people or corporations they're trying to stop. What role does respect or compassion play? Once you've got the footage of the dolphin slaughter, do you feel any responsibility to fair play—to confronting the perpetrators directly with your intentions?

DB: For better or worse, controversy is a terribly important part of educating the public. It gets their attention. No one's going to watch a football game if neither side tries to win. In the case of Sam and the tuna fleet, I think you have to build a power relation before you can hope to get anywhere. *Power* is a bad word, but nobody will pay attention unless there's enough fuss on the other side.

It's a complex issue, and I don't have the answer. In Nepal there are two sins: one is to make your child cry and the other is to embarrass someone. In our culture, we've made a virtue out of embarrassing people. As far as compassion is concerned, we have a lot to learn about that.

Living by Gaia

L YNN MARGULIS's resume is a thirty-page, single-spaced, small-print epic. She has written over 140 scientific articles (with titles such as *Ancient Locomotion: Prokaryotic Motility Systems* and *Homeostatic Tendencies of the Earth's Atmosphere*), fifty reviews, and eight books. Her first book, *Origin of Eukaryotic Cells,* was published in 1970, with its third version appearing in 1993 as *Symbiosis in Cell Evolution.* Several of her recent books, including *Microcosmos, Mystery Dance: On the Evolution of Human Sexuality,* and *The Garden of Microbial Delights* (a science book for middle school students and teachers), were coauthored with Dorion Sagan, Lynn's eldest son.

Lynn was born in Chicago in 1938, the eldest of four daughters. At age fourteen, she enrolled in an undergraduate program at the University of Chicago, where she was introduced to the natural sciences. After graduating, Lynn pursued an M.S. in zoology and genetics at the University of Wisconsin. In 1965, she received her Ph.D. in genetics from the University of California at Berkeley. In 1970, Lynn moved to Massachusetts where, over the following twenty-two years, she raised four children and rose through the ranks to professor at Boston University. She now teaches at the University of Massachusetts at Amherst.

Lynn is the reigning queen of the microcosmos, and especially the biological kingdom Protoctista, which includes an estimated 250,000 algae, seaweeds, amoebas, and other little-known life forms. It's here that she learned her lessons in radical scientific thinking. In the sixties she started looking for DNA where no microbiologist thought it could be found: outside the nucleus of the algal cell. She found it, and her discovery supported a revolutionary theory of symbiosis in the origin of the cell. There are four parts to the theory, three of which are now accepted in mainstream science.

The historian William Irwin Thompson once said of Lynn, "If you wish to carry on as a 'child of Gaia' or a 'healer of the planet,' one interested in getting back to nature, . . . then hold on to your environmentalist virginity, cross your mind, heart, and thighs, and don't read Margulis! . . . But, if you want to understand the intricate, fundamental systems by which life creates and maintains itself, then you just might find Margulis the right place to start all over again: from the ground up."

I flew into Amherst on the crest of a December storm. Lynn had had a party the night before with over a hundred guests, celebrating the release of *Concepts of Symbiogenesis*, by Liya Nikolaevna Khakhina, which Lynn had edited with a colleague. As usual, she had several conversations going at once. Before getting started on the interview, Lynn suggested we walk down to Nancy Jane's bakery to collect a batch of fresh muffins. Roosevelt, a midsized gray mutt Lynn had rescued from the animal shelter, was anxious to join us, so we followed him out the back door. Just through the hedge, we stumbled on the garden and red-brick home of Lynn's favorite poet, Emily Dickinson. "Do you know the poem about the hummingbird?" she asked, never skipping a beat. Off we went, pulled by Roosevelt and the poems and stories of a woman who, like Lynn, was a phenomenon of brilliance, energy, and love for life.

J ONATHAN WHITE: To get started, would you give a brief description of the Gaia hypothesis?

LYNN MARGULIS: The Gaia hypothesis states that certain conditions that sustain life are regulated by life itself. More specifically, the atmosphere and the sum of all life on the planet behave as a single integrated physiological system. The traditionally viewed "inert environment" is highly active, forming an integral part of the Gaian system.

The strongest evidence for Gaia comes from the study of atmospheric chemistry. The composition of the earth's atmosphere differs radically from our nearest neighbors, Mars and Venus. Both of these planets have a carbon dioxide–rich steady-state atmosphere. The composition of their atmospheres makes perfect chemical sense. The earth, however, is different. Loaded with reactive gases, its atmosphere makes no chemical sense whatsoever. For example, our air contains high levels of oxygen, nitrogen, and methane, among many other gases, which are violently reactive with each other. There is no way to explain this by chemistry alone. James Lovelock, the British atmospheric chemist who invented the Gaia hypothesis, puzzled over these atmospheric anomalies for a long time, concluding that the co-presence of such reactive gases are evidence that the atmospheric composition on Earth is actively regulated. The atmosphere is an extension of life. If the surface of the earth were not covered with oxygen-emitting algae and plants, methane-producing bacteria, hydrogen-producing fermenters, and countless other life forms, its atmosphere would long ago have reached the same steady state of Mars and Venus.

Another argument for Gaia comes from astronomy. According to accepted models, our sun is 30 to 70 percent hotter today than it was in the early history of life on the planet. If the earth's temperature were consistent with this increase in solar radiation, we would now be at a boiling point. But the temperature of the earth has remained relatively stable and conducive to life for all this time! Some argue that this stability is just geochemical coincidence. We think that exponentially growing populations of gas-producing organisms have actively maintained surface temperatures within a range suitable for life.

J W: You're always insistent that the Gaia hypothesis is James Lovelock's, but you're often regarded as co-creator of the theory. Lovelock himself claims you were the only scientist who would talk to him about the hypothesis. When did you first meet, and how did your collaboration evolve?

L M: I met James Lovelock in 1969, but he had developed the Gaia hypothesis before then. In 1965, Jim was hired by NASA to evaluate the experiments for detecting life on Mars. In his evaluation, he and his colleague Dian Hitchcock found that the NASA experiments were inappropriate. They were designed to detect life in a place where life as we know it may not exist. "It seemed," Jim said, "that we were sent on an expedition to find camels on the Greenland ice cap, or fish among the sand dunes of the Sahara." In re-visioning the NASA experiments, Lovelock was convinced that he could use the principles of his hypothesis to detect life on Mars without ever going there. All he needed to know was the rate of gas production and removal in the atmosphere, and if these rates could be explained by physics and chemistry alone, there would be no life. If the Martian atmosphere could not be explained with physics and chemistry alone, then the chances of finding life would be much greater.

Lovelock considered calling his theory the "Biocybernetic Universal System Tendency/Homeostasis." He was talked out of this name by William Golding, author of *Lord of the Flies* and Lovelock's walking companion. What Lovelock needed, Golding said, was a good four-letter word to get the attention of his colleagues. He suggested that the theory be named after the Greek goddess of the earth, Gaia.

Meanwhile, my own work in reconstructing the history of early life on the planet was revealing that bacteria produce and remove all sorts of atmospheric gases. It was well known that plants produce oxygen, but what about the other gases? What about nitrogen oxides, hydrogen sulfide, carbon dioxide, methane, and ammonia? One or another of these gases is emitted by every lineage of bacteria I studied. I kept asking, "Why do scientists agree that oxygen is a product of life, but never discuss the thirty-five or forty other atmospheric gases? Are they a product of life too?" About six scientists with whom I talked said, "Go talk to James Lovelock. He agrees with you." And I'd say, "What do you mean he agrees with me?" I didn't pay any attention to this for a long time, but finally I wrote him. He wrote back saying he'd be coming to Massachusetts soon, so we could talk in detail then. He also wrote that, according to his calculations, the amount of methane in the earth's atmosphere is off by an enormous factor. Given the temperatures, pressure, amount of oxygen and other gases in the atmosphere, and their known chemical reactions, there should be a virtually undetectable amount of methane. Yet methane is present in one or two parts per million everywhere. So, Lovelock asked in his letter, "Do you know of any biological process that could produce methane?" I was amused, because anybody who studies bacteria has heard of the methanogenic bacteria that live in anaerobic mud, cow rumen, and termites, among other places. They take in carbon dioxide and hydrogen and emit methane. I wrote Lovelock explaining this and he wrote again, confirming our meeting on his visit to New England. This was in 1972. And I remember the day he came to our family house in Newton, Massachusetts. When we answered the door, he said, "Hello, how are you? I answer to the name of Jim." He was very sweet and friendly. After a few minutes, he said, "You know, we've met before." And I said, "No, we haven't." "Yes," he said, "I'll tell you exactly when," and he pulled out a book called *The Origins of Life,* which I had edited in 1969. The book grew out of a very small meeting in Princeton that I had wheedled my way into because I was so fascinated by the topic. I think I was pregnant with my daughter, Jennifer, at the time. We looked at the list of attendees and, sure enough, Jim had been there. He had only spoken three sentences during the entire meeting. "Preston Cloud, the geologist, was so rude and aggressive to me," he said, "that I couldn't get my ideas out. I never said a word after the introductory session."

We had a wonderful meeting, and from then on we kept up a regular correspondence. Jim sent chemical queries asking for biological processes that would account for them. He was less conversant in microbiology than I, so I helped him bring microbial awareness to his work.

It took at least two years before I understood what Jim's Gaia hypothesis really meant. In 1972 a fortuitous thing happened. Stewart Wilson of Polaroid invited Jim and me to his interactive lecture laboratory to tape a conversation on Gaia. For hours we talked back and forth. Jim asked about methane, and I'd answer by explaining how methane was produced by bacteria. He'd ask why the earth is alkaline when our neighboring planets, Mars and Venus, are acidic. I'd suggest that ammonia, which is alkaline in water, is a common waste product of nitrogen metabolism. He asked if organisms could change the color of surface waters or sediments or if they could alter cloud coverage. He explained that the Gaia idea means that the earth's surface is controlled and regulated by the organisms. "You mean organisms adapt to their environment?" I'd say. "No," he'd answer.

At the end of four hours of dialogue, Stewart rewound the tape so we could hear how it came out. He pushed the playback button and sat down. There was no sound, nothing. Stewart had forgotten to turn the recording switch on! "Oh my God," says Lovelock, "what are we going to do? I'm only going to be here another two days." And Stewart says, "I either have to abandon this whole project or we tape all over again." As it turns out, having to retape the session was probably the most important thing that ever happened to the early development of the Gaia hypothesis. It took two days of sessions and the time in between for me to understand something about what Lovelock was trying to say. The tape of the second dialogue served as the basis for three important papers: two technical and one popular summary that was published in the *CoEvolution Quarterly* in 1975.

J W: There are some points of the Gaia hypothesis on which you and Lovelock disagree. What are they?

L M: A recent article in *Science* magazine said, "Margulis is well known as the fervent supporter of the controversial hypothesis that the earth is a single living organism." This kind of thing makes me angry because I never say the earth is a single, live organism. Lovelock might, but not me. It's a bad metaphor. It leads to goddesses, mysticism, and other misconceptions about Earth. The earth is an ecosystem, or the sum of many ecosystems. I see a big difference between a single organism and an ecosystem. For example, an organism produces gases, but it can't recycle its gaseous waste. It relies on the ecosystem for that.

J W: Lovelock likes to compare the earth with a giant redwood tree. The interesting thing to remember, he says, is that the middle of the tree is dead wood with just a thick skin of living tissue around the circumference. Beyond that there's another dead layer, the bark, which protects the tree from the environment. Lovelock says the earth is very much like that. You have the middle, which is molten and dead, a thin skin of living tissue around the circumference, and beyond that, the atmosphere, which is just like the bark of a tree.

L M: That's an interesting comparison that helps make my point. A tree is an extraordinarily complex community. It not only includes the life you can see—the bugs and worms and birds—but also the myriad of microorganisms that live on the tree and in the soil below. What we see is a composite organism but not an ecosystem. The tree needs the rest of the ecosystem of which it is a part to deliver its carbon dioxide and water and recycle the oxygen it produces as waste. I agree that a tree is a better analogy for the earth than a person, but there are still significant differences.

Lovelock would agree to all this, but he doesn't see a problem with using the metaphor of a living planet, particularly when speaking to the general public. He's a brilliant mischief maker, and realizes that people respond much more sympathetically to the image of a living planet than to a term like *ecosystem.* If the earth is alive, it's harder to justify kicking it around the way we do.

Our differences are probably just a matter of how we approach the public. Lovelock is much more negative than I toward the academic establishment. He thinks academics tend to do anything to keep themselves in business. Consequently, he doesn't trust them and prefers to take his case directly to the public. I am more circumspect about this, perhaps because I work within academia. I think we're much better off if we express ourselves carefully and enlist scientists who can help develop the hypothesis. Lovelock is certainly right when he says the image of the earth as an organism is far more moving than thinking of it as an ecosystem. But unscientific presentation alienates the very people we need most—the scientists, particularly geologists and biologists.

One of Lovelock's arguments for a life-centered metaphor is that we've lived too long with mechanistic metaphors. We think of life as a machine. We talk about the mechanisms of heredity, and we use defense analogies when we talk about fighting disease. I agree with Lovelock when he says, "What's wrong with having a living metaphor when the other metaphors are dead?" It's really just a matter of emphasis.

JW: Since the introduction of the Gaia hypothesis in 1972, both you and Lovelock have discovered that the idea is not necessarily new. Scientists such as Hutton, Lamarck, and Humbolt were emphasizing interdependence and relatedness in nature back in the eighteenth and early nineteenth centuries. Will you give a brief history of this kind of thinking?

LM: After the 1974 and 1975 publications, Jim and I started getting letters from all over the world with information about this way of thinking. We were both aware of the history of science, of course, but these letters brought to our attention a lot of unknown or previously obscure material.

James Hutton was one of the first persons to recognize that the proper study of the environment included the study of living organisms. He was a Scottish geologist, farmer, and natural philosopher who lived in the mid eighteenth century. Describing the earth as a "superorganism," Hutton compared the churning of soil and the cycling of water between the oceans and land over time with the circulation of blood. Coming out of the age of the lifeless mechanical sciences, Hutton's view of a cyclical, organic earth seems all the more revolutionary. He is the one who introduced the idea that life itself is a geological force, and that you can't study geology with only physics and chemistry.

The French naturalist Jean-Baptiste Lamarck, who lived about the same time as Hutton, also understood the planetary role of life, insisting on the link between geology, meteorology, chemistry, and evolutionary biology. "Living phenomena [do] not stand alone," he said, "but ha[ve] to be seen as part of a larger whole, nature; indeed, they [are] only comprehensible when their constant interaction with the nonliving world [is] recognized." Lamarck is better known for his work in botany and zoology, and especially evolutionary theory, but his scientific philosophy is a precursor to our modern ecological worldview. His theories are largely rejected and trivialized to "inheritance of acquired characteristics."

Most of these early ideas are completely ignored or misconstrued. Hutton is celebrated as a geologist, but his views on "geophysiology" and the environment are all but unknown. Lamarck is passé. He gets one or two negative lines in a large college textbook of biology, and that's it. Unfortunately, much of the advancement of science has come through the last two centuries by compartmentalization. The specialized disciplines paid little or no attention to each other, much less to the unity of nature as a whole. This was particularly true of the earth and life sciences, which ended up in separate buildings at the university, developing separate languages to address their separate fields. Lovelock calls this "academic apartheid," a phenomenon still prevalent today. Among the few scientists opposing this fragmentation of knowledge was the German geologist Alexander Von Humbolt, who lived and worked a little later than Hutton and Lamarck. He was a wonderfully dedicated scientist, working every day from the age of fourteen into old age. He was an accomplished cartographer too, and drew up plans for all kinds of weather instruments. The historian Jacques Grinvald says, "The evolution of living organisms, climate, ocean, and the earth's crust is in fact a grand scientific idea deeply rooted in the nineteenth-century scientific world view associated in particular with Humbolt." The wide influence of Humbolt's work can be seen in early American studies of biogeography and ecology as well as in the thinking of other prominent scientists such as Charles Darwin.

The work of Vladimir Vernadsky, the most significant predecessor of these ideas, was not known to me at all until about 1978, when Stewart Brand sent me a piece of his work. I nearly flipped when I read it. With the exception of a few fragments like the piece Stewart had, none of Vernadsky's work was available in English until the very skewed publication of *The Biosphere* in 1986, an edition I cannot recommend. This was nearly fifty years later than the original French publication in 1929, *La Biosphère*. In that book, Vernadsky presents the notion of the whole earth as an extraordinary single living phenomenon. He gives credit to the geologist Edouard Suess for having coined the term *biosphère* in 1875, but then takes the concept much further. To Vernadsky, the biosphere comprised the coevolution of "living matter" and the planetary environment of life. *Bio* means life and *sphere* means place, so *biosphere* is the sum of all life, including its environment. We owe our concept of the biosphere to Vernadsky.

In his wonderful book, *Traces of Bygone Biospheres,* A. V. Lapo says that Vernadsky's ideas were essentially unknown in the West except by G. Evelyn Hutchinson and Heinz Lowenstam. It was Vernadsky's son George, a Russian scholar at Yale, who introduced his father's ideas to the eminent ecologist Hutchinson in the late 1920s. Hutchinson was deeply impressed and helped to publish a summary of Vernadsky's work in the *American Scientist*. Ironically, the publication came out in January of 1945, just a few days after Vernadsky's death in Moscow. The geologist Heinz Lowenstam dedicated his life's work to the study of minerals made by living processes. In the early 1940s, it was said that silica and calcium carbonate—the materials that make up animal shells and coral reefs—were the only minerals made by life. Using Vernadsky's notions of life as a geochemical force, Lowenstam showed that over fifty minerals are the result of living processes.

These are just a few of the scientists who have influenced our present thinking about the earth. As I said earlier, their contributions concerning the earth as an integrated system that demands an interdisciplinary approach are not what you'd call mainstream ideas.

J w: The Gaia hypothesis, with its emphasis on mutualism and the reciprocity between life and the environment, appears to be a radically different view of evolution than Darwinism, which stresses natural selection through competition. Are these two theories really as incompatible as they seem?

L M: No, they're not. Lamarck, who was really the first evolutionist, said life is connected by common ancestry through time. *Evolution* means unfolding, literally, and refers to change through time. Astronomers talk about stellar evolution when describing the changes predicted for stars, and anthropologists speak of the evolution of cultural artifacts. When we talk about organic evolution, however, we're talking about the change in living organisms over the course of Earth's history. All modern biologists agree that evolution has occurred and that organisms are related. It's when we start talking about how evolution works that we get into big trouble.

It comes down to the question of how some beings survive and leave offspring and others don't. Who or what is doing the selecting? There are surely artificial selection pressures, such as the breeding of animals by human beings. In this case, humans choose traits they like, such as cuteness or meatiness or docility, and breed animals with those traits, over and over again. But what happens when there isn't an artificial selection process? Who or what does the selecting in the natural world? Is it God? Is it the environment? Is it the biota, the sum total of life on Earth?

Darwin, who was a Lamarckian, emphasized that evolution happens by "natural selection," which has come to be understood as the "survival of the fittest." These are the prevailing Western terminologies, but even the most devout followers of Darwin admit that evolution is not a single, simple process.

An example of one aspect of this process is the potential for runaway population growth that is present in every organism. Some fungi produce one hundred thousand spores per minute. Dogs can have six or seven puppies per litter three times a year. If two elephants can have four elephants, and all of them live, it wouldn't take long before the world would be completely populated with elephants. These organisms don't often realize their reproduction rate, but the potential is absolutely intrinsic to living phenomena. So why is the potential never reached? Numerous environmental factors prevent this from happening. Usually, over 99 percent of offspring die because of restrictions such as lack of food, space, water, predation, disease, and so on. Darwin called these checks, and these checks are the essence of natural selection. The fact that the potential for runaway population growth is present but never fully realized is natural selection. This selecting process works on all organisms at every stage of their lives.

Up to this point, there is no contradiction between Darwinism, or even neo-Darwinism, which is the combination of Darwin's views and modern population genetics, and the Gaia hypothesis. What people miss is that it's Gaia, the ecosystem of the earth, that keeps any given population potential in check. Life regulates life. Gaia itself does the "natural selecting." Our critics don't understand this at all. Some insist that evolution is contradictory with Gaia. The truth is, the Gaian view simply includes the environment as an evolutionary factor.

j w: Are you saying that Darwin is misinterpreted?

L M: Yes, both Darwin and Lovelock are misinterpreted. Darwin was a wonderful biologist, but he was also full of contradictions. So full of contradictions, in fact, that you can find evidence in his work to support almost anything. Although he was anthropocentric at times, he also acknowledged the ancestral connection between human beings and other mammals. He discouraged the use of judgmental terms in evolution, such as describing one form as better or higher than another. Instead, he preferred to say that one form is more suitably adapted to a particular environment than another. One criticism of Darwin is his lack of consideration for the environment. In his view, organisms adapt to the environment as if it were some independent entity with a capital *E*. There is no acknowledgment whatsoever of an active, mutually constructive exchange between any given life form and its living environment. The Gaian view, which accepts this mutual exchange, does not contradict Darwin's vision but takes it a step further.

It's no longer sufficient to study only biology in the pursuit of how evolution works. We need other sciences, especially geology and chemistry, if we're going to have any hope of understanding the whole system. The neo-Darwinist view, which is our present paradigm for scientific thinking in the West, denies the need for chemistry, climatology, geology, comparative planetology, and the like. Instead, it promotes the capitalistic view that organisms succeed over time just because they leave the most progeny or are better at outwitting their neighbors.

J W: Richard Dawkins, author of *The Selfish Gene,* is an outspoken critic of the Gaia hypothesis. He claims that life is made up of a network of small, self-interested components. A neo-Darwinist, Dawkins says, "Entities that pay the costs of furthering the well-being of the ecosystem as a whole will tend to reproduce themselves less successfully than rivals that exploit their public-spirited colleagues, and contribute nothing to the general welfare." Along with Dawkins, other scientists such as Ford Doolittle and Stephen Jay Gould insist that regulation of the planet by the biota would require foresight and planning—a kind of global-scale altruism that could not evolve through natural selection. Because the earth itself does not reproduce, there would be no pressure for it to evolve as "the most fit planet." How do you respond to these criticisms?

L M: Neo-Darwinism's current funk over altruism reflects a failure to comprehend that every organism is part of a larger ecosystem, a system on which it depends for respiratory gas, water, food, and a sink for waste products. Are bacteria "public-spirited" in ridding themselves of their waste, which happens to be the oxygen necessary for the other organisms in the system? Are those bacteria that don't produce oxygen "cheating" and thus at a reproductive advantage? I don't think so. Dawkins's claim that the Gaia hypothesis cannot be true because there is no evidence for competition between Earth and its neighboring planets reflects a preoccupation with the romantic, Victorian conception of evolution as a prolonged and bloody battle. Life, according to the neo-Darwinists, is a collective of individuals who reproduce, mutate, and reproduce their mutations. These mutations are assumed to arise by chance. The life-centered alternative to this view recognizes that, with the exception of bacteria, individuals with single genetic systems don't exist. All other living organisms, such as animals, plants, and fungi, are complex communities of multiple, tightly organized beings. What we generally accept as an individual animal, such as a cow, is really a collection of entities that together form an "emergent domain." The hind-gut of a termite, for example, is loaded with over twenty-five different kinds of bacteria and protists. Each of these organism types evolved over millions of years to perform a role in the "domain" that we recognize as a "termite." Without them, the termite would starve to death, because it alone is unable to digest wood. Yet termites acquire their vital supply of bacteria and protists not through their genes but in a peculiar ritual of feeding on the anal fluid of their fellow termites. There are dozens of examples of this mutual reliance, or what the philosopher Gail Fleischaker would call nestedness, in nature.

In this view, organisms do not compete in the neo-Darwinian sense—"nature, red in tooth and claw"—nor are they selected by God or some other "higher intelligence." It's not the individual but the community of life that evolves by cooperation, interaction, and mutual dependence. Life did not take over the globe by combat but by networking. As the philosopher David Abram says, "The interaction of life and the environment is more a dialogue where the environment puts questions to the organism and the organism, in answering those questions, puts new questions to the environment. The environment, in turn, answers with further questions."

J W: Some argue that while the Gaia hypothesis is a good idea, promoting a much-needed shift from a human-centered to a life-centered perspective, it is not—and never will be—provable. What is the current status on the search for mechanisms that demonstrate the existence of planetary regulation?

L M: Some work is being done, but it's a slow and complicated process. A current example is the study on cloud formation and temperature regulation over the ocean. Robert Charlson, an atmospheric scientist from the University of Washington in Seattle, has found that certain marine algae produce compounds that enter the atmosphere. Once there, they serve as particles around which clouds form. In warm temperatures, the algae bloom, causing more clouds. The increasing clouds reflect the sun's light and warmth back up into the atmosphere, causing cooler temperatures and fewer algae. Fewer algae means fewer clouds, and fewer clouds mean a rise in temperature. With that, the cycle begins again. The net result is temperature regulation. Although this is an oversimplified presentation, it's a good example of how organisms affect the environment without sitting around in a committee and deciding what or how to regulate. I've seen satellite photographs of these tiny algae on the ocean's surface that extend fifty by two hundred kilometers.

Any mechanism that's regulating life has some sort of sensor that sends a signal to an amplifier. This is part of any feedback system, whether it be Gaian or manmade. The thermostat in your home is a sensor that sends a signal to the furnace, which amplifies the signal by turning on and generating heat. In the example I just gave of cloud-temperature regulation over the ocean, light or temperature is the signal these tiny algae receive. The amplifier is the potential for runaway population growth, which we talked about earlier. With lots of light and warm temperatures, these algae grow exponentially until, as a result of their growth, their conditions change again. The new signal, generated by more clouds, is less light or cooler temperatures. Thus the cycle reverses itself. This is the essence of a positive and negative feedback system. Now, what's the difference between a manmade and a Gaian system? A manmade system is modeled by an engineer; in the Gaian system, feedback is an intrinsic property of the living system itself.

I see two basic approaches to the search for natural feedback systems. The first approach uses a model that results from the observation of global phenomena, like the temperature regulation by algae that I just described. The second approach attempts to remove the living elements of a miniaturized system in order to measure the effect their absence has on the rest of the system. Schwartzman, a geologist from Howard University in Washington, used this method in his studies of weathering. Until he proved differently, the breakdown of rock was considered only a physical and chemical process, primarily involving erosion by water and wind. Nobody who studied weathering needed to know anything about biology. By removing the organisms in a miniaturized system, Schwartzman found that the rate of weathering was reduced by a factor of a thousand! This is a great example of how the Gaia hypothesis, whether it's true or not, is promoting new scientific inquiry. Because of the obvious problems of miniaturizing a system or isolating elements within it, these experiments are not done often. Biosphere projects, like Biosphere II in Arizona, are another good example of this kind of approach.

When it was first stated, the Gaia hypothesis had three parts to it: temperature regulation, chemical regulation (oxygen, nitrogen, methane, and so on), and acidity/alkalinity (pH) regulation. New research, generated by the hypothesis itself, has revealed that the regulation and distribution of heavy metals such as gold, iron, manganese, and copper may be added to that list. Water salinity in the oceans may be regulated by Gaia, too. We know that tons of salts are deposited there each year by streams and rivers. With no mechanism for removal, the salinity of the oceans should steadily increase, yet it has remained relatively stable for over five hundred million years. Why? I'm convinced that we'll eventually discover a Gaian mechanism for salt regulation. And, in that process, my suspicion is that we'll find evidence to support the argument that life influences lateral plate movement also.

A most striking current possibility is that life may play a role in retaining water on this planet. Venus and Mars are both very dry. Why? Because the elements—principally hydrogen—that water comprises escape from the atmosphere into space. In fact, it looks like a whole ocean's worth of water has escaped from Mars and Venus! The ozone layer in our atmosphere, which is made by life, prevents the loss of water to the upper atmosphere. That's one way life might be regulating the retention of water, but there are other ways, too. For example, the scum that grows over the surface of ponds and lakes helps to prevent evaporation.

Ultimately, it doesn't matter whether the hypothesis is proved or not. The fact that it has generated new thoughts and new work is the best evidence of its value. It may be that all these experiments will show that life makes no difference at all, that the surface of the earth is run completely by nonliving properties. That's one solution. Another solution is that life determines *all* regulation. The answer, of course, is probably somewhere in between. For example, no one claims that the amounts of neon, krypton, helium, and argon in the earth's atmosphere are regulated by life. These gases, unlike carbon, nitrogen, and hydrogen, are not reactive.

J W: In *Microcosmos,* you say that the ancestor of all life first appeared in the form of bacterial cells 3.5 billion years ago. These earliest forms of life learned almost everything there is to know about living in a system, and what they learned is, principally, what we know today. These bacteria are still with us, you say, in our DNA and in our consciousness. We are surrounded by them and composed of them. This not only challenges the way we look at ourselves as individuals, but also the way we look at time and history.

L M: The past is all around us. Darwin's biggest contribution was to show us that all individual organisms are connected through time. It doesn't matter whether you compare kangaroos, bacteria, humans, or salamanders, we all have incredible chemical similarities. As far as I know, no one disagrees with this. Vernadsky showed us that organisms are not only connected through time but also through space. The carbon dioxide we exhale as a waste product becomes the life-giving force for a plant; in turn, the oxygen waste of a plant gives us life. This exchange of gas is what the word *spirit* means. Spirituality is essentially the act of breathing. But the connection doesn't stop at the exchange of gases in the atmosphere. We are also physically connected, and you can see evidence of this everywhere you look. Think of the protists that live in the hind-gut of the termite, or the fungi that live in the rootstock of trees and plants. The birds that flitter from tree to tree transport fungi spores throughout the environment. Their droppings host a community of insects and microorganisms. When rain falls on the droppings, spores are splashed back up on the tree, creating pockets for life to begin to grow again. This interdependence is an inexorable fact of life. As Vernadsky said, without this interdependence, no organism can hope to survive.

The fact that we are connected through space and time shows that life is a unitary phenomenon, no matter how we express that fact. We are not one living organism, but we constitute a single ecosystem with many differentiated parts. I don't see this as a contradiction, because parts and wholes are nested in each other.

J W: Biologically speaking, does all this mean we're not different than our hunter-gatherer ancestors of ten thousand years ago?

L M: We're somewhat different, of course. The corn seed you plant today is not exactly the same as the one you planted last year. There are differences and similarities, both.

We think of change in qualitative, hierarchical terms. We think of life as starting from a single cell and becoming more complex until we arrive at humankind, the pinnacle of evolutionary accomplishment. Most accounts of evolution don't even begin until a few hundred million years ago. But life began long before that. Of the 3.5 billion years that life has existed on Earth, the entire history of human beings from the cave to the condominium represents less than one-tenth of 1 percent. Feeding, moving, mutating, sexually recombining, photosynthesizing, reproducing, overgrowing, predacious, and energy-expanding symbiotic microorganisms preceded all animals and all plants by at least one billion years. Our powers of intelligence and technology, then, do not belong specifically to us but to all life. As Lewis Thomas says, "For all our elegance and eloquence as a species, for all our massive frontal lobes, for all our music, we have not progressed all that far from our microbial forebears. They are still with us, part of us. Or, to put it another way, we are part of them."

Life is a continuous phenomenon. You can't point to any of the great global catastrophes, like the one that wiped out the dinosaurs during the Cretaceous period sixty-five million years ago, and say that it extinguished *all* life. It's true that thousands of species are now extinct, and that life itself has undergone huge changes in composition and detail. But in spite of all this, life's connection through space and time remains essentially unbroken.

J W: Apparently there have been over thirty of these catastrophic events in Earth's history, all of which were thousands of times more severe than anything humans can generate, including an all-out nuclear war. If the Gaian system is not threatened by these events, doesn't that shed a new light on the movement to "save the earth?"

LM: Absolutely. It's not the earth that's in jeopardy, it's the middle-class Western life-style. Soil erosion, loss of nutrients, methane production, ozone depletion, deforestation, and the loss of species diversity may all be Gaian processes, but surely our behavior has accentuated them to the point of near catastrophe. It's quite possible that our ecocidal environmental policies and our insidious overpopulation will stress the system to such an extent that the earth will roll over into another steady-state regime, which may or may not include human life.

The idea that we are "stewards of the earth" is another symptom of human arrogance. Imagine yourself with the task of overseeing your body's physiological processes. Do you understand the way it works well enough to keep all its systems in operation? Can you make your kidneys function? Can you control the removal of waste? Are you conscious of the blood flow through your arteries, or the fact that you are losing a hundred thousand skin cells a minute? We are unconscious of most of our body's processes, thank goodness, because we'd screw it up if we weren't. The human body is so complex, with so many parts, yet it is only one infinitesimally small part of the Gaian system, a system which is far more complex than we can fully imagine. The idea that we are consciously caretaking such a large and mysterious system is ludicrous.

Many things we must do are more simple and straightforward than steering the planet into the future. We must stop using plastics for packaging or throw-away products such as fishing nets and champagne cups. We must stop using paper and plastic plates and tiny bottles of shampoo. We must use more silk, which is strong and durable as well as biodegradable. We could distribute grains grown in the Midwest to countries that need them. We must vastly improve the education of our children. So many things we can do are simple and tangible, yet living in an anti-intellectual country, we seem to lack the political will.

We need to recognize that humans have a large effect on the environment but relatively little effect on any idealized planetary system.

Ultimately, it's the quality of life for humankind and other large animals that we affect most profoundly by our behavior. I don't think we should feel embarrassed or ashamed to show concern for our own survival. The earth will live on until the sun dies—it's just a question of whether we'll be a part of its future.

Life-Ways of the Hunter

RICHARD NELSON is a writer and cultural anthropologist who has been studying native peoples and their relationship to nature for nearly thirty years. In 1961, as a sophomore in biology at the University of Wisconsin, Richard joined a summer expedition to study fish and intertidal fauna off the coast of Kodiak Island. It was his first venture North, but one that led him back two years later as a research assistant on an archaeological project in the Aleutian Islands. His increasing fascination with the North and Northern cultures turned his interests at the university from biology to anthropology. "After all," he says, "it was not nature in and of itself that intrigued me, but the way people interacted with it."

Over the following fifteen years, Richard traveled and lived among many native people of the North, including Inupiaq Eskimos, Gwich'in people (inland Athabascan Indians), and the Koyukon. Four books grew out of these experiences: *Hunters of the Northern Ice* (1969), *Hunters of the Northern Forest* (1973), *Shadow of the Hunter* (1980), and *Make Prayers to the Raven* (1983).

Richard's newest book, *The Island Within,* is a more personal exploration of his relationship with nature and home. It received the John Burroughs Award for Nature Writing in 1991. Richard is currently working on a book about North American deer. Since receiving his Ph.D. in anthropology in 1971, he has taught at the University of Hawaii, the Memorial University of Newfoundland, the Universities of California at Santa Barbara and Santa Cruz, and the University of Alaska at Fairbanks.

The following interview took place on a small island just off the coast of Richard's home in southeast Alaska. Though we were in the middle of a dark, cold, wet Alaskan winter, Richard was out hiking, surfing, hunting, and exploring the coast. I followed along with as little complaint as possible, pausing to join him for an occasional peanut butter and salmonberry sandwich or a candy bar, and then moving on. As it happened, we came to rest on two soaked logs in the muskeg, talking between bites of sandwich and watching for deer.

~·~·~

JONATHAN WHITE: What first led you to live with native people?

RICHARD NELSON: I was studying at the University of Wisconsin when a professor who knew of my interest in northern cultures asked me if I wanted to go live with the Inupiaq Eskimos on the Arctic coast. It was part of a project funded by the Air Force to learn how these people hunted, traveled, and survived on the sea ice. With that information, the Air Force wanted to write a manual to aid pilots who might crash on the ice. I was twenty-two years old at the time and I felt that if I was going to write about how Eskimo people hunt and travel, I would have to learn how to do those things myself. So I bought dogs, made a dogsled and harnesses, and learned how to drive a dog team. I also bought a rifle and Eskimo people taught me how to hunt in their way. I spent a year doing that, and it was really my first year living away from my home in Madison, Wisconsin.

My ideas about how to live, and especially my ideas about hunting, completely changed in that year. Not only had I never hunted, but I was always emphatically opposed to it. That year I found myself living with people whose whole lives were completely focused on hunting. We hunted seals and caribou in winter and bowhead whales and walrus in the spring. I went along with them and hunted just exactly as they did.

J W: What were your strongest impressions—particularly the ones that changed your own views—of living with Eskimo people?

R N: What struck me most forcefully was how much the Eskimo people know about the animals and about their environment. I had never encountered that level of knowledge, especially not in the biology department of the university. Professors and university scientists don't know animal behavior and ecology in the same way people do when their everyday life centers around animals. Eskimos study animals as intensively as any biologist, but their knowledge is not as esoteric; it's based on hunting these animals for survival. As a consequence, they have tremendous practical knowledge and insight into animals.

The second thing that impressed me about the Eskimos was the passion with which they pursued animals, not just in the hunt, but also in the pursuit of knowledge about them. There again, I don't think I had ever experienced anything like the intensity with which they lived in relationship with animals.

The greatest hunter in the village where I lived was an old man named Wesley Ekak. His sense about animals was so profound that the distinction between his humanness and the animal's animalness seemed blurred. One spring, for example, we were camped out on the edge of the ice while hunting for whales. We hadn't seen one in three or four days because apparently the ice was closed up somewhere south of us. There were six or seven of us inside the tent, and the old man—he must have been about seventy at the time—was lying on his caribou skin mattress with his eyes closed, smoking a cigarette. Suddenly he said, "I think a whale is going to come." Then, after a short time, he said, "I think it's going to come up really close." To my amazement, all the men got up in a hurry and went out to get their hunting gear ready. As the last guy left the tent, I felt so ridiculous that I got up, too. I remember saying to Ekak, who was the only person who hadn't moved at all, "Well, I guess I'll go out and see if you're right." Before I got five steps out of the tent, a whale blew right in front of me, just off the ice edge.

There was no normal way Ekak could have known the whale was around. It was the only one we saw in three days. No one mentioned a word about it except Ekak, who said later, "There was a ringing in my ears."

Another thing about hunting that struck me was a personal thing. For the first time in my life, I found myself engaged in the entire process of keeping myself alive, and it was a tremendous breakthrough in my understanding of where my life comes from. I remember wondering why this hunting life was so satisfying. Part of it was that I was involved with the whole process of keeping myself alive, from the often laborious and lengthy process of finding an animal to killing it, taking it apart, and then learning how it becomes food. I had never done any of that before. Food had always come out of the store. The deep sense of satisfaction I discovered in that process has never changed.

J W: By the time you went to live with the Koyukon people of the Alaskan interior in 1976, you were quite a bit older and had had several other experiences living with native peoples of the North. What had changed for you in your approach to that study?

R N: By the time I went to live with Koyukon people, my orientation toward working with Native Americans had changed a lot. I felt it was not ethically justifiable to go and live in a community, study the people, and then just take away the knowledge. That approach leaves them with essentially nothing in return except the entertainment value of having a buffoon living in their community. As an anthropologist living in a Native American community, I had to have something more specific and practical to give them in return to justify my being there.

The research I did with Koyukon people was designed to provide the National Park Service with information on the traditional uses of the Koyukon homelands. Specifically, I wanted to show the National Park Service how people used these lands that were about to become parks so that the native people wouldn't be evicted once the park was established. That was the first and most important work with Koyukon people. The work I did in gathering information on their spiritual life was something I did more for myself.

JW: It's clear from ethnographic studies that there is much we can learn from native cultures. But do we tend to idealize them? Are the native people you lived with really as conscientious about environmental issues as is commonly believed?

RN: It's fashionable among certain academics and highly rational skeptics to try to prove Native American people were just as bad as we are. As an anthropologist, I think there is enormous ethnographic evidence supporting the fact that Native American people did and still do have a very strong sense of conservation. The principles that the Koyukon people follow in their relationship with the natural world are essentially universal. You find these principles practiced by traditional people everywhere in the world.

We also have to remember that in any culture there are individuals who follow the moral code to the letter and there are individuals who completely disregard it. Secondly, cultures or communities don't always follow their beliefs to the letter. In any traditional culture, you'll find times when people don't behave as their own culture says they should. Almost any Koyukon person can tell you about a time when he or she violated the code of respect toward an animal and suffered for it.

We generalize when we expect people in other cultures to behave like automatons. That's not how human society works. But even if it could be shown that Native American people routinely violated their own rules, we can still learn from their principles of respect, restraint, and responsible conservation toward the natural world. It wouldn't matter if no one had ever followed these principles. They're there, and they've worked beautifully over the whole face of North America, expressed in millions of different ways.

The Koyukon people have a very sophisticated, empirically based system of conservation, of so-called resource management. In Western culture, we are discovering the same thing. It's a *re*discovery, really. What's wonderful is that, by a different route, we're coming back to see the resounding wisdom in these older ways. I see it as strengthening the position in favor of conservation among all the cultures. One truth demonstrates and reinforces the truth of the other. It's a good complement.

J w: If it's true that our sense of nature—and indeed our *experience* of nature—is determined by our cultural bias, can we ever fully understand, much less follow, the example of native people?

R N: I don't think we can ever trust the idea that we really understand what someone from another culture thinks or believes or how they perceive the world. I don't even know if we should try. We're deeply different groups of people. Perhaps the only way to truly understand another culture is to be raised in it. As an ethnographer, I was always struck by how little I could understand. I found that really frustrating. I wouldn't want anyone to read an ethnography and believe it represented the whole truth about another culture. But when we look at the premises on which a balanced relationship to the natural world is based, it seems to me that we can find a common sense of what is right and wrong.

The natural world responds to us in a universal language. If we're behaving badly, the world will tell us. If you're a trapper, for example, your luck will disappear if you trap out all the beavers and beaver houses in your trapline. You'll get a message back the next year that you made a mistake. A Koyukon hunter once told me with great pride, "I've trapped this country for the whole fifty years of my life, and it's just as rich today as it was when I first started hunting here." So, if you overuse or disrespect the environment, you'll get a message back. And isn't that exactly what's happening to us now? On a much larger scale, aren't we getting messages back that what we're doing is wrong? The message comes to us in the form of cancers that invade our bodies, in the changing climate, in the erosion of soil, in the progressive diminution of the capacity of the earth to sustain us. So, in the sense of feedback, the same experiences that have been happening to native people all over the world for thousands of years are now happening to us, only on a larger scale. The message is that we can't go on living like this.

J W: In *Make Prayers to the Raven* you write that the Koyukon believe the world is alive and ever aware. Because of this, a proper spiritual balance between the human and nonhuman world is essential. Will you explain that further?

R N: The most essential fact of Koyukon people's relationship to the natural world is that everything in nature has a spirit—every plant, every animal, the physical earth, everything. This spirit has power that gives the world an awareness of what people do in relation to it. If you do something disrespectful toward an animal or plant, for example, you will offend its spirit. The offense will bring you bad luck, and for a hunter that generally means bad luck in hunting. The animal you offend won't allow you to take it. It's as if the animal becomes invisible. If you see it, it's just a fleeting glimpse; or if you get a chance to shoot at it, you'll miss.

In our culture, we believe if you treat other people disrespectfully, it will come back to you in some way. We often talk about it in terms of bad karma. If you're disrespectful toward a person, that person won't like you and will avoid or shun you. The exact same principle applies for Koyukon people, only it applies to the whole world, not just to other people. The Koyukon people have taken the principles of morality and ethics and respect to include the entire world in which they live, rather than just other humans.

The Koyukon world is surrounded with spiritual power. They are never removed from this spirituality, whether they're dealing with a brown bear, a shrew, a tree, or a raven. That's why I've always had this image of a forest of eyes. When you're out in the forest, the Koyukon believe that all the trees know you're there. The tree you're leaning against knows you're leaning against it, and the animals on this island know what you're saying.

From the Koyukon view, animals possess qualities that westerners consider exclusively human. They have a range of emotion, for example, and distinct personalities. They communicate among themselves and they understand human behavior and language. Animals are constantly aware of what people say and do and their presiding spirits are easily offended by disrespectful behavior.

j w: You've written about the many rules that govern conduct and preserve the spiritual balance between nature and the Koyukon. Can you give some examples?

r n: For Koyukon people, bears are among the strongest animals spiritually. And the strongest and most dangerous of all bears is the brown bear. In a place like this, a Koyukon person would be careful not to say anything bad about brown bears. In fact, for fear of causing offense, they'd be reluctant even to say the name of brown bear in this place.

Stephen and Catherine Attla, two of my most important teachers, came to visit me once in a little village in southeast Alaska. We were out in my boat, floating down a river, when all of a sudden Catherine started acting really strange. "There's something over there, there's something over there," she said. Several minutes later, Stephen and I saw that there was a brown bear right across the river. We hadn't seen it, but she had. In the Koyukon way, it was bad manners for her to look at it, point at it, say its name, or in any way indicate to us where or what it was.

Another aspect of this is the Koyukon belief that life leaves an animal slowly. It doesn't die the minute it becomes still on the ground. And with powerful animals like bears, it can take years for all the life to go out of it. During that time, its life lingers. It's aware of you, and there are certain rules that need to be followed.

For example, a bear hide keeps its power for a long time, and so Koyukon people as a rule don't take them. When they kill a bear, they leave the bear's hide out in the woods. When they used black bear hides in the old days, they would leave them out in the woods for often as long as a year. It would take that long for the life to drain out of it, and only then would it be safe to be around.

An old man once told me that every hair on a brown bear's hide has a life of its own. He meant this literally. "The brown bear's hide is so full of life, so full of physical and spiritual power," he said, and that's one of the reasons they have such a vitriolic temper.

J w: So an animal doesn't just represent spirit, it is spirit.

R N: When a Koyukon person tells me, "When you say an animal's name, you're calling its spirit," I can't say I know exactly what that means. I don't know if they do either. It's hard for someone from Western culture to understand this way of seeing the world. I spent only a few years with the Koyukon, only long enough to understand a small part of their beliefs. It's like asking a minister in our culture about Christian theology. You could spend a lifetime studying and still feel like you understand only a small part of it.

If I make an insulting remark about brown bear, people might say, "Good grief, you're going to pay for that." The point is that the invisible spiritual life that surrounds the bear is just as real as the physical things that surround it.

I was sitting out on the edge of a muskeg once with an old man named Grandpa Joe. We were talking quietly when a bird landed on top of a nearby tree and started making a lot of noise. I picked up a pair of binoculars and walked out onto the muskeg to get a closer look. I had never seen a bird like it before, so I asked Grandpa Joe what kind it was. He looked and then listened for awhile. Finally he said, "I don't know!" Perplexed, he got up and walked closer. Then he started talking to it in the Koyukon language, saying, "Who are you? What are you saying to us?" He was deeply concerned because for Koyukon people strange events in the natural world have the potential of being an omen. He talked to it for awhile, and then referred to it by some kinship term, and said, "I wish you would surround us in a circle of protection."

Throughout most of human history it would have been perfectly normal to see a man talking to a bird and asking it for protection. Yet to me it was one of the most powerful and astonishing things I had ever experienced.

The Koyukon understand that nature interacts with us and that we're a part of the whole community, and to talk to nature is perfectly normal. The lack of this understanding in our own culture is where the depth and poignancy of our loss lies. Losing the recognition of spirituality in nature may be the most important transformation of the human mind in all of human history. Surely it has the greatest consequences. That's why I believe that regaining respect is the most important thing we could ever do.

J W: If everything is so aware, when you hunt for deer is there a sense in which it, too, is choosing to be taken? Is the deer giving itself to you?

R N: Both Koyukon and Eskimo people say that animals give themselves to the hunter. Koyukon people say that when a hunter has a long history of respect toward a particular kind of animal, those animals will give themselves to him or to her. The Koyukon people wouldn't say, "I'm a good hunter." In the first place, that would be bragging; in the second place, it would be taking credit for something given to you. If your friends give you a lot of nice gifts at Christmas, you don't say, "I'm really good at Christmas." You say, "I'm lucky to have friends who are so generous to me." Similarly, the hunter among Koyukon people will say, "Well, I had luck; I was lucky," or some people will even say, "I am lucky with a certain kind of animal."

There's a word in the Koyukon language, *bik'uhnaatltonh,* which means, "something took care of him." If a hunter goes out and has good luck, gets a good moose or a bear or something, people will say, *bik'uhnaatltonh,* "something took care of him." Now isn't that different from our own tradition—including our own traditional hunting—where we take personal credit for our skill in getting what we get out of the earth?

These same ideas are the basis of my own life as a hunter. I won't say I absolutely believe there's a spirit in everything in the natural world, but I believe that I should behave as if there were. One of my favorite quotes is from Robert Aitken, who writes in his book *Taking the Path of Zen,* "Even if it could be shown that Shakyamuni never lived, the myth of his life would be our guide." That's the principle I follow with respect to Koyukon beliefs: these things may or may not be true, but I should behave as if they are. I try to follow the lessons I learned from the Koyukon as carefully as I can.

J W: When hunting, it seems that you can't focus too much on any single thing, but that you must be aware of many things at once.

R N: The best lessons I learned about attention are from Eskimo people. When they hunted seals on the sea ice, they taught me how it was dangerous to focus all your attention on one thing. On the sea ice, for example, you never know when the ice is going to move or crack. If it does, it could be fatal. Also, a polar bear could be stalking the same seal you are. On the island here, the same thing is true for me.

Hunting is the most focused activity of my life. Nothing I do, whether it's bird-watching, picture-taking, or hiking through the woods, can draw the same level of attention out of me. I can come out here and spend all day hunting and have several hours at a time pass without ever noticing. I'm a really fidgety person—not the sort who can sit around—but hunting for me can be almost hypnotic. It's like a walking meditation. But my attention is not exclusively on deer, because here on the island I always need to be aware of whether there's a bear around. That's much more important to me than knowing if there's a deer around, because out here I'm not necessarily on top of the food chain. There's one animal here that could be hunting me. So, it would be foolish to focus entirely on my own hunting and forget that something else might also be hunting me.

I don't know of anything in my life where I use my eyes more intensely than in hunting. I'm always looking at the bushes to see if a branch has been nipped off, or at the ground to see if there are any tracks or fresh droppings, or I'm watching my dog, Keta, to see what she's doing. I'm also watching ravens, because Koyukon people say ravens tuck their wing and roll halfway over in the sky when there's an animal below. They'll make a particular sound, too, that goes *gaaga! gaaga!* The Koyukon people say that sound is the word *ggaagga*, which means animal. I follow a raven if it's doing that because more often than not I find a deer there.

J W: Hunting seems both a physical and a spiritual seeking—an invitation to encounter our own mortality, our own animalness.

R N: I think most of my sense about being connected to the natural world of animals and plants is because of being a hunter. I want to say again that I grew up thinking that hunting was a wrong thing to do. But I feel now that when you take responsibility for the taking of a life to nourish your own life, you're engaging yourself fully in your own connectedness to the natural world. It's important to remember that all of us are just as connected to the natural world as every other person. An Australian Aborigine, a pygmy, or a bushman living with stone tools and hide clothing sewn with sinew is no more connected to the natural world than a person living in the middle of New York City. Every one of us is 100 percent connected to the natural world during every instant that we're alive. The difference is in the level of ignorance and denial. We've forgotten our connection to the natural world in part because we have delegated the responsibilities of killing our food to someone else.

When you go out and harvest your own food, you get a deeper awareness of what your body is made of. The body that I harvest comes into me and becomes my body. I don't know anything else that teaches that lesson better than actually going out and fishing or hunting or gathering foods or growing a garden. Although I do all those things, nothing teaches these lessons with the force and power that hunting does. When you hunt it's so much more evident that the life you take into yourself is the same kind of life you possess. The fact that a plant can fully nourish my biological life and that my biological life, in turn, can serve as nutrients to sustain the life of a plant, demonstrates that the plant and I have exactly the same kind of life. Because we can pass it back and forth between us, there's no difference in the quality of our living nature, the plant and me. It happens that in my case a lot of the plant food comes to me through deer. The deer eats the plant and I eat the deer.

As a culture we have largely forgotten that each of us lives by taking other life. There isn't any alternative. What I think is more important than wringing our hands over this fact is simply to live in daily awareness of it, to sit down at the table and let our mind have at least a moment of gratitude for the other lives that nurture our lives and to recognize that the process of life and death is a beautiful thing in which we are all fully engaged. There is no life of *any* kind without death. Each life is nourished by thousands of little deaths, and then that life in turn becomes one of the many deaths that nourishes other life. That's the way it is. If we'd stop worrying about it and immerse ourselves in the beauty of that process, I think we'd be much healthier as a culture.

JW: Causing death challenges our conscience. Why is it so much more difficult to cause the death of a warm-blooded, furry animal than a plant?

RN: When we kill an animal, that death is in a sense our own death. We look at it and we can't help but see our own mortality. The death of a warm-blooded, furry animal is particularly vivid and poignant. I don't think anyone can take an animal's life without projecting themselves into it.

JW: You talk about the Koyukon sense of respect, which encourages awareness of and direct participation in the cycles of life and death. Yet many in our culture are not only physically removed from this cycle but have developed the perverse notion that *any* kind of death is wrong.

RN: Death is viewed as destruction. We feel we are destroying something when we kill an animal or a fish or a plant, or anything. I think people in the Native American tradition had a better awareness that life is not destroyed, but only passed along.

I get a great deal of pleasure from knowing that my body is made in no small measure from deer. I am passionately in love with deer but I also kill them. I appreciate the fact that I am made out of the animal I love. Somewhere, both literally and physically, a deer looks out through my eyes; and some day my body will feed deer, too. Then they will live from me and the whole cycle will come around. We don't own life, we just take its shape and then pass it on.

I'm not saying it's easy for me to hunt deer. It's very hard, both psychologically and emotionally, for me to cope with it. But I feel a responsibility to confront the process of my own life through hunting.

Most people in this country don't realize how involved they are in the lives and deaths of deer. Each year millions of deer are killed in this country in order to protect many different crops such as corn, grapes, and lettuce. In fact, almost any time an American sits down at the table for dinner, there's a fair chance deer have been killed to protect some of the food that's on the table. Because deer are killed to protect grapes, you can't drink a glass of wine made in the United States today without participating in the lives—and the deaths—of deer.

Although animal rights activists will say otherwise, there isn't the tiniest shred of evidence to indicate that we could sustain agriculture in many parts of the United States today without some kind of predation on deer. Both deer populations and their nonhuman predators were nearly wiped out by the turn of the last century. In the absence of nonhuman predators and with new hunting laws in place, deer populations have increased tremendously. In some parts of the country, their populations are so high they cause severe damage to crops. There's good evidence in Wisconsin, for example, that the agricultural economy would be wiped out in as short a period as three to five years if deer hunting were stopped.

JW: When we were out the other day and you killed a deer, I was struck by the responsibility of it all. After it was gutted and cleaned, we carried it with us and I felt its presence strongly all day. What are some of the thoughts you have after you kill an animal?

RN: After I take an animal, it hangs for a few days in my basement, and whenever I go down there I think about it. I don't think of it as a senseless conglomeration of bones and meat and fat; I still think of it as an animal. I try to talk carefully around it and to treat it with respect. People think of hunting as simply going out and killing animals. That's one part of it, and certainly it's the most emotionally powerful and compelling part of it; but working with an animal and making it into your food, or using the hide and making it into things that you use, is also a strong thing. The process of taking an animal apart—what they call dressing or butchering it—is a really beautiful process. I love doing all of that. There is a lot of learning and skill involved in this process, and it takes a long time to learn how to do it well.

I feel a strong need to use everything I possibly can from the deer. After the meat is taken off the bones, I take the bones up to the woods behind the house where there's a big old stump and I put the bones up there for the ravens to find. I'll put fat up there too, and when I do that I always say, "I'm leaving this for the other animals," or "I'm leaving this back here behind the house for the raven," or if there's one around I'll say, "I'm leaving this for you guys." That's something Koyukon people do. They're always careful that any part of an animal they can't use is put in the woods in a respectful way. They say the parts are never thrown away "as if they were nothing."

For Koyukon people meat is a sacred substance. My teacher, Catherine Attla, never used to walk around outside with meat on a plate in the open air. She always covered it. "You don't want to act as if you don't care about it," she would say. So every bit of the process is sacred.

This sense of respect shouldn't end with animals or with people who hunt. The same kind of humility and gratitude should be shown when anyone sits down at a table that is arrayed with living things that died to feed them. I think we should be more mindful toward all life that comes to us.

JW: In *The Island Within,* you talk about hunting as a means of finding your way home. In the light of this, it's significant that the deer you hunt are not just random deer but deer that live in the same community where you live.

RN: One of the ethical dimensions of hunting is that you live in the community where you hunt. The fact that you live there binds you with the plants and animals and the other people who live there, too. There's a commitment that perhaps wouldn't be there if you did your hunting and fishing and gathering some place thousands of miles from home. It would be more difficult to feel that reciprocity. A man from Honolulu once pointed out to me how tourists completely ignore traffic laws there. He said they treat the streets of the city as if they were a mall where people go around on foot. They'll walk out in front of traffic; they ignore crosswalks; they ignore everything.

I've noticed that here where I live, too. When you're in another place, all of a sudden the rules don't seem to apply anymore. When you commit yourself to a place and you draw your livelihood from that place, you're more likely to develop a sense that there are rules that impinge upon you. I like the way Wendell Berry speaks about this commitment to place as marriage. This feeling of "marriage" contributes a lot to my sense of having a participating membership in a community that includes a lot more than just people.

JW: Is it possible to gain this same sense of authenticity and "marriage" in an urban environment?

RN: Since I don't live in an urban environment it's a little hard for me to speak with authority about that. But I think there are two things you can do anywhere. One is to work on an awareness of where your food comes from and how that connects you with the total environment of our continent. The other thing is to establish a personal relationship to your place and to the other kinds of animals that are a part of your community.

Even if you live in a city, the fact that you live on corn and wheat that come from the fields of Iowa and Indiana engages you in an ecological relationship to nature. The relationship is less obvious, so it requires more conscious thought. As I was saying earlier, when you sit down at a table full of food, no matter where you are, you can remember that you're a natural part of an ecological interchange.

Choosing to pay attention to some particular part of the environment is another way to develop a sense of belonging to nature. For me, it's an island near my home. But if you live in a big city maybe there's a park nearby. It doesn't have to be a wild park, but any park where squirrels and birds and other animals live. Pay attention to that place, go there as often as possible, maybe five, six, or seven days a week, and throughout the year and over a period of years to see how the place changes. Repeated experiences of a place are really important. There's a book by an excellent writer named Donald Knowler called *The Falconer of Central Park,* where he tells the story of a year spent watching the people and animals of Central Park in the middle of New York City. It's a wonderful natural history and it's a good example of what anyone could do in an urban place.

A person could pay attention to their own backyard too, or to one tree and what lives in it. There's nature everywhere. I remember being in New York and taking note of all the birds and animals around. There are a lot of them.

J W: There's a passage in *The Island Within* where you refer to yourself as a stain on the landscape. What do you mean by that, and has your perspective changed since you wrote it?

R N: Yes, it has. Sometime after *The Island Within* was published, I was reading through something or other and I saw where I had referred to myself as an irrelevant flaw on the island's face. It really caught me by surprise, and I thought, "Why in the world did I say that?" When the book came out in paperback, I changed flaw to fleck. Recently I discovered how I referred to myself as a stain, as you point out, and I'd like to change that, too, because it relates to an older way in my thinking.

For a long time I thought of myself as a negative element in the environment, and there was some vague sense of embarrassment about being human in the natural world. Unfortunately, I think many of us grew up with this perspective. Because of the damage we're doing to the environment, we seem to feel that there's no right place for human beings on the earth. I don't believe that at all. Human beings are marvelous creatures with a tremendous capacity for harmonious relationship with the environment. We just happen to be wildly off the track right now.

I don't have any interest in focusing on the negative side of what's happening with respect to the environment and the natural world. I grieve for the destruction of nature but I don't want to spend my energy grieving. I want to use my energy to try to look for solutions and for positive courses to follow.

j w: I find it revealing that otherwise sensitive people respond to the environmental crisis by condemning the entire human race. As you say, there's an underlying embarrassment and shame about being human. The guilt we feel can be debilitating. This attitude only seems to intensify our estrangement from nature.

r n: It's dangerous to think of ourselves as loathsome creatures or as perversions in the natural world. We need to see ourselves as having a rightful place and to rediscover that rightful place. We take pictures of all kinds of natural scenes and often we try to avoid having a human being in them. A natural place with human habitation blended into it is beautiful, too. In our society, we force ourselves into a greater and greater distance from the natural world by creating parks and wilderness areas where our only role is to go in and look. And we call this loving it. We lavish tremendous concern and care on scenery but we ignore the ravaging of environments from which our lives are drawn.

Until we as a culture understand that nature is not just scenery, that this natural world is our community and that we live in ecological relationship to it, I think we're going to continue to go in the wrong direction. I'm a big supporter of national parks and national monuments and scenery of all sorts. I love it as much as anybody does but I also think it's dangerous to consider nature simply as scenery.

When you have a better sense of your personal ecology and the way in which the environment flows through your own body, you're liable to work harder at taking care of the environment. You learn to appreciate, for example, that the corn fields of Iowa are what you're made of. If poison is put on those fields, then that poison is running through your body. If the soil of Iowa is flowing off into the Mississippi River, it's taking something away from your body and your children's and your grandchildren's bodies.

Coming Back
from the Silence

C AN ONE find a common denominator in the work and thought of Ursula K. Le Guin?" asks writer Theodore Sturgeon. "Probably not; but there are some notes in her orchestrations that come out repeatedly and with power. A cautionary fear of the development of democracy into dictatorship. Celebrations of courage, endurance, risk. Language, not only loved and shaped, but investigated in all its aspects; call that, perhaps, communication. But above all, in almost unearthly terms Ursula Le Guin examines, attacks, unbuttons, takes down and exposes our notions of reality."

With over three million copies of her books in print, Ursula Le Guin is not only one of the most widely read writers in North America but also one of the most prolific. During one of her intense writing periods, between 1966 and 1974, she published seven science fiction novels, nine poems, three fantasy novels, sixteen short stories, five book reviews, and sixteen essays. For these and other works she has received numerous awards, including the Boston Globe-Horn Book Award in 1969 for her first fantasy novel, *A Wizard of Earthsea*. She received the Hugo and Nebula awards for *The Left Hand of Darkness* in 1970 and was a finalist for the National Book Award for Children's Literature in 1972 for *The Tombs of Atuan*. In 1985, Ursula was the National Book Award runner-up and Kafka Award recipient for *Always Com-*

ing Home, and in 1973 she received the National Book Award for *The Farthest Shore.*

Ursula was born in Berkeley, California, in 1929, the daughter of Alfred Kroeber, one of the founders of modern anthropology, and psychologist/writer Theodora Kroeber. The family, including Ursula's three brothers, spent winters in Berkeley and summers in the Napa Valley sixty miles north of San Francisco. In 1951, Ursula graduated from Radcliffe with a B.A. in French, and in 1952 she received her M.A. in Romance Languages from Columbia. Fulbright scholarships allowed her to spend a year in Paris (1953) and two years in London (1968 and 1975). In 1953, she married the historian Charles Le Guin, and they eventually made their home in Portland, Oregon, where they raised three children.

In answer to my request for this interview, Ursula wrote, "Greed compels me to ask first if you live near that wonderful New Mexican restaurant with the garlic custard. Ooh. That garlic custard. I wish I lived on Phinney Hill. . . . Excuse me. Yes, an interview would be fine (could you bring some custard?)."

Custard in hand, I showed up on Ursula's doorstep in northwest Portland a few months later. We drank tea and sat in her living room until the early evening, recording the following conversation. With only momentary interruptions by Lorenzo the cat or chimes from the grandfather clock, Ursula demonstrated that coyotelike skill for which she is famous: making up worlds with words.

~·~·~

JONATHAN WHITE: It's clear from your work that language and writing have become sharp tools for re-visioning human society and humanity's place in the larger household. Much of that re-visioning, at least in the last thirty years, has been inspired by feminist principles. Your goal, you say, is always to subvert, creating metaphors for the future "where any assumption can be tested and any rule rewritten. Including the rules of who's on top, and what gender means, and who gets to be free." Let's begin with the question of how you were introduced to the feminist movement and the role it has played in your writing.

URSULA LE GUIN: My introduction was slow and late. All my early fiction tends to be rather male-centered. A couple of the *Earthsea* books have no women in them at all or only marginal woman figures. That's how hero stories worked; they were about men. With the exception of just a few feminists like Joanna Russ, science fiction was pretty much male-dominated up to the 1960s. Women who wrote in that field often used pen names.

None of this bothered me. It was my tradition, and I worked in it happily. But I began coming up against certain discomforts. My first feminist text was *The Left Hand of Darkness,* which I started writing in 1967. It was an early experiment in deconstructing gender. Everybody was asking, "What is it to be a man? What is it to be a woman?" It's a hard question, so in *The Left Hand of Darkness* I eliminated gender to find out what would be left. Science fiction is a wonderful opportunity to play this kind of game.

As a thought experiment, *The Left Hand of Darkness* was messy. I recently wrote the screenplay version, where I was able to make some of the changes I wish I could make to the novel. They're details, but important ones, such as seeing the main character, Genly, with children or doing things we think of as womanly. All you ever see him doing are manly things, like being a politician or hauling a sledge. The two societies in the book are somewhat like a feudal monarchy and Russian communism, which tend to be slightly paranoid. I don't know why I thought androgynous people would be paranoid. With twenty years of feminism under my belt, I can now imagine an androgynous society as being much different—and far more interesting—than our gendered society. For instance, I wouldn't lock the people from the planet Gethen, where the story takes place, into heterosexuality. The insistence that sexual partners must be of the opposite sex is naive. It never occurred to me to explore their homosexual practices, and I regret the implication that sexuality has to be heterosexuality.

I gradually realized that my own fiction was telling me that I could no longer ignore the feminine. While I was writing *The Eye of the Heron* in 1977, the hero insisted on destroying himself before the middle of the book. "Hey," I said, "you can't do that, you're the hero.

Where's my book?" I stopped writing. The book had a woman in it, but I didn't know how to write about women. I blundered around awhile and then found some guidance in feminist theory. I got excited when I discovered feminist literary criticism was something I could read and actually enjoy. I read *The Norton Book of Literature by Women* from cover to cover. It was a bible for me. It taught me that I didn't have to write like an honorary man anymore, that I could write like a woman and feel liberated in doing so.

J W: Your mother, Theodora Kroeber, was an accomplished writer. Her book *Ishi in Two Worlds* is an ethnological classic. What kind of encouragement did her life and work offer you?

U L: My mother wasn't really a feminist. She didn't even like the word. She called feminists "those women's lib people." But she also asked me questions like, "Why do you always have men heroes?" And I'd answer, "I don't know, Ma. Ask me an easy question!" So, I got a lot from her. But toward the end of her life, we were in some conflict.

My mother also led me to Virginia Woolf, who has given me a life-long education. As a novelist, Woolf is a much more important writer than the keepers of the canons of English literature want to admit. In fact, they're still afraid of her. And quite rightly. She's deeply subversive, and a great novelist! I still turn to her for guidance.

J W: What was it that attracted you to the science fiction genre?

U L: I didn't exactly choose science fiction. I went where I got published, which took a long time because my work is so odd. For the last fifty or sixty years, literature has been categorized as "realism," and if you weren't writing realism, you weren't respectable. I had to ignore that and say to myself that I could do things in science fiction that I could never do in realism. I tend to be prickly about this subject because I get tired of being put down as a science fiction writer. The fact is, in the postmodern era, all the barriers are breaking down pretty fast.

I've been editing *The Norton Book of Science Fiction,* which has inspired some new thoughts on this matter. For instance, I've learned that science fiction is a child of realism, not of fantasy. A realistic story deals with something that might have happened but didn't, right? Many science fiction stories are about worlds that don't exist, but could exist in the future. Both realism and science fiction deal with stories that might be true. Fantasy, on the other hand, tells a story that couldn't possibly be true. With fantasy, we simply agree to lift the ban on the imagination and follow the story, no matter how implausible it may be.

J W: Didn't you say once that fantasy may not be actual, but it's true?

U L: Wouldn't you say any attempt to tell a story is an attempt to tell the truth? It's the technique you use in the telling that is either more or less plausible. Sometimes the most direct way to tell the truth is to tell a totally implausible story, like a myth. That way you avoid the muddle of pretending the story ever happened, or ever will happen.

Who knows how stories really work? We're so used to stories with all the trappings of being real that we've lost our ability to read anything else. When you read a Native American story, you have to relearn how to read. There's nothing in them to draw you in. There's no sweetening of the pill. Maybe there's a coyote, but there's no description. We're used to a lot of fleshing out, and we're used to being courted and drawn into the story.

J W: Nora Dauenhaeur, a Tlingit woman and coauthor of *Haa Shuka, Our Ancestors,* reminded me last summer that Native American stories are usually told to an audience that already knows them. In fact, they've heard the stories over and over again, through many winters. As a result, the storyteller often uses shorthand—a single word or phrase—to remind the audience of a larger event with many details. She pointed out that we are telling stories like this all the time, particularly among friends and family with whom we share a history. We may say, "Remember that time we were caught in a dust storm outside of Phoenix?" And that's the story, all of it.

U L: Yes, exactly. You don't describe the sky or the clouds or what you were wearing. There isn't any of this scene-setting in Native American stories. It bothers me when I read gussied-up Native American stories. They're no longer sacred.

J W: What is it, exactly, that makes a story sacred?

U L: I don't know. But when we embellish a Native American story, it turns into just another story. Our culture doesn't think storytelling is sacred; we don't set aside a time of year for it. We don't hold anything sacred except what organized religion declares to be so. Artists pursue a sacred call, although some would buck and rear at having their work labeled like this. Artists are lucky to have a form in which to express themselves; there is a sacredness about that, and a terrific sense of responsibility. We've got to do it right. Why do we have to do it right? Because that's the whole point: either it's right or it's all wrong.

J W: We tend to have such a linear, cause-and-effect way of looking at the world. I wonder if one of the things that attracts us to stories is their ability to change our way of seeing?

U L: The daily routine of most adults is so heavy and artificial that we are closed off to much of the world. We have to do this in order to get our work done. I think one purpose of art is to get us out of those routines. When we hear music or poetry or stories, the world opens up again. We're drawn in—or out—and the windows of our perception are cleansed, as William Blake said. The same thing can happen when we're around young children or adults who have unlearned those habits of shutting the world out.

The tribal storyteller is not just providing spiritual access but also moral guidance. I think much of American writing today is an exploration of ethical problems. I'm thinking particularly of novels by black women such as Paula Marshall, Alice Walker, Gloria Naylor, and Toni Morrison. The stories these women write are gaining literary praise, but they're also doing something terribly important for their people, who are not just black Americans but all Americans. In a sense, these women are fulfilling the ancient role of tribal storytellers, because they're trying to lead us into different spiritual and moral realms. They're intensely serious about this, and that's why they're so beloved as novelists.

J W: Stories can also help us remember who we are. In *The Book of Laughter and Forgetting,* Milan Kundera says, "What is the self but the sum of everything we remember?"

U L: Yes. To *remember,* if my Latin is correct, actually means to put the parts together. So that implies there are ways of losing parts. Kundera talks about this aspect of storytelling, too. In fact, he says that history, which is another kind of story, is often deliberately falsified in order to make a people forget who they are or who they were. He calls that "the method of organized forgetting."

History is one way of telling stories, just like myth, fiction, or oral storytelling. But over the last hundred years, history has preempted the other forms of storytelling because of its claim to absolute, objective truth. Trying to be scientists, historians stood outside of history and told the story of how it was. All that has changed radically over the last twenty years. Historians now laugh at the pretense of objective truth. They agree that every age has its own history, and if there is any objective truth, we can't reach it with words. History is not a science, it's an art.

There are still people who insist on teaching history as a science, but that's not how most historians work anymore. My husband, Charles, who is a historian, says, "I don't know the difference between story and history. I think it may not be a difference in kind, but a difference in their attempts to be truthful."

The history of the last hundred years still has a tremendous intellectual bias toward the white European point of view. Defined by historians as the written record, it conveniently illegitimizes all oral traditions and most indigenous people right from the start. In fact, in its view, everybody but white Europeans are "primitive." If you don't have a written language, you aren't part of history.

J W: Are the current changes in how we look at history also changing the way we look at indigenous cultures?

U L: Absolutely. It's a de-centering process. We've been pretending that Europe was the center of the world for too long. With the help of anthropologists, and now historians, we are finding that there is no center, or that there are many centers. Nobody has "the answer." It's amazing how much resistance there is to this. Everybody wants to be "the people," everybody wants to be "the center." And everybody *is* the center, if only they'd realize it and not sneer at all the other centers.

J W: Because history, as it has been practiced, concerns itself only with the written record, language acquires a loaded role in terms of our perception of reality. Like history, language can become a tool of forgetting, a tool of estrangement. As a writer, how do you work against that?

U L: This is a tricky area. As a writer, you want the language to be genuinely significant and mean exactly what it says. That's why the language of politicians, which is empty of everything but rather brutal signals, is something a writer has to get as far away from as possible. If you believe that words are acts, as I do, then one must hold writers responsible for what their words do.

One of the strangest things about our culture is our ability to describe the destruction of the world in exquisite, even beautiful, detail. The whole science of ecology, for instance, describes exactly what we're doing wrong and what the global effects are. The odd twist is that we become so enamored of our language and its ability to describe the world that we create a false and irresponsible separation. We use language as a device for distancing. Somebody who is genuinely living in their ecosystem wouldn't have a word for it. They'd just call it the world.

We can't restructure our society without restructuring the English language. One reflects the other. A lot of people are getting tired of the huge pool of metaphors that have to do with war and conflict. The "war against drugs" is an obvious example of this. So is the proliferation of battle metaphors, such as being a warrior, fighting, defeating, and so on. In response, I could say that once you become conscious of these battle metaphors, you can start "fighting" against them. That's one option. Another is to realize that conflict is not the only human response to a situation and to begin to find other metaphors, such as resisting, outwitting, skipping, or subverting. This kind of consciousness can open the door to all sorts of new behavior.

I am struck by how much we talk about rebirthing but never about *rebearing*. The word itself is unfamiliar to most people. Yet both women and men are capable of rebearing, women literally and men metaphorically. A door opens just by changing the name. We don't have to be reborn; we can *rebear*. This is part of the writer's job, either to rebear the metaphors or refuse to use them. Gary Snyder's lifelong metaphor is *watershed*. How fruitful that is! Another of his is *composting,* which is a lovely word that describes the practice of creating.

J W: The use of language to name the world seems to have two sides. On one hand, things are given names as an expression of intimacy and respect; and on the other hand they are given names to create distance and separation. In your story, "She Unnames Them," for example, barriers are broken down as the names for animals are taken away.

U L: "She Unnames Them" is really an Adam and Eve story that I subverted. Eve takes all the names back because they were either wrong from the start or they went wrong. As she does this, the barriers between herself and the world are dismantled. At the end of the story, she has no words left. She's so close to the animals that she feels vulnerable and afraid, yet full of new desire to touch, smell, and eat.

Why do I feel like the way we give names is wrong? I don't want to flog that little story to death, because it was meant partly as a joke, but we do use names to cut ourselves off. Talking about a dog is different than talking about Rover. In the language of war, we don't talk about killing or even casualties anymore. We use strange euphemisms instead, like "body count" and "friendly fire." The language of pretended objectivity is often used this way, too. We manipulate names as categories of reality, and the names then become screens between ourselves and the world. The names become a tool of division rather than of community.

My father worked with the Yurok Indians of California, among other tribes. If you read his Yurok myths, you learn that every rock and every tree had its name. It was a small world they lived in, not a planetary one. They were in intense community with it, and their naming was a way of respecting their interdependence. But anything is reversible, and naming can become the destruction of community, where we hide from the real world by using more and more words. I know people who refuse to learn the names of trees. They have a concept of "tree," but the names simply get between them and the real tree.

I grew up in the Napa Valley without learning the English names for many of the plants and animals. When I started writing *Always Coming Home,* which takes place there, I had a wonderful time learning the flora and fauna of the area. For a while, I knew the name of every wildflower. But what you learn late doesn't stick. Now when I come across a flower whose name I've forgotten, I say, "How do you do, little yellow flower, whatever your name is." I used to crave to know the names, and I enjoyed learning them. It's funny, by naming a thing, do we think we get control over it? I think we do. That's how magic works. If you know the name of a thing, then you know its essence. At some level, I think we all must believe that.

We're naming creatures, but we need to respect that some things are beyond names. Like the mysterious essence of an animal in the wild. If our names make them appear tame or petlike, as in Walt Disney's world, then it's degrading. Some of the California Indians knew that when you name an animal, such as a deer, you are addressing its metaphysical nature. They called that universal quality "Deerness" or "The Deer." It's a profoundly mysterious and important matter, and very hard to put into words, but I feel I know what they're talking about. When these Indians hunted, they asked Deerness to help them. The deer that comes to the hunter is related physically to all other beings, but it is also an embodiment of Deerness. It's the gift of Deerness. This way of looking at the world can apply to every living being. When we name something we are naming its essence, and therefore its sacredness.

J w: You often mention Rilke's "Eighth Duino Elegy" as the poem that has taught you the most about animals. What is it about that poem that touches you so deeply?

U L: Rilke knew a lot about the sacredness between humans and other animals. When you look in an animal's eyes, what are you seeing? What are they seeing? Rilke says that what the animal sees is pure being, the truth. The animal doesn't know its own death, it looks through it:

> . . . What is outside, we know from the face
> of the animal only; for we turn even the
>   youngest child
> around and force it to see all forms
> backwards, not the openness
> so deep in the beast's gaze. Free from death.
> Only we see that. The free animal
> has its dying always behind it
> and God in front of it, and its way
> is the eternal way, as the spring flowing . . .

Again, this is profoundly mystical, and it sounds sort of silly to talk about it outside of poetry. But I think Rilke is right. That's why contact with animals is a sacred thing—because they know something we don't. We know a lot, but we had to give up something in order to know what we know. That's why we must not lose contact with the animals, and why I'm spooked by people who have.

J w: In *Buffalo Gals,* you say that all creatures talk to one another, whether we are able to hear or not. But this conversation—this community—is not a simple harmony: "The peaceable kingdom, where lion and lamb lie down, is an endearing vision not of this world." What do you mean by that?

U L: The vision of the "peaceable kingdom" denies wilderness. In the Christian tradition, the denial of violence, of the fact that we eat each other in order to live, removes you from this world. Heaven is supernal bliss where there is no violence, no eating, and no sex. When lions and lambs lie down in the wilderness, the lamb ends up inside the lion. That's how it is. You can deny that in order to gain another world. But if the only world you want is this one—and this one seems quite satisfactory to me—then the myth of the "peaceable kingdom" is only a charming painting.

J w: You continue in *Buffalo Gals:* "Some rash poets get caught in the traps set for animals and, unable to endure the cruelty, maim themselves to escape." You give the example of Robinson Jeffers. Was Jeffers maimed because he took too personally his disappointment in the dark side of nature?

U L: Jeffers was a very strange man and poet, with an enormous component of cruelty and violence in his work. He had incredible sympathy with animals. He could give you an animal in a word or two like very few poets can. I think he honestly felt them, even though he often perceives them through violence. I can't explain Jeffers, he has always awed and annoyed me. I'm grateful to him as one of my predecessors writing about California. Even as a teenager, I knew he had California right.

The poem that most reveals Jeffers's self-hatred is the one about the early cavemen who torment a mammoth to death. They trap it and roast it alive. He's full of this kind of disgust for humanity. Yet he soars out into a great vision; never a happy vision, but a great vision. He's a difficult case when you're talking about animals.

J W: The trap of shamefulness seems like an easy one to fall into. If we want to be alert, we have to take all this in—the violence, the killing, the cruelty—

U L: Yes. But since we're capable of compassion, we know it hurts. This causes all sorts of difficulties. My aunt was a biologist, and I watched her drop an artichoke into a pot of boiling water and say, "I wonder if it can feel that?" She was a very hardheaded biologist. Other animals, like the cow, certainly don't wonder if the grass hurts. Humans have to think about these things, whether we like it or not. It's the nature of our humanity to feel uncomfortable and full of guilt and shame and confusion. But we still participate, because we have to eat. Much of what animals do naturally we have to do consciously. That's our gift and our curse. All we can do is be conscientious about it—do it rightly, not wrongly.

J W: In *Always Coming Home,* hunting for food and skins was primarily done by children and adolescents. Under the supervision of adults, young girls and boys were allowed to hunt rabbit, possum, squirrel and other small game, and deer. Why was hunting considered inappropriate behavior for adults?

U L: You're supposed to outgrow it. The same thing is true of war. In one chapter, I describe a small war with the Pig People. It's modeled on the warfare of the Northern California Indians, which was usually just a matter of standing on a hill and shouting insults. Sometimes people got mad enough to hurt each other, and occasionally someone was killed. Mostly it was the young boys who engaged in war, not the whole tribe. What comes up in the chapter on the Pig war is the report that there were adults involved in the war. That's a shameful thing in the Kesh society. Both hunting and war are looked upon as occupations for adolescents, adolescents who are already a little out of control and needing to prove themselves. You can continue to hunt into adulthood if you're really good at it, of course, but I was implying that it's something most people outgrow.

J W: That's interesting. Human ecologist/writer Paul Shepard and anthropologist/writer Richard Nelson are outspoken in their support of hunting. For them, it's a way to experience their inseparable connection to life.

U L: I'm sorry, I don't buy that. I don't see that you have to kill an animal in order to connect with nature or landscape or your life or anything else. If that's what you think, there's something wrong with you. If you're hungry, that's another matter. If you were lost in the woods and needed food, knowing how to hunt would be a valuable skill to have.

There's a tremendous mystique around hunting and fishing. I've gone out with a fisherwoman friend. She fished faithfully while I sat by the creek, and I think I was just as connected to the landscape as she was. I hunted for a couple of years as a child, so I know something of the incredible visceral emotion involved.

J W: Neither Paul nor Richard hunts for sport. I think it was Paul who said that he doesn't know of a better way to confront the intensity of the life-death cycle than hunting.

U L: It's a short circuit. People should be able to figure out their place in the life-death cycle without killing animals. The trouble is that it relates to what Hemingway said: "You can't be a man until you've killed another one." I say bullshit! Why don't you try it without the gun? Maybe there's a gender difference there. Maybe a woman can do it and a man can't. I hate to say that, but you wonder.

It isn't built into women to be hunters in our culture. Even a fisherwoman is unusual. I found that out when I went fishing in the Sierras with my friend. We were among the few women on the river, and the men gave us rather unfriendly stares, as if to say, "This is a man's sport, a man's country." But perhaps the different gender responses to hunting are culturally induced; perhaps what men have learned to get from hunting women get from watching a sparrow fly, or an old cat walk across the room.

Having a close relationship with an animal, particularly one that lives a short life, can be an intense, constant reminder of mortality. Cats only live ten years, so most of us see a lot of cats die in our lifetime. Going through the death of a pet, particularly for children, can put us through the same emotional process that hunting does. We don't have to kill an animal to get there. It's a very interesting subject, and I hope the difference is cultural and not inherent to gender.

J w: Another angle on the hunting issue is that it teaches us where our food comes from.

u L: That's a different subject. That's not a spiritual process but a matter of facing up to the facts. What are you willing to do for your food? Most of us would kill an animal to eat it, if we had to. I could, and would, if I were hungry or defending myself. I'm not saying I would enjoy it, but for those two reasons I would kill an animal. I have Buddhist friends who don't even swat flies. I can't go that far. If something is biting me, I squash it. A pest is a pest.

J w: In your essay "Women/Wilderness," you say that civilized man considers himself the master of the world. Everything else is Other: "I am that I am, and the rest is women and the wilderness, to be used as I see fit." This is changing, you say: "The wilderness is answering back. Those who were identified as having nothing to say, . . . those who were identified with Nature, which listens, as against Man, who speaks—those people are speaking. They speak for themselves and for other people, animals, trees, rivers, rocks. And what they say is: We are sacred. . . . They do not say Nature is sacred. . . . They distrust that word, Nature."

u L: This is the naming thing again. As soon as you call it nature, you immediately create a dichotomy between you and it. But just a little word of caution before I go on. I wrote "Women/Wilderness" for a

talk I did for Gary Snyder's class at the University of California in
1986. It's a polemical piece, overstating its case deliberately. I don't believe all that it says.

J W: In that talk you bring up a fascinating diagram used by the anthropologists Shirley Ardener and Edwin Ardener. They started out
with two circles largely overlapping, but not completely. You write:
"One of the two circles is the Dominant element of the culture, that is,
Men. The other is the Muted element of the culture, that is,
Women. . . . Both the crescent that belongs to men only and the crescent that belongs to women only, outside the shared, central, civilized
area of overlap, may be called 'the Wilderness.' The men's wilderness
is real; it is where men go hunting and exploring. . . and it is accessible
to and structured by language." Women know about men's wilderness because it has become part of the history and mythology of the
culture. So, you say, "men's 'wilderness' becomes Nature, considered
as the property of Man. . . . But the experience of women as women,
their experience unshared with men, that experience is the wilderness or the wildness that is utterly Other—that is in fact, to Man, un-
natural."

U L: That is a fascinating image, isn't it? Many feminists have used it,
but as far as I know no one has taken it any further.

Part of the women's experience is shared with men and part of it
isn't. Experiences that are only women's, like childbirth, have been described a thousand times, mostly in novels by men. These descriptions
have nothing to do with the actual experience. Generally, I don't think
men in our culture want to hear from women about childbirth because
men want to have it their way. So, women's stories have been cast in the
form of men's stories. All my early books are men's stories, with male
heroes. A women's story has a different shape, different words, different rhythm. Theirs is the silent crescent of experience that we are just
beginning to find words for. As Linda Hogan writes,

Daughters, the women are speaking.
They arrive
over the wise distances
on perfect feet.

The incredible upsurge of woman writers and poets in the 1980s is a sign that women are finding their voices. They're beginning to talk about their experiences without using a male vocabulary or meeting male expectations. It's sticky, because the language is so male-centered that it excludes much of the feminine experience. Sex, for instance, is always described from a male point of view, as penetration, insemination, and so on. A lot of women still deny that their experience is different than a man's. They do this because it's scary to realize you don't have the words to describe your own experience. The few words we do have we get from our mothers and the women who taught us when we were young. Virginia Woolf says, "We think back through our mothers."

One of the functions of art is to give people the words to know their own experience. There are always areas of vast silence in any culture, and part of an artist's job is to go into those areas and come back from the silence with something to say. It's one reason why we read poetry, because poets can give us the words we need. When we read good poetry, we often say, "Yeah, that's it. That's how I feel." Storytelling is a tool for knowing who we are and what we want, too. If we never find our experience described in poetry or stories, we assume that our experience is insignificant.

JW: The natural landscape is another one of those vast silent areas you speak of. As a writer, are there certain landscapes that have had a particularly strong influence on you?

UL: Mostly, I don't know where my writing comes from. Experiences are composted, and then something different and unexpected grows out of them. In 1969, my husband and I spent a couple nights in

French Glen, the mountainous area of southeastern Oregon. It was my first sight of that sagebrush high desert terrain, and it got into me so instantly and authoritatively that a book grew out of it, *The Tombs of Atuan*. The book isn't about the desert but about a community surrounded by a terrain similar to what you find in southeastern Oregon. The desert is a buried metaphor in the book. I have no idea of the reason for the emotional economy of it, but I know the book came to me as I was driving back from French Glen.

The central landscape of my life is the Napa Valley in Northern California. I grew up there and I consider it my home. I've often thought, "How can I get this beautiful valley into a book?" That was the main impulse of *Always Coming Home*. I wanted to write about people living in the Napa Valley who used it a little more wisely than we do now. When I was a child, it was the most beautiful and diversified agriculture you ever saw. There were vines and orchards and truck gardens. It was the way a cultivated valley ought to be. But there was too much money in vines, so they pulled up the orchards and truck gardens. The only thing growing there now is money.

Both the Oregon desert and the Napa Valley gave me books. One of them I've known since I was born, a landscape that is deep in me. The other I saw for two days. Of course, I've gone back to visit often. Once you go to southeastern Oregon, you tend to go back.

j w: What role has your interest in indigenous people played in your work?

u l: I wasn't aware that it played any role at first. Although my father was an anthropologist and an archaeologist, my entire formal training in this area amounts to one physical anthropology class. Obviously I have some temperamental affinity with my father, but I often say that he studied real cultures and I make them up. He had an eye for exact concrete detail, and an interest in it. He also had a respect for tools and the way things work. I got a lot of that from him.

When I started thinking about *Always Coming Home* I took a lot of time to discover what the book was going to be. Once I realized I wanted it to grow out of the Napa Valley I looked around for a literary precedent. I couldn't find anything except a couple of swashbuckling romantic novels about Italian wine-growing families. The only literature of that earth was Native American oral literature. The people of the valley itself, the Wappo, are gone. Even the name they used for themselves is gone. There are people with a little Wappo blood, but there is no language, no tradition, and there are no stories left. So I read other Northern Californian myths and legends and songs. There's a good deal of information available there. My father collected much of it himself. I read widely from traditions all over the United States. My problem was to find a way to use the literature without stealing or exploiting it, because we've done enough of that to Native American writing. I certainly didn't want to put a bunch of made up Indians into a Napa Valley of the future. That was not what I was trying to do. What I got from reading California oral literature was a sense of a distant and different quality of life. You can't hear the voices but you can pick up the feeling.

JW: So in *Always Coming Home,* the Napa Valley is as it is, but the people are of the future: "Real gardens, imaginary toads," as you say. The Kesh, who live in the Valley of the Na, are both hunter-gatherers and agricultural farmers. Is that right?

UL: They're highly agricultural people. They have herds and flocks and they live in towns. They do hunt and gather, but you couldn't call them hunter-gatherers. What I did there is slightly suspect from an anthropological view, although I did it quite consciously. You see, there's a gospel that defines people as either hunter-gatherers or agricultural farmers, but not both. Actually, there are lots of places where the two mix, so I didn't see any reason why they shouldn't mix in my book. Living in California, where there's wild food growing everywhere, why shouldn't you do a little of both? It seems dumb to rely on cultivated food alone.

JW: The Kesh communities are saturated in ritual. They had festivals of the moon, water, summer, wine, and grass to celebrate the natural cycles. They danced together at the equinox and the solstice. Where did you get your understanding of ritual, and what role do you see it playing in a healthy culture?

UL: What I know about ritual I learned from books. I've never lived in a culture like the one in *Always Coming Home.*

What we're talking about here is partly a matter of literary tactics. The book is made of words. The Kesh have to have a lot of verbal rituals so that I could write about what they did. And their rituals had to be lively and interesting so that they could be told through stories and poetry. I wasn't conscious of these processes when I was writing the book, but I know that's the way it works. These rituals are part of the context of the book, but they also show a society living well, doing no harm, while at the same time not sitting on their hands and doing nothing. Like a climax forest, the Kesh society is in good balance. They have a refined technology, but not a growth technology. They may change the details and the style in the way they do things, but not quickly or radically as in a society built on growth technology such as ours. One way to demonstrate the difference in the way the Kesh lived is to show them involved in the ritual of repeated activities and festivals. The rituals of the season reveal the Kesh embeddedness in the texture of existence, environment, culture. Everything flows in one direction.

There seems to be a profound ritual aspect in most healthy Native American cultures. I used the Pueblo and the Hopi to some extent as models. They have a lot of ritualized behavior, which is all taken very easily and informally. I'm always impressed when I go to pow-wows by how casual they seem. It's ritual, and yet people are talking and laughing and babies are running around. It all seems appropriate. The ritual of organized religion is a different kind of thing. It's something separate, hierarchical, and male-centered. If everybody's doing ritual all the time, as they were in Native American cultures, religion and life are absolutely inseparable.

JW: Did your appreciation for ritual change in the process of writing the book?

U L: One reason I hated to finish the book was that I had to wean my-self from going through the year as a Kesh person. I enjoyed it, and I felt very much at home in that kind of round. Living with a fairly con-sistent cycle of activities, ritual relationships, ceremonies, and festivals is the way most people in most cultures have lived throughout human history.

J W: The historical period, which followed the Neolithic era for some thousands of years, is referred to by the Kesh as the time when people lived "outside the world." What do you mean by that?

U L: What I was doing there is playing with the idea of our present growth technology from the Industrial Revolution on through the present—the last two hundred years. We don't know when this pe-riod will end, but it will. We tend to think of our present historic era as representing the highest evolution of human society. We're convinced that our exploitive, fast-growing technology is the only possible reality. In *Always Coming Home,* I put people who believe this into one little capsule where the Kesh could look at them as weird aberrations. It was the most disrespectful thing I could do, like wrapping a turd in cello-phane. That's sort of a Coyote metaphor.

J W: Speaking of Coyote, she wanders in and out of much of your recent work. How did you meet up with her?

U L: She trotted through a project of mine in 1982. It was an essay on utopia called "A Non-Euclidean View of California as a Cold Place to Be," and when the tracks of utopia and Coyote crossed, I thought, "Yes, now I'm getting somewhere!" The idea of utopia has been stuck in a blueprint phase for too long now. Most of the writing you see is similar to Callenbach's *Ecotopia,* which is another "wouldn't the fu-ture be great if we did this or that?" Or, in science fiction, it's been *dys-topia:* utopia gone sour. These blueprints aren't working anymore.

Coyote is an anarchist. She can confuse all civilized ideas simply by trotting through. And she always fools the pompous. Just when your ideas begin to get all nicely arranged and squared off, she messes them up. Things are never going to be neat, that's one thing you can count on.

Coyote walks through all our minds. Obviously, we need a trickster, a creator who made the world all wrong. We need the idea of a God who makes mistakes, gets into trouble, and who is identified with a scruffy little animal.

Animal Presence

T HE BRILLIANT and mischievous psychologist James Hillman
is perhaps the most widely known Jungian analyst in the world
today. His numerous books include *Suicide of the Soul* (1964), *The
Feeling Function* (1971), *The Dream and the Underworld* (1979), *A Blue
Fire* (1989), and *We've Had a Hundred Years of Psychotherapy, and the
World's Getting Worse* (1992, with Michael Ventura). His major post-
Jungian work, *Revisioning Psychology,* was nominated for a Pulitzer
Prize in 1975.

In an *L.A. Weekly* interview entitled, "Could Psychology Be Part of
the Disease, Not Part of the Cure?" Michael Ventura says, "Just who
is Hillman? A psychologist, some say. . . . A wild old man, I say, who
throws thoughts the way a potter throws pots, the way a hunter throws
spears, the way a ventriloquist throws his voice, the way an angry lover
throws you out of the house. Some of Hillman's thoughts are vessels
you can put stuff in and drink from; others, weapons you can go into
battle with. Some . . . well, you'd best get out of their way. Hillman
knows that the work of thought is one of the most ancient and useful
activities of humankind. To generate thought is to create life, liveli-
ness, community. Consensus isn't important. What's important is how
the generative power of our thought makes life vivid and burns out the
dead brush, dead habits, dead institutions. For me, Hillman's the most
inspiring and disruptive thinker at work now in our country."

James Hillman was born in Atlantic City, New Jersey, in 1926. He attended Georgetown University, the Sorbonne, Trinity College, and the University of Zurich, where he received his Ph.D. in philosophical psychology in 1959. He stayed another twenty years in Zurich, ten of which he served as acting director of studies at the C. G. Jung Institute. In the late 1970s he returned to the United States to become a founding fellow of the Dallas Institute of Humanities and Culture, continuing his role as publisher and editor of *Spring Publications,* an expansion of the Jung Institute's *Spring* magazine. In recent years, he has taught at men's workshops and lectured at clinics and conferences throughout Europe, Japan, and North America. He now lives and works in rural Connecticut.

James Hillman joined the schooner *Crusader* in southeast Alaska to teach a weeklong seminar entitled "Come into Animal Presence," named after Denise Levertov's poem. With twelve other participants, we sailed in the waters of Frederick Sound and Chatham Straits. Evenings and mornings were spent in sessions on deck, with a little sailing, hiking, dancing, and fishing in between.

＞·＞·＞

JONATHAN WHITE: Let's start with where we are. What influence does this boat and these waters have on the contents of your seminar, "Come into Animal Presence"?

JAMES HILLMAN: Well, the first thing I feel is that this boat doesn't disturb the world it's in. I don't know if that's because it's old or funky or wood or what. But there's no slickness to it. And because it doesn't disturb the world it's in, it makes the feeling right. Getting the feeling right is very important in the primitive world, the wilderness world, or what I would rather call the world of tribal people. Tribal people spend an immense amount of time making sure the feeling is right, either by sweats, rituals, dances, or feasts. There are anthropological studies that say tribal people spend about 30 percent of their time doing what we would call working and the rest of the time preparing and performing rituals, dances, and ceremonies. Why do they do that? They do that so their feeling is in right relation with the world they're in. And we do none of that, we don't even think about it. So, this boat provides the right container for the feeling. That's the first thing.

J W: I often think of the spring maintenance on *Crusader* as a form of ritual. It's a tremendous effort to keep an old wooden boat in good shape, but that's only a small part of the whole project.

J H: No, it isn't a small part of it, and that's the point. It's not the talk, and it's not the people, because you can have talk and people anywhere. In our culture, we forget the importance of the place. You go somewhere to hear a talk on the Greek gods and goddesses, and you find out it's in the basement of a church with fluorescent lights, hideous folding chairs, and no windows. The place is absolutely ruinous, and you're supposed to talk about individuation or beauty or something.

I've talked about animal images in dreams for thirty years, and given seminars in many, many places, and this is the only place where it's really appropriate. Because the animals are right there. You have to be careful you don't say something stupid, because the animals are listening. You can't interpret them; you can't symbolize them; you can't do something that is only human about them. Their presence is felt.

If the boat is ignored, or just treated as a vehicle to get you here, the whole relation wouldn't work. How do we know that the whales, who come as close to the boat as they did on this trip, don't also appreciate it? How do we know that? We don't know that. The main thing is, we don't know any of that—how they perceive us, how they pick up our vibes. We know their sensitivities are extraordinary, that their hearing and communication methods are physiologically beyond ours in many ways. So how do we know they don't pick up the boat as well, and that your attention to the boat is not just keeping it in ship-shape and comfortable but something else.

J W: As we prepare the boat for the season, we do it with much of the memory of the things that happen out here each summer. There's a sense in which the adventures of every season are always present. The atmosphere seems to contain them.

J H: Suppose that, instead of the word *atmosphere,* we used the word *soul?* Suppose this boat has soul—the way people used to say, "This boat really has soul," or, "That old woman, she's got soul," or the way blacks use the word for *soul brother, soul food, soul music.* So this boat, it's a soul boat. I think that if the seminar participants and teachers who come on board bring their souls, that adds soul to the boat. You don't want religion, or "new age," or something that's going to make it . . . well, you don't want to lose the animals.

J W: I'd like to hear you talk more about the whole idea of preparation, of getting the feeling right.

J H: Getting the feeling right in relation to animals, let's talk about that. In order to go about a hunt, or to fish, or to bring the quail closer, you learn the quail songs or the buffalo songs so you can draw them in. You need those songs in order to be successful in the hunt and to feed yourself, your tribe, and your community. The hunters had to get their feeling right, or the quail and the buffalo wouldn't come; they wouldn't allow themselves to be hunted. When you're preparing the boat for a trip, you are also getting your feeling right, which is different than management.

Management is information: making sure the connections are right, that you've got everybody's addresses right, and the tickets, and the fuel. All of that is the management of a successful thing. But if you're sitting, looking out, thinking about the portholes or the lines, or you're walking through town and you see something that would go wonderfully on the boat, like a brass fitting or whatever, then your soul's engaged. It's like a writer who gets a thought and, wherever he or she is, puts it down in a notebook. Or painters who see something that moves their vision, and when they begin to paint again it comes into the painting. I think that's what must happen if your mind is meditatively on the boat. The boat becomes a vehicle for soul, like a book for a writer's soul or a canvas for a painter's soul. And that's tremendously important. It makes the whole activity more of a ritual. And then you're also not fighting the boat [*whining voice*] "Oh, this thing, I've gotta fix that, oh I don't want to . . ." You couldn't write a book that way; you couldn't paint a painting that way. You work fourteen hours a day, but it's because your soul's in it.

j w: In an article called "Trails of Meaning," Robin Riddington writes about how the Dundze, a tribe from interior Alaska, hunt. Part of their preparation is to wait for a dream, and, when it comes, the dream instructs them on how to proceed. The actual event of finding and killing the animal is understood as a re-enactment of the dream. So, when the hunter returns to the village to tell the story, it's the dream he tells.

j h: That's the whole difference between soul and management. If you were thinking about management, you would come back from this trip and say, "Well, that was a successful trip, nothing went wrong. We had one little problem with the toilet, but it all worked pretty well, and everyone was happy and they wrote a little note saying they were." It was a clean job: management. Close the book. But the dream would be something else.

And the dream has an echo that goes on in memory, in resonance, and in other souls. The best thing that could happen from this trip, for me, would be that the animals benefit. Not only that the people benefit, that the ten people all learn something, fine, they can learn something. But if something happened in the soul of these people that can reach the animals, that would be the best thing of all, because these animals have done so much for us for thousands of years. They've brought us food, they've brought us dances, they've brought us wisdom, they've brought us technical skills. Who taught us to make a halibut hook? See, this is the way people think, "Oh boy, some smart guy named Joe Jones, he invented the hook so that we could catch halibut more quickly this way than that way. What a good idea." So we call it the Joe Jones hook.

But originally, the people who lived with halibut and whose life depended on them watched the halibut, and it taught them how to make the hook. So we owe the halibut for the instrument to catch it. And we owe the deer for the way to hunt it—walking stealthily, walking downwind. They taught us all those things. We owe them so much.

From the dreams we've been working with on this boat I've tried to point out again and again that the animals come in our dreams as guides, helpers, and saviors; as teachers, again. We still are inflated to think we're saving them, but they may be teaching us about saving. What happens to our hearts when we see them wounded or hurt? That's a turning point, when the animal is hurt. They teach us something through their woundedness; that they're threatened and endangered and wounded. They're beginning to convert the world! The animal rights movement and the efforts to save endangered species have all sprung up in the last thirty years, but they've changed our consciousness enormously. The images of dead elephants, whales, seals, and birds affect us deeply. The spotted owl is saving the forest. Take it as a myth, don't take it as a law. Of course, it's a legality in that it's the only way we could get through the court system. But if we were telling the tale, the spotted owl is saving our forest. Jesus, it's there!

J W: Most psychologists tell us that when animals come into our dreams, they come as representations of some aspect of ourselves. But you're saying they come into our dreams for their own sake—to teach us something.

J H: Yes, they teach us something, but they're not part of us. They correspond with part of us. The bear dream that one man had corresponds with his own earthy, shaggy nature, and therefore he can feel an affinity. But that bear is not his own shaggy nature. That reduces the bear to just a piece of himself and insults the bear—it interprets the bear away. The presence of the bear in the dream corresponds with qualities of the human soul but is not reducible to it.

J W: How do you know when an animal is in your dream to teach you something on its own account or when it has appeared because its qualities correspond to something in your soul?

J H: I think they go together. I wouldn't want to make it an either-or. I would rather say the animal in the dream is a presence that corresponds with some interiority of your own self—your own wolf, for instance, or your relation to Wolf, whether it's insatiable appetite, or constantly tracking and pursuing, or loneliness, or something of that wolf quality. And at the same time it's a presentation of the divine wolf, the wolf god, the wolf totem, the wolf ancestor, who may be bringing you to more intensity in regard to those qualities.

So the question is, What does the wolf want? Why did it bother to come to me? Is it trying to remind me of my own wolfishness? If the animal is an ancestor, then it's going to bless those qualities. It's going to give them an archetypal background. My loneliness, my constant trekking and feeling an outsider, is blessed by the wolf's appearance. That's a nice thought.

Or take the fox. My cleverness, my sneakiness, and my trying to raid everything that happens and getting into all the chicken houses—instead of saying "this is my psychopathic shadow, this is my sex complex," the fox comes and says, "this is part of nature, this is where we connect." Then you have more respect for that part of yourself and you begin to try to live it right.

J W: By acknowledging the animal's presence on its own account, we are saying that the unconscious is not just a private place where everything that happens is ultimately about our own ego. The animal de-

mands our respect and attention, and I imagine this way of looking at
it is part of what it means to "get the feeling right" in relation to the
world around you.

J H: "Morality," "Being right," and having the "true" sense of
things—those words that are moral words in our world—come out
of religious texts or from priests. In the tribal world, those words come
out of the behavior of animals. In that world, you're not going to be
able to eat if you don't do it right. So morality is like a craftsman's morality. You have to have a "true" line, or a "right" angle. Those words,
true and *right,* are craft words, skill words.

J W: You've talked about animal presences in dreams, but what about
actual encounters in the wild? For instance, over this last week we've
been with whales, bears, salmon. . . .

J H: Eagles, seals, orcas. My goodness, it's remarkable how many
animals we've seen on this trip, and how close we've come to them!

J W: And porpoises playing off the bow! Nobody really knows why
they do that, but they sure look like they're having fun.

J H: Yes. What I tried to say yesterday had to do with corresponding
emotions. If we feel moved by the porpoise leaping and playing on the
bow, as we all did, then our emotion is corresponding to the animal.
Do you remember how everyone on board was imitating the movements of the porpoise—jumping up and down, laughing, being playful? Those emotions tell us the truth about something. When we're
afraid, emotions give us significant information about fear or desire or
anger or insult. Your emotion is corresponding to the act, the external
world. That's called the significance theory of emotion. Your emotion
is telling you about the significance of something. You look at a big
dark forest and you feel melancholy. It's telling you something about
the gestalt there.

So why not imagine that there's a correspondence between the joy we're feeling and what the porpoise is feeling? When you hear the whales blow or see them leap and turn over slowly, you get this heartfelt beauty and sadness and wonder. Why couldn't that correspond to something the whales feel about themselves? That they too are depleted; their environment is noisy; they can't communicate as they used to; and they're not appreciated. Who knows what goes on in the whale's soul? But why not read it through our own feeling? You see those eagles, you have a certain feeling of awe and terror—you don't feel warmth in your heart.

J W: No, it's more like respect.

J H: Respect, right. Amazement when they're flying up high, and respect. So why not read those emotions the way tribal people did? We would call that anthropomorphism; we use that term way too much.

The reverence that people feel, the excitement when they see the actual animal, is much more powerful than the talk or the dream or the poem, usually, because it's so unfamiliar to most of us. It's synergistic. It brings together the two, the word and the physical thing.

J W: Last night we were talking about some of the physical and spiritual challenges imposed by the need to kill in order to live. It's interesting to consider that the spiritual challenge of killing can be so intense for a culture that it can outweigh many of its other material concerns. Some ethnologists suggest that the spiritual problem of killing and eating large animals in the far north may pose a more difficult problem than dealing with the extreme cold.

J H: The Inuit people told Rasmussen that the tragedy of their life was that they were always eating other souls.

J W: Richard Nelson and Paul Shepard, among others, suggest there may be no better way to feel our connectedness to nature than to kill our own food. Although Ursula Le Guin acknowledges the necessity of killing, she says hunting is something we should outgrow. She believes she can get the same sense of connectedness by watching a sparrow fly or an old cat walk across the room. Is there something unique that we gain, and that we can't get any other way, from killing an animal?

J H: We need to be very careful, very reserved talking about killing. Our American civilization rests upon killing—animals, trees, Native Americans, Africans, Mexicans, and of course directly or indirectly people and life all over the globe. I think Ursula Le Guin is right about her cat, but she may be avoiding the issue of killing. Paul Shepard and Richard Nelson are saying that to eat, we kill. It's better to recognize this fact concretely than to deny it with supermarket-packaged meat. Nature eats nature, and we are no exception, so let us have rituals that remind us. Hunters like Richard Nelson and Paul Shepard are asking us to restore the sacramental feeling to the necessary killing that sustains life. And not only killing animals: carrots, wheat, cherries from the tree, are all killed that we may eat them. Maybe, if we were more ritualistic, more directly concrete about the killing that goes into daily eating, we might be less extravagantly mad in those other killings— the twenty thousand murders an adolescent will have watched on television, the Vietnam, Iraq, and Panama bombings, and so on. There is a horror with blood letting, and only the most serious and communal rituals can encompass this horror—like what goes on in surgery or when an animal is slaughtered and dressed for winter eating.

Practically, I don't see how we can even begin to kill, each of us, the food we need to eat daily. But we can stop for a moment when buying food, preparing food, and eating food to thank the Lord. But the Lord is not an abstraction in Heaven; the Lord we need to thank is the animal itself—a little belatedly of course—who is giving itself to our delight. Sometimes I think, I've eaten tons of meat by now. I owe the animals one helluva debt. When and how will they ask me to pay up?

J W: Are there other ways to approach this inevitable death and killing?

J H: Well, I think we can be closer to the killing of animals.

J W: What do you mean by that?

J H: We put our pets away, or put our sick horses down, and nobody sees it or knows anything about it. We don't bury our animals, we don't hold them dead in our arms. We know nothing about butchering or slaughtering any longer. We see road kills, but that's about it. The wounded, dead animal evokes a tremendous feeling.

What else can we do? We can take trips on the *Crusader*. That is, we can move to places where one is with the animal and watch it. We can be much less involved with pesticides and insecticides and allow ourselves to get in quandaries about things like that.

For example, I have chickens, and raccoons come in night after night and steal the chickens. I'm in a tremendous quandary about that. In the springtime, raccoons feed their young. This is the time when they need the chickens. But I don't want them to take *my* chickens. So I'm caught in the borderland. What do I do? That, magnified, is exactly what the Massai or the tribes of northern Kenya feel. They want to keep the wild animals away from where they're grazing their cattle. It's the same problem worldwide: what is the relation between my territory and theirs? What do I do, slaughter a chicken once a week and throw it out where the raccoons will get it? Or do I start feeding the raccoons, which would then set up a whole other system of them going into the garbage?

This is a neighborhood problem, because it involves alley cats and street dogs as well as humans. It's an important problem, because it gets us all thinking about these issues of living together. I don't have an answer—think locally and feel globally, or whatever they say.

And it means the loss of the human's position. We have to give up more territory. If I want to keep raccoons in the world, I have to give up something. So when I left, I closed my chicken house. I gave my chickens away to the guy I got them from. It wasn't right to let them get slaughtered, either. So I gave up my territory. I don't think that's the only solution, but you have to come to some terms.

When I said people should take trips on the *Crusader,* I mean people should have more direct contact and thereby feel the wonder, which is the beginning of the feeling of religion. Swedish ethnologists have said that religion began with the circumpolar people's experience with bears. That was the first feeling of religion and the beginning of doing things to propitiate the animals—to dance, to sing, to worship, to think about the bear.

We're usually taught that religion begins with burial, with death and wonder about the afterlife. But my theory is that religion grew out of the human relationship to the animal. That keeps you earthed, rather than thinking about the afterlife and beyond. I think that's a very important thought.

J W: In *Pan and the Nightmare* you describe how Pan, the goat-god of nature, died with the rise of monotheism. "What had soul, lost it; lost was the psychic connection with nature. When Pan is alive, then nature is too, and it is filled with gods, so that the owl's hoot is Athene and the mollusc on the shore is Aphrodite—how better to participate in them than through their concrete natural presentations?" Later you say that to restore our relationship to nature, both "in here" and "out there," we must start in part from Pan's point of view. "But," you say, "Pan's world includes masturbation, rape, panic, convulsions, and nightmares. The re-education of the citizen in relation to nature means nothing less than a wholly new relationship with the 'horrors' and 'moral depravations' and madness which are part of the instinctual life of the citizen's soul." Isn't this proposal in direct opposition to everything our modern culture prides itself on? How would one go about this process, and where would we find support for such a re-education?

J H: You bet those remarks in my book on Pan oppose "modern culture." Psychoanalysis from its inception opposes modern culture. Analysis is subversive. It's mainly on the side of what Freud called the *id*—at least as I understand it. This is because an analysis starts with psychopathology. It says, come along with me and explore Hell—the horrors, peculiarities, and cruelties that exist in your nature and all nature. You see, remembering Pan means remembering that nature is wild, hairy, savage, frightening—a nightmare. Pan was, after all, the god of nightmares. As children of nature we are each children of Pan. We are already performing the hell in our civic life, in our foreign policies. So the task is to find rituals and times and places and mentors who can give to wildness its due rather than have wildness take us over and turn us into adolescent savages, as in William Golding's *Lord of the Flies.*

J W: In *News of the Universe,* Robert Bly says that each time a human being's desire-energy leaves the body and goes out into the hills or forest, it whispers as it leaves, "You know, one day you will die." Bly says we need this whisper in order to be grounded. Is this the reality of seeking a relationship with nature? Is this part of the danger and the fear, that ultimately we are facing our own mortality in the act?

J H: That's a very deep thought from Bly. I think he's right on. Alone in a field or at the seashore we do feel closer to the natural boundaries set by death. We feel closer to the mystery of life and death than when actually at risk crossing the street or riding in a fast car, when death may be literally just around the corner. Then we feel fear and panic but not mystery. So we go to nature, the field, the seashore, or these Alaskan waters to feel more alive by feeling the death that nature insists we not forget. Nature seems to want us to remember death. Is that why it's so hard to get out of the house, out of the car, off the boat? I may be "dying to get out of the house," but in fact getting out of the daily routine brings you face to face with the whisper Bly hears.

J W: How do we gain access to these natural boundaries if we live in the city?

J H: Some people are doing it by watching animal movies. There's a tremendous amount more of that on television now than there was when I was a kid, or even thirty years ago. You can also get access to those feelings by engaging in the life and death of your pet, as I said earlier. Or leaving the city for periods of time. But I don't have a real solution.

J W: It's tricky, I think. Although I'm up here five months of the year, it's not my home. There's a sense in which I feel like a guest.

J H: Yet it is your neighborhood.

J W: Yes.

J H: I don't know why you have to give up either of those positions. Maybe the feeling of being a guest is an important one in the world. Suppose we're all guests. In his biography, George Santayana gave a tribute, or a memoir: "To my host, the world." He was a guest in the world. Now, that means you treat everything with great respect, if you're a guest.

J W: It has always struck me as odd that our culture fosters such extreme positions in regard to the environment. On one hand, we have the greatest leaders in conservation and the most devoted protectors of wildlife in the world, and on the other hand, we're the most consumptive and ecologically destructive. What do you think accounts for these two extremes?

J H: These two positions seem diametrically contradictory, but they stem from the same psychological ground. Neither group feels it *is* nature. The first group is the good shepherds, the caretakers, basically moralists, and moralists are always above what they are judging. The second group is the conquerors, Promethean and Herculean in their ability to overcome nature. But both groups stand apart, forever doing something *to* or *for* or *with* nature. If you feel yourself to *be* nature, no different from it, then you simply are like a tree or a squirrel in the tree, and you move along without an attitude of one kind or another. Of course, this is a very romantic view, but why not? It's no more mad than the two ways you just described in your question.

Hanging Out with Raven

BORN IN San Francisco in 1930, Gary Snyder spent most of his childhood years on a family farm in Lake City, Washington. There he raised cows and chickens, tended orchards, learned carpentry and mechanical skills, and spent summers in logging camps and forests. He also was an avid reader of books, from the age of seven on, and devoured the Seattle Public Library.

Inspired by the trees, rivers, and mountains of the Pacific Northwest, Gary began writing poetry at age fifteen. By the time he was in his late teens, he had climbed all the great peaks of the Northwest: Mt. St. Helens, Mt. Shasta, Mt. Hood, Mt. Adams, Mt. Baker, and Mt. Rainier. He later said of these climbing experiences, "It was an initiation by all the great gods of the land here."

Gary attended Reed College in Portland, Oregon, between 1947 and 1951, where he earned a reputation for brilliance in poetry and anthropology, particularly in his studies of Northwest Coast Indian myths. His undergraduate thesis, *He Who Hunted Birds in His Father's Village*, was published in 1979.

After graduating from Reed, Gary spent the following six years among poet friends such as Allen Ginsberg, Kenneth Rexroth, and Jack Kerouac in San Francisco's North Beach. During the summers of these years, he worked as a fire lookout in the forests of California and Washington. In the winter he studied oriental languages at the University of California at Berkeley. His growing interest in and affinity for oriental culture led him to Kyoto, Japan, in 1956, where he spent the following ten years studying at Daitoku-ji Sodo, mostly as a lay student. In 1968, Gary returned to Marin County, California, where he lived for two years before moving to his present home in the foothills of the Sierra Nevada.

Among Gary's books of poetry are *Riprap and Cold Mountain Poems* (1965), *Turtle Island* (for which he won the 1975 Pulitzer Prize), *Axe Handles* (1983), *Left Out in the Rain* (1986), and *No Nature* (1992). His collections of essays include *The Real Work* (1980) and *The Practice of the Wild* (1990).

Catherine Ingram writes of Gary, "Here is a backwoodsman who is familiar with everything that runs in the streams and creeks of his 'bioregion'; a man who is comfortable hiking and camping alone in the mountains for months on end; a man who chops wood, plants trees, changes diapers, dances, and sings; and here is a scholar and poet bent over centuries-old Chinese texts, pondering the words 'One the Way and One Its Power.' Here also is a man trained for more than thirty years in zazen."

This interview took place aboard the schooner *Crusader* in southeast Alaska. We had just returned from a week of sailing on the outer coasts of Baranof and Chichagof Islands. One evening on that voyage, twelve of us put on silly hats and danced on the deck. I had always read how Gary recommended such things, but never witnessed it until that evening. I looked up from my chart in time to catch Gary dancing on top of the forward anchor winch. He was gripping the forestay, keeping his balance as the bow lifted and fell over large, foamy Pacific swells. He had a mischievous sparkle in his eye and, looking back, signaled with his thumb to turn up the volume.

~·~·~

JONATHAN WHITE: You've been telling a lot of stories this last week, particularly ones from native cultures of the North Pacific rim. Why tell these stories here and now? How do they speak to us?

GARY SNYDER: The great thing about stories is you can tell them anywhere. And a good storyteller can get people into the imagination of almost any place to some extent. So you can hear Kipling's *Just So* tales, and even though you've never been to India you can get some strong sense of it. So you're not limited to telling stories in a place. But to tell a story in its own place is to get another dimension. One of the dimensions is seeing what it is in the story that comes out of that particular place.

Stories are uniquely based in every locale but at the same time they have themes and motifs that are universal to the human spirit and to cultures everywhere. This is something scholars are well aware of. What people are not quite so attentive to is how certain aspects of myth are specific to the place and to the culture. As the Jewish saying goes, "God is in the details." So there's a dimension that might easily be overlooked, which is very potent, the dimension of the place itself speaking through the folktale. You can even think of it as a mode in which animals speak to the human world through fairy tales and myths. They speak to the imagination and the imagination puts it into folktale and myth. This is the concrete side of mythology, rather than the universal side of it. So I like to bring that forward and see what the experience of the story is in its own locale, and that gives it a place-based dimension.

JW: What do you mean when you say animals speak to people through the imagination?

GS: They speak to us through the creative imagination and outward into art and myth. How do animals manifest themselves in the human world? They manifest themselves by our interpretation of them, by how we take them in and how we put them forward. For thousands of years this process has been demonstrated in cave paintings, primitive drawings of animals, little prehistoric sculptures of animals, and fish designs on early pottery. These are all real beings that are reflected in that. Our art is full of animal and plant motifs. All art is full of it. And all storytelling and song is full of animals and plants. One can ignore this and look at it as simply art, or one can say, "Ah, this is also a way that nature has entered into human culture." And what does that tell us about the human mind and about each plant or animal? There's some way in which each animal has spoken to the creative mind that it should take such form.

J W: When an animal comes into our dreams, we tend to think of it as a projection of our soul. Psychologist James Hillman says that's demeaning to the animal, because it might be coming into our dream for its own sake.

G S: Yes, that's also very much what I'm saying. Animals come into myth or dream not as projections, but as a way to speak to the human mind. In one sense, you can say that's a projection, but the fact is we couldn't have animals in our dreams if there weren't real animals. There is some kind of information that is exchanged there.

J W: What is the role of mythological stories in native cultures, and how are myths useful, particularly in the lessons they reveal about our relationship to the wild?

G S: This is a question that could be asked not just of the local performance literatures or oral literatures, as they are called, but of all literature everywhere. What is the role of literature? People have been working on that question for a long time now.

There are several basic answers. One is that when a story becomes an accepted expression of the group, it reinforces the culture, too. The stories give you a cultural identity: "These are *our* tales." They tell you both who you are and where you are. They locate you in terms of clan, local history, and the creation mythology of your region. Stories about the rocks and hills of your area give you a mythological history of why that's all there. A story may tell the origin of the name of a house, which is an explanatory tale of a certain sort. There are many, many kinds of roles. As an exercise of the imagination, a story shows how the phenomenal world is given many levels of interpretation.

Stories often have less obvious statements buried in them about the culture's stresses and tensions, its contradictions, its hidden angers, its play with power. The stories reveal the dynamics of ownership, money, prestige, status, sexuality, the body. All of these are contained in the narratives of literature, and it is the narratives of literature that become big models for what to do, what to be, how to be. Like a hero is an image of what you can be. A demon is an image of evil. A beautiful woman is a model of what women might aspire to be. All of these things become archetypalized, so to speak.

So just as we say that narratives, myths, and tales are among the biggest shapers of our imaginative life, they also shape our lives on very concrete levels of human social struggle. This is true everywhere. You could narrow it down and say, "Well, what's at work globally in these isolated maritime cultures of the North Pacific?" And, as I found out when I did my study on the Haida story, "He Who Hunted Birds in His Father's Village," not only are these stories very specific to a place but they also contain motifs and themes that are worldwide and are ten to fifteen thousand years old. So there's a dimension in which these isolated maritime cultures are participating in some very ancient cosmopolitan internationalism.

Then there's the sheer pleasure of performance. The fact that these stories were performed with mime, with masks, with dance movements, and in dramatic situations means that they're just sheer magic.

The stories are also what keeps a culture happy and vivid. It's a great pleasure to go to a good play or a really good performance of anything—a dance or a good storytelling performance or a poetry reading are all very vivid events. So these are the kinds of things that have been happening in everybody's life for tens of thousands of years.

Retelling these stories today allows us to step out of the cosmopolitan urban lives we are living and jump into a totally different imagination, within a totally different place, and yet discover how much of our imagination can still meet it. Then when we see killer whales, for example, it's good to know that they sometimes steal women and marry them and go live with them under the sea. That wouldn't come up if you were studying only their natural history. The imagination of this place is strange and new, and at the same time it's strangely familiar. That's what's fun about it.

JW: I once participated in a discussion with you and several others where you proposed an exercise in response to the question, "Where do you live?" We happened to be in Seattle, Washington, and you asked us to describe how to get there to someone coming in from outer space. After we all fumbled around for a while, you said, "Well, first you'd want to identify the Northern Hemisphere as the area with the most land, then zero in on the place where the two largest land masses almost join: the Bering Strait. Next you'd have them follow the coastline down to Vancouver Island and into the Puget Sound basin," and so on. Once we've arrived, how would you describe our feeling about this place?

GS: This is where we *live*. We are the people who are at home here now, along with a lot of other people. And as one who was born and raised on the West Coast and who went to school around Puget Sound and Portland, visiting these locations and retelling these stories is not exactly a venture into the strange and the new for me. It's part of my education and continuing enlargement within the region. And I'm fascinated with the oldness and the newness of it. Its newness is in that the maritime Northwest and North Pacific is one of the last places on Earth to have been transformed by Euro-American civilization. Parts of this countryside were not contacted until the 1840s, several centuries later than European contact on the Atlantic seaboard. And so, from the standpoint of Euro-American culture, it's new.

From the broader standpoint of humanity, this region has a long history of intense cultural activities. The region is biologically very potent. The biological wealth of the coastal waters and mountains is extraordinary, just extraordinary. And the beauty of the mountains and the glaciers and the fjords of Alaska, the volcanoes of Washington and Oregon, and the uniquely diverse botany and climate of California as a continuation southward—it's all quite wonderful.

The big rain forests of British Columbia, Washington, Oregon, and Northern California are the densest, richest temperate rain forests in the world and the only ones that have survived until modern times. The European and Asian temperate forests were cut down some centuries ago. As I wrote in *The Practice of the Wild,* the big forests of the Northwest had the highest biomass—the most tons of living matter per acre—of any forest in the world, including all the tropical rain forests. The coastal redwood forests of California have the highest biomass of any place on Earth. There's no tropical rain forest that has as much *stuff* growing.

So this countryside is wonderfully powerful and rich. And it's also where we live. Every place is unique, each in its own way. But this is where *we* are. Part of my exercise as a writer and a person living in this century and place is to intuitively and intellectually pick up both the echoes of this region from the people who lived here before the Euro-Americans came and the echoes that speak of its own presence, through its own nature. That's an exercise in knowing my place in every sense.

For people of North America and Canada, the exercise of knowing where you are is the beginning of making a culture of this continent, which we call Turtle Island.

The stories that come from here are not just Aleut, Eskimo, and Athabascan tales. They are a heritage of the classical literature of twenty-first-century America. They are classical tales that will be absorbed in the future by civilizations who will appreciate the North Pacific. These stories are laying the groundwork for a new round of classics. They'll be in the curriculum, one of the things kids will grow up with, alongside Greek, Chinese, Japanese, and Indian mythologies. If they live here, they'll say that these are *our* stories, and not marginalize them by calling them the stories of native people.

These old stories touch *our* lives, too. If an eagle is flying outside the window, that is the same eagle that is in these myths, not just a twentieth-century eagle. And so, to know what Eagle or Raven is doing in the myth is to know what they are doing today.

J W: So myth time is somehow both present and past. The eagle that just flew by is not different than the one in the stories.

G S: Well, everything is still the same. The way the clouds look out there and the way the light looks—they looked exactly the same to the Tlingit people. We're seeing the same view.

It came to me down in the Sacramento Valley last year that the breeze in the oak trees and the song of the black-headed grosbeak was that of a long time ago. I was hearing exactly the same song that California Indian people heard five thousand years ago. *Lots* of things are still right here, we're living in the same realm, actually. So if those old stories have something to say about Raven or about Black-headed Grosbeak, that is *real*. It's not something that's only in the past; it's also in the present. Just like the light and the mist on the water are in the present.

J W: You've said a number of times that we don't have to look at this landscape as a fantastic wilderness area, that this is the way it's supposed to be.

G S: I tend to speak highly of the biological wealth of the waters and the region up here. In part, it's because it has survived or, in the case of the protected sea otter and seal populations, actually come back. When you read early Spanish accounts of California, you learn that the California grizzly was as large as the Kodiak brown bear; it went up to eighteen hundred pounds or a ton. The streams were full of salmon. There were deer and pronghorn running this way and that. You can see the same view in the early literature of Ireland, Scotland, France, Germany, even the Mediterranean. There were literally more animals and more birds and more fish. They've been severely depleted all over the world. When we come to some place like Alaska, we think, "Oh, this is fantastic." But it is *normal*. It's the way the rest of the world was. And so we can look at this and remind ourselves that this is how it's supposed to be. This is not something fantastic; this is a kind of goal for our future planet. That's a helpful thing to do. I think some people respond to the riches of wildlife you see up here because it touches some kind of archetypal chord that goes beyond mere reason. There's a fundamental human delight in seeing creatures, enjoying their movement, their flight, their beauty. There's great strength in that.

J w: You've often talked about how the first step in getting to know a place is getting to know the plants. You've called that step nature literacy. How does the process of getting to know a place proceed from there? Would you explain why you're so adamant about knowing the plants?

G s: Well, really I'm not so adamant about it. In fact, I'm not nearly as good with plants as I'd like to be myself. But it's an interesting and really fundamental notion that to be acquainted with a place is to be acquainted with its natural vegetation. That acquaintance is something people take for granted in most of the world. Knowing the plants is part of everyone's cultural heritage.

And this isn't something just for hunting-and-gathering people or wilderness culture people. We should all have at least a nodding acquaintance with most of the plants in the landscape. The fact that we don't even realize that knowing plants is part of what most people know when they live somewhere is an indication of how far removed we are from understanding our place.

This is what I call nature literacy. Because the word *literacy* is a popular word, and it's considered a bad thing to be illiterate, I say this to make people aware that maybe they are illiterate about nature.

And it isn't just plants. Nature literacy is being tuned to the weather and to birds and animals. It's having a sense of what your particular climatic type is. It's knowing what river you're living on or where your drinking water comes from. That leads right into the processes of one's own household. Where does your fuel or firewood or energy come from? An overall nature literacy touches on these kinds of things. And maybe it goes farther, into a certain amount of regional environmental history: When were these forests first logged? Is this second growth or third growth? Does the vegetation we see here represent the original vegetation, or has it been changed? What was the effect of grazing around here? When was the last forest fire? Has this ever been under a big flood? Those are all really interesting questions that are a pragmatic part of living in a place.

So there's nothing esoteric about nature literacy. It's not like becoming a scientist or a fanatic. What can we be expected to know? I like to use it that way. And then a person could say, "Well, I don't know as much as I should."

J W: Does this literacy extend to the cities? Is it possible to achieve a sense of place or home by getting to know an urban landscape?

G S: Yes. This is not only important in nature or in rural areas. It makes no difference whether you're in the city or in the suburbs. So, as the urban bioregional people say, "What are the steps by which your city water comes to you? Where does your solid waste go? What are the energy pathways by which you live?" The larger housekeeping and the smaller housekeeping. Your very house has its own little ecology, as your city does. There is an ecology of energy, waste, water, food coming in in trucks, and garbage going out in other trucks. This should not just be information for engineers and urban planners; it should be part of our understanding. Life becomes more real.

Most of the rhododendrons and camellias found in urban and suburban gardens of the world come from plants that were carried out of the mountains of southwest China in the early nineteenth century.

The British loved them. They arranged to have horseback loads packed out from Yunnan Province. They sailed them around to England, planted them in English nurseries, played with them, crossbred them, propagated them, and got them into gardens as far away as British Columbia. Portland, Oregon, and Seattle are full of rhododendrons that came via England from southwest China.

So there's all kinds of urban and agricultural ecology to know. It's a pity to consign that to experts. There are situations where people don't even know how to find their own house, or which way is north. We live in a time of surprising ignorance.

In the ideal curriculum, there would be more of this kind of familiarity with the way things work, starting in grade school. And all of that is like the groundwork for my imaginary civilization of the late twenty-first century, in which Aleut tales are part of the classics.

J W: Will you talk about some of your own experiences in getting to know a place? Are there times when a place makes itself known to us?

G S: You see things differently by actively studying plants, flowers, weather, birds, over a long period. At my place, I've begun to have little recognitions of things that have been there all along but I haven't noticed them before. They come clear in a different way than they do when you simply go out and study them. There's a big, old live oak down in one end of the meadow I have walked by hundreds of times. I knew what it was—an interior live oak. I've crawled under it on several occasions. It was no mystery to me. But one day last spring, I stopped and took a look at it, and I really *saw* it. In a sense, it showed itself to me. No woo-woo about it. It wasn't anything particularly magical or anything, it's just that I really *saw* it. I could see that it was very old and that it had been through maybe one full fire that had burned it down, its base thickened by a rebuilt root stalk. Its wonderfully complex arm structure was sheltering a horde of birds. I saw these forms as though for the first time.

It's a gift; it's like there's a moment in which the thing is ready to let you see it. In India, this is called *darshan*. *Darshan* means getting a view, and if the clouds blow away, as they did once for me, and you get a view of the Himalayas from the foothills, an Indian person would say, "Ah, the Himalayas are giving you their *darshan*"; they're letting you have their view. This comfortable, really deep way of getting a sense of something takes time. It doesn't show itself to you right away.

It isn't even necessary to know the names of things the way a botanist would. It's more important to be aware of the *suchness* of the thing; it's a reality. It's also a source of a certain kind of inspiration for creativity. I see it in the work of Georgia O'Keeffe. She had that eye, you know.

J W: My understanding of what you're talking about grows more out of my experiences on this boat—underway on this coast—than it does in being in a specific locale. There are subtle discoveries that seem to be given with time. For example, sometimes I can tell how fast the boat is moving through the water—often within a tenth of a knot—by the sound and shape of the bow wave.

G S: Those things gradually come to you. Those are the kinds of craft and skill knowledges that make people able to do all the great things they're able to do. Whether it's fishing or hunting or running a kayak or anything else, you get it by practice. There are some things that only come by doing them enough times. So living in place is also something that takes practice. *Practice,* as we use the word in Buddhism, means doing it, and doing it a lot of times. There's no substitute for that. As in *The Practice of the Wild,* getting intimate with nature and knowing our own wild natures is a matter of going face to face many times.

J W: In *The Practice of the Wild,* you talk about our attraction to being out in nature because it's where the unknown happens, where we encounter surprise. I also feel a longing to belong to the out-of-doors, to somehow meet it, to appreciate it, and also to feel appreciated by it. I'm challenged by my experiences in nature to stand up and to be more centered and alert. The natural world is a community I want to be a part of, because I have more respect for myself when I'm engaged with it. When I walk through the woods in bear country, I have mixed feelings about warning bears of my presence. On one hand, I need to be cautious and prevent an accidental and potentially dangerous encounter, but on the other hand I want to see them and be as close to them as I can.

G S: You find both kinds of people. There are many people who don't want that closeness at all and couldn't care less about it. And then you find people for whom there's a powerful attraction to get closer. I think there may be some fundamental differences in human character there. I have a friend who says there are wild people and there are tame people.

And it is, as you say, an ambivalent or possibly dangerous attraction, because you want to get closer when maybe you shouldn't, when maybe you're being an intruder. I long ago learned to control my desire to go to certain Indian ceremonies—out of respect for them, actually. I felt it was better that they happened without me intruding, and that I could enjoy them from afar. I feel that way about grizzly bears, that their space should be their own. And yet I would love to hang out with them, *ideally.* But maybe one of the ways we hang out with them is in stories, since it's not a good idea to try to do it too literally. So we take it away from a literal context and internalize it and have a story of "The Woman Who Married a Bear." It's another way of closeness. Getting close with bear-ness inside ourselves. But we must not forget our concern for the welfare of endangered bear species. James Hillman would like that.

There's another angle that's interesting, too. People, myself included, are drawn to the powerful, the outstanding in nature—the bear, the mountain, the forest. We put our little boots and packs on and go out into it. There's a whole lot to be gained that way. I was a fanatic mountaineer for many years, climbed many snow peaks, and I just loved it. But I gradually learned to see the more ordinary things as well, the not-so-spectacular, the not-so-big and dramatic, and to appreciate that there are little processes equally wild but less dramatic going on all the time. I think there's a refinement that's possible as we grow, and also as we practice, which is recognizing that in small ways around us there are things equally mysterious, equally beautiful, not so remote, maybe not even so threatening. An interesting challenge is how to deal with mosquitoes. There's wild nature! Many angles.

The Chinese say that the raw person delights in the gaudy and spectacular; the cooked person delights in the ordinary.

J W: So being familiar is like getting cooked?

G S: Yes. When things are really familiar and boring to you, maybe *then* is when you'll really start seeing. And you'll be surprised by what you see once in a while. Familiarity could breed contempt, but if familiarity leads to further respect, things open up. That's really true in human relationships, too. A real key to getting deeper with somebody is to keep your familiarity respectful.

J W: When I spoke with whale biologist Roger Payne, I asked him whether wild animals are interested in us. Once in a while they behave in ways that seem extraordinarily friendly or curious. When I was sailing off Vancouver Island some months ago, a pod of orcas approached our boat. We spent several hours with them, and they with us. They could have swum away at any time, but they stayed very close, within yards.

G S: Well, it's great that the world is that way. The difference between having seen that kind of thing and not is the difference between people who assume the natural world is some kind of mechanism to be exploited and people who see it as extravagance and performance and reality and mystery. To the latter, the natural world has its own kind of consciousness, something you wouldn't want to wreck. For people who see that—like seeing porpoises breaking off the bow for the first time—it may be enough to change them inside. I would hope that's the case—that people are touched in small ways, more than they realize.

J W: In *The Practice of the Wild,* you say that American society "operates under the delusion that we are each a kind of 'solitary knower'—that we exist as rootless intelligences without layers of localized contexts. . . . In this there is no real recognition that grandparents, place, grammar, pets, friends, lovers, children, tools, the poems and stories we remember, are what we *think with*." Would you talk more about what you mean by the delusion of the solitary knower?

G S: That term, *the solitary knower,* is another way of talking about the myth of the hero or the individual ego that people in our culture seem to imagine as having no parents, no community, and no other connections. In a psychological sense, it's the delusion that the self is forever set apart and has no real association with the rest of the world. It also can be seen as the Western scientific and philosophical stance toward objective truth. That is, the belief that you can come up with ideas about the world as though you weren't part of it. In physics, the Heisenberg Uncertainty Principle tells us that there is no such thing as an objective view. The act of observing changes what we observe.

The other way of understanding this is to realize there is no "knowing" without the rich web of connections into which we are all born. We don't have solitary, pure, personal ideas. All of our thoughts have been given to us by the context in which we live. As Teilhard de Chardin says, the knower is how the environment gets to know itself.

J W: There seems to be a number of ways of looking at this. The biologist Lynn Margulis says that we are connected with every other living being through time and space.

GS: Yes. It doesn't surprise me that this is coming up in other places. The Buddhist way of talking about the delusion of the separate self is to say "no self." That's what my phrase "no nature" means—no inherent predictable characteristics.

JW: In *The Practice of the Wild,* you also talk about taking a different approach to evolution than the paradigm offered by Social Darwinism. There are other creative possibilities, you say. For example, a food source can bring a form into existence, like the way huckleberries and salmon call for bears. You said, "The sperm whale may be sucked into existence by the pulsing, fluctuating pastures of squid."

GS: You know, I didn't invent that idea. There's an interesting book by G. Evelyn Hutchinson called *The Ecological Theater and the Evolutionary Play,* in which he makes the point that evolutionary and ecological processes work together. That evolution does not take place except in a context of ecological forces, and vice versa. And so you can look at the evolutionary model as a species running through time, changing through competition or stimulus-response relationship to other species or individuals, but not necessarily to the environment. And then the story is of the *species.* Or you can look at it in terms of the *habitat*—the ecological theater. From this perspective, the theater or habitat sets the limits and shapes the behavior of what the species can do. For example, if there is a food source and nobody is eating it, some organism will evolve to have the capacity to eat it. From the evolutionary standpoint, this is an opportunistic venture on the part of that species to go and utilize the resource. But from the ecological standpoint, the resource made the species happen, and the species is simply the victim of the condition. If I create a condition out there, I will make people run into that condition and shape themselves to it. If I open a pulp mill, for example, I will create a generation of men who spend their lives working in a pulp mill. They will think, "*I* chose to work in a pulp mill." From my standpoint, I will think "*I* created a bunch of guys who are pulp mill workers."

So those two dynamics are at work in nature, too. And it's good to see it from both standpoints. It's good to understand that the range of the world itself has made things happen, that there would be no orcas without seals, no seals without salmon, and no salmon without little pink plankton.

Why are there so many Inupiaq people living on the shores of the Arctic Ocean? Why were more people living there in pre-European contact times than in central Utah? From the ecological point of view, the answer is that colder northern waters lock in more oxygen. The chain of events goes like this: colder water means more oxygen, which means more nutrients, higher plankton population, more fish, more seals, and then more people who live off seals.

We may think we're the masters of our fates, but from another standpoint we are entirely at the mercy of the conditions that created us. There's a certain pleasure in allowing ourselves to learn what the conditions that brought us into existence are. So Buddhist whales would be putting plankton on their altar and making a little bow to them. A little whale bow. That's what they have those big flippers for, so they can go like this. *[Gary puts his hands together and nods his head.]*

J W: In this context, is there a sense in which a landscape will call for a certain kind of language, the way cold water will call for more nutrients? Can a poem be a kind of echo of place, a way the place speaks to us?

G S: I wouldn't say literally a language. Languages seem to have their own ways of moving from place to place. Languages travel with human beings. But they obviously pick up vocabularies and strategy and become transformed in some way by the locale. What you're talking about is how the literature or the literary imagination grows out of a place.

With my background in anthropological linguistics, I would definitely avoid saying there is a language that belongs to a particular place. In a poetic sense there is a language of place, which is a language of flowers and seasons, such as haiku. Haiku, with its convention of always belonging to one of the four seasons and having different plants come forth, can be said to be a poetry that has become a language of place. There are specific cases where you can see that at work. And the language of myth is the same. The vocabulary of myth, the animals and creatures that are chosen to speak in myth, are part of the way language takes shape. Raven is part of the language of the Northwest Coast, so to speak, because it's a figure in the mythology. There are creatures that live here that have not entered into the mythology, which is also an interesting question. Why some birds but not others? Some things get passed over; other things become strong presences. Nobody I know of knows why.

J W: Does a place call out for a certain way to be in or near it? Is there a sense in which we learn how to be in the forest by the example of the forest? Or to be on the ocean by the example of the ocean?

G S: Usually people don't go out into the forest just for fun. They don't do what they do on the ocean just for fun, they go out to fish. Or they go in the forest to gather plants or to hunt or to sing. It's interesting how our archaic relationship is always a practical one.

My wife Carole and I like to go for walks. And when we walk, I also like to look for food. I try to bring back some manzanita berries or some mushrooms. I make it into a foraging trip. All walks should be foraging, and that's a pleasure. Because you see better. It sharpens your eye in another way. That's the way the old-time people did it. And if they didn't bring something back home, they'd remember what they saw that might be useful later. If they noticed a downed oak or a certain kind of plant, they'd remember where to go when they needed those things for firewood or food. They memorized the landscape that way.

We learn as we participate, and one way we participate is by looking for food. It's a primary activity. The environment teaches us in subtle ways around that activity. When we notice the skunk cabbages have been dug out, we know a bear has been through. This is an interpretation, a kind of reading. You know the signs; you read them. Knowing that a certain kind of shimmer on the surface of the water is actually a school of fish is a learning thing. So you learn exactly in that way, by doing what you have to do, traditionally, historically. It's the oldest and strongest way to learn.

Mountains Constantly Walking

IN THE WORDS of Raymond Mungo, Dolores LaChapelle "is a lithe, lean woman who is both a walking encyclopedia of earth lore, authoritative and scholarly, and a wild pixie-ish spirit eager to run off to waterfalls and forest glens for joyful invocations and tiptoe dancing."

Dolores, her two sisters, and her mother and father moved to Denver, Colorado, shortly after Dolores's birth in Kentucky in 1926. Her father, of Cherokee descent, stayed at home with the three girls during their early years. He took them on long walks at dawn, teaching them the names of plants, how water flows, where rocks come from, and how to rescue spiders from the household bathtub.

Although Dolores learned to ski and climb trees early, it wasn't until age seventeen that she climbed her first mountain. Joining the Colorado Mountain Club, she climbed the fourteen-thousand-foot Pikes Peak by moonlight, making the final ascent at sunrise. The morning light, she says, made the mountain look as beautiful as Heidi had described it in Johanna Spyri's famous novel by the same name, a favorite of Dolores's childhood. That morning on Pikes Peak convinced Dolores that she would need to climb mountains for the rest of her life. And she has, throughout the western United States, Canada, Europe, and Japan.

After graduating Phi Beta Kappa from Denver University in 1947,

Dolores took a job teaching elementary school in Aspen, where she could ski on weekends and climb mountains in the summer. Two years later she met her husband, Ed LaChapelle, while climbing in the Canadian Rockies. They married in 1950 and moved to Switzerland where Ed finished his studies at the Swiss Federal Avalanche Institute. Two years later, with a new son, they moved to Alta, Utah. For the following seventeen years, Dolores worked as a ski instructor in winter and spent summers conducting research with Ed on the Blue Glacier in Washington's Olympic National Park.

Dolores now lives in Silverton, Colorado, where she teaches Tai Chi, writes, climbs, skis, and directs the Way of Mountain Learning Center. Her first book, *Earth Festivals,* was published in 1976, followed by *Earth Wisdom* in 1978 and *Sacred Land, Sacred Sex: Rapture of the Deep* in 1988.

Dolores joined us in southeast Alaska for a week aboard the schooner *Crusader.* One afternoon we took a skiff across Wrangell Narrows and walked among the thick spruce and giant skunk cabbage of Kupreanof Island. We picked a few of the first ripening salmonberries and sat down on the stairs of a newly framed cabin by the water. We talked until late, watching the tide go out and the sky darken. It wasn't until midnight that we were rowing back across Wrangell Narrows.

~·~·~

JONATHAN WHITE: The term *deep ecology* appears frequently in your work. Could you talk about what this means and where the term comes from?

DOLORES LACHAPELLE: You can't talk about deep ecology without talking about the Norwegian philosopher Arne Naess. He's not only an expert on Gandhi and Spinoza but he's also an accomplished mountaineer.

Arne first described the difference between deep ecology and the more prevalent shallow ecology at the Third World Futures Conference in Bucharest in 1972. Shallow ecology, he said, is the fight against pollution and resource depletion. Its central objective is the health of people in developed countries. Deep ecology, he said, rejects the man-in-environment image in favor of the relational, total-field image. Deep ecology's objectives are to uphold the rights of every form of life—both human and nonhuman—and to promote diversity, symbiosis, local economy, and decentralization.

In 1979 Arne wrote a paper called "Essentials of a New Philosophy of Nature" in which he says, "Certain kinds of systems-thinking or gestalt-thinking are necessary tools for understanding the holistic character of nature. . . . What is needed is a 'deep' conception and plan of action going down to the roots—societal, political, economic—of the present impasse."

Back then Arne wasn't using the term *deep ecology* much because he didn't believe it was comprehensive. He preferred *ecosophy,* a combination of the Greek words *oikos* and *sophia,* meaning "wisdom of the household." This term is too abstract for most people, and Arne now recognizes that deep ecology is probably the best term for this perspective.

J W: You're one of the original proponents of deep ecology in the United States. How did you get involved?

D L: I met Arne Naess in 1977 and, while hiking on the lower slopes of Mt. Baldy in California, I had the chance to discuss ecological matters with him for the first time. There were many of us working on these concepts. Joe Meeker and Paul Shepard were working together on a possible new program for International College titled New Natural Philosophy. Joe and Paul both wrote me about it after seeing my first book, *Earth Festivals.* Arne came over from Norway to meet with them on the same project. I met George Sessions later, but he had been teaching a course at Sierra State since 1975 called "Rationality, Mysticism, and Ecology." He met Arne in the spring of 1978 when Arne was teaching at UC Santa Cruz and called together a group to discuss Spinoza. Gary Snyder had been using deep ecological principles in his poetry long before Arne defined the term. There were others who were working on these ideas about that time, too, like Bill Devall and Michael Zimmerman. Later, Dave Foreman of EarthFirst! became an advocate of deep ecology principles.

As the 1980 tenth anniversary of Earth Day approached, I received an invitation to submit a paper to the University of Denver Colloquium. I thought the invitation was an accident, because I had never gotten a call for papers before. I sent an abstract along and, to my surprise, it was accepted. While I was working on my paper and feeling depressed by the mainstream, anthropocentric, Christian environmental literature I was reading, I got a big packet of newsletters called *Eco-Philosophy* from George Sessions, whom I had not yet met. George had been documenting the growth of what Arne Naess originally termed Eco-Philosophy since 1974. George's paper had been selected for the Denver Colloquium too, so we met at the University and gave our presentations. We used the term *deep ecology* to describe what we were talking about, and there was a lot of interest and discussion about it, especially among the academic types.

As a result of the friendships made at that conference, Bill, George, Michael Zimmerman (who is now head of the Philosophy department at Tulane University) and I got together in Colorado to walk in the mountains and talk. We called it our "Heidegger in the Mountains" conference, because both Michael and I had done a lot of thinking and writing on Heidegger. That's when we first started talking seriously about deep ecology in this country.

It wasn't too much later that George Sessions and Bill Devall began thinking of putting a book together. I agreed, and bought a book on cooperative publishing. Then Bill found some interest at Dream Garden Press. From then on, the story is long and complicated. But essentially, what happened is that two books by the same title—*Deep Ecology*—came out at once, one by George Sessions and Bill Devall (ultimately published by Gibbs Smith) and one by Michael Tobias. Because neither of the books was put together well, and neither represented deep ecology accurately, the movement got off to a confusing start.

J W: I'm not sure anyone knows what it is, still.

DL: It's easy to see why many academics and intellectuals have such a difficult time with deep ecology. If it can't be defined within the narrow Eurocentric tradition then it simply doesn't exist. What they don't realize is that it's not limited by the Greek, Christian, humanistic tradition. It's based on the essential nature of all beings. Arne Naess says that in order to clarify the discussion one must avoid looking for one definite philosophy or religion among its supporters. I agree. Fortunately there is a rich variety of interpretations that can be derived from the principles of deep ecology. Arne sometimes uses the word *biocentric,* meaning "life-centered." But there are those Greek words again. Why not just say life-centered?

Arne's term *ecosophy* is a good one—if we must have a Greek word—because it allows for all these different ways of looking at it. Many aspects fall under "wisdom of the household," so you don't have to fight these dumb battles of who's right and who's wrong and who's not deep enough.

In an interview in *Ten Directions,* from the Zen Center in Los Angeles, Arne asks the critical questions that are essential to living deep ecology: "We ask whether the present society fulfills basic human needs like love and security and access to nature. We ask which society, which education is beneficial for all life on the planet as a whole, and then we ask further what we need to do in order to make the necessary changes."

I began my Way of Mountain newsletter in 1982 in response to these questions and principles, and each year since then I've tried to note the most important books and essays on the subject.

JW: The deep ecology movement has been criticized for its antihuman position. For example, in Al Gore's book *Earth in the Balance,* he says the problem with deep ecology is "that it defines human beings as inherently and contagiously destructive, the deadly carriers of a plague upon the earth." He goes on to say that the logic of deep ecology points to only one cure: eliminating people. Gore's criticism is particularly harsh and perhaps misguided, but I believe it reflects the general perspective toward deep ecology.

DL: No, deep ecology is not antihuman. It's larger than the human. It includes humans within the whole of life, not setting them apart from life or above life. There's some talk that we humans need to become humble, artificially humble. But that's not the point. As soon as you pay attention, you are at once humbled by what you do not know. Take our bodies, for example. The bacteria inside us are constantly working to sustain life, yet we have little or no awareness of it.

Deep means going deeply into the human. Perhaps some of the confusion over this question comes from the criticism deep ecologists direct at our modern industrial growth society. It's becoming obvious to everyone that this modern system cannot continue. Well, the answer is not to use more of the same tactics. The only way out is to relearn or just remember the techniques that made us human in the first place. Those are the techniques that governed humankind and our relations with the earth for the past fifty thousand years. If these techniques hadn't been successful, we wouldn't be here. It's as simple as that.

JW: What *are* the techniques that made us human in the first place?

DL: What is it that you most like to do? Chances are it's some variation of hunting, dancing, racing, conversation, or flirting. This is the life of primitive hunter-gatherers who, like the aristocrats of all cultures, made no distinction between leisure and life. Primitive tribes are the original affluent society. The primitive !Kung San bushmen, who live in the most inhospitable desert in the world, work an average of twenty hours a week. The rest of the time is devoted to dancing and storytelling and ritual.

Primitive man is not the sick, beleaguered, pre-scientific creature we've been taught to believe he is. Instead, he is a highly social, responsible being who lived in some degree of harmony with his environment.

Cultural man has been on Earth for over two million years, and for 99 percent of that time he's been a hunter-gatherer. Only in the last ten thousand years have we turned to farming. We're fooling ourselves by thinking we can draw on some new potential here. We and our ancestors are the same people. That's who we are! We still have the sophisticated body and highly complex brain of the hunter, yet in the last four hundred years we've been trying to force this body/brain into the tight, dull, limited, violent view of modern industrial culture. The breakdown is showing up all over the place—in stress-related diseases, alcoholism, suicide, devastation of land, and so on. The end of this modern system does not mean the end of all life, it means the return to real living and responsible relationship.

The "old ways," thanks to Gary Snyder, has come to mean our rather sudden and recent remembering of who we are and what we should be doing on Earth. And it turns out to be exactly what we want to be doing.

J W: When you say "the end of this modern system," do you mean that literally? Can we use our present technology and science to undo the problems it has caused, as David Brower suggests, or do we need to find entirely new tools to rediscover "real living and responsible relationship"?

D L: The titles of books these days, such as *Reweaving the Sacred Web, Healing the Earth,* and so on, imply that we think we can accomplish the necessary work by still more planning and ideas. But it's not the earth that threw us out. We threw ourselves out. Rational, human planning is part of the problem, not part of the solution.

Just before he died, Gregory Bateson said the biggest task ahead is reinserting humanity back into nature. That's not going to happen through philosophy or science. It happens through direct experiences where you know you are part of nature with no questions asked.

Long before I heard of any of the concepts we're talking about, I was experiencing them while skiing and mountain climbing. For years I skied deep powder and had come to know the bliss of interacting with snow, gravity, and humans in a group. It was an experience of ritual long before I had any words for it. One of the first times I thought about this was on a day in Alta, Utah, when it was snowing graupel, which are hard, round pellets the size of marbles that roll down the hill. Most skiers don't know about graupel because it happens rarely and under miserable weather conditions, but it combines the best of powder and corn snow for skiing. So on this particular day most everyone was in the lodge except six of us. It was miserable on the chair lift. We had to hold on for life and bury our faces in our hoods. But once on top, it was total bliss all the way down. All together, all the way. We had to ski in the trees because that was the only place where we could see. Later in the afternoon I began to wonder what was going on. My friend on the chair ahead of me looked like he was suffering unbearably, yet actually we were in sheer bliss. I couldn't figure it out except that it had something to do with the effortless flow of all of us skiing together down the mountain. It wasn't a matter of thinking about turns or avoiding a collision with another skier or a tree. We were all moving together with no thought. Humans get a chance to move like this together only rarely. Like the flock of wild geese Barry Lopez describes at Tule Lake, we were each part of the group yet also part of something larger. "I never saw two birds so much as brush wingtips in the air," he says. "They roll up into a headwind together in a seamless movement that brings them gently to the ground like falling leaves."

J W: So you're not skiing the mountain, it's skiing you?

D L: Yes. Bach once answered the question of how he could play so beautifully by saying that he didn't play the music, it played him. Whenever something is going very well with no effort I think most of us have the feeling that we're not the one doing it but that it's being done. That's an experience of the sacred.

One spring I experienced the difference between right- and left-brain skiing when a group of us were asked to ski in a Warren Miller film. Each time we came down the mountain Warren would say, "I want you to turn over there in front of that tree or over there," and so on. So we would ski down the same slope with the same snow, but the bliss wasn't there. It all looked good on film, but nothing was happening. That's when I first asked, "What's going on here?"

As I paid attention to my skiing, I noticed that I set the first turn and from then on the snow and the valley did the turning. When Warren Miller asked me to turn in a certain place, I'd have to start thinking, and as soon as I did that the rhythm was broken. It's still fun, but it's a whole different thing: more left- than right-brain skiing. And I got tired fast, too; whereas when I'm letting the mountain and the snow do the turning, I can ski in two to three feet of powder all day without being tired. This is where I first learned about this feeling.

j w: I worked in Poland with a group of people at Jerzy Grotowski's Institute for Actor Research in 1974 and 1975. As a group of ten we did a lot of physical exercises together, including running in the forests and mountains for hours or days at a time. It was all nonverbal work designed to invoke the experience of what Grotowski called an "essential connectedness" to ourselves, each other, and the forests and mountains around us. I think the feeling we were working toward is similar to what you describe in skiing. It's not an intellectual process but some other kind of knowing in the body.

d l: Yes, that's deep ecology! You can experience this in a lot of different ways. I often have this experience while climbing the mountains in Colorado. One spring morning, for example, I took off with my old friend George to climb Mt. Snowden, a 13,077-foot peak. I figured we would climb the easier side since neither of us had been out for awhile, but George arrived that morning with all his hardware.

We started up the trail with me leading to set the pace (George is thirty years younger). As we got higher, we moved more carefully and eventually roped up for the 5.8 sections. I thought it was going to get too difficult, but the mountain kept opening up. Later, as we climbed down the next buttress, George kept checking on me. "Don't forget it's a long fall," he yelled. Even though it was fourth-class rock, we didn't need to rope up.

Then the bliss took over—a state of total relaxation, total alertness, total joy and thankfulness that the mountain is allowing you to do this. It's being at home—completely at home, like nowhere else. Friends say, "Oh yeah, you're just addicted to adrenaline." But that's the point, there is no adrenaline when you feel so safe, so good, so flowing. And, as it turned out, I was healed on that day from a back injury that was causing a lot of pain in my groin. I don't even remember when the pain left me, but it was somewhere on that mountain.

Later I came across a beautiful piece by D. H. Lawrence that reminded me of these experiences in the mountains. He was watching porpoises off the bow of a ship and apparently dictated this to his wife, Frieda: "Mingling among themselves in some strange single laughter of multiple consciousness, giving off the joy of life. . . . togetherness in pure complete motion, many lusty bodied fish." He goes on and then at the end he says, "This is the purest achievement of joy I have seen in all my life. . . . What civilization will bring us to such a pitch of swift laughing togetherness as these fish have reached?"

Gregory Bateson says that there is a larger mind of which the individual mind is only a subsystem. "Our consciousness, especially our left brain activity, is just a sampling of the events and processes of the body and of what goes on in the total mind," he says. "This larger mind is what some people may mean when they say God. Another way to look at it is to realize that the lines we draw between us and the environment are artificial. They are not boundaries of the thinking system." Bateson's great example of this is the blind person walking down the sidewalk with his white stick. Where do his "eyes" end? Where his hand touches the stick? Halfway down the stick? Where the stick touches the sidewalk? Where do his senses end? Nowhere. His "eyes" are the connection between the brain, the hand on the stick, the stick tapping the sidewalk, and so on. It's a systemic circle.

I don't think any of this is particularly new. Before modern times the interaction between nature and primitive people was probably like this much of the time. We experience the total alertness and joy of this large mind only sporadically, and it feels a little bit like magic. But as the anthropologist Paul Radin says, primitives lived "in a blaze of reality." They distinguished the things of their world down to the finest detail, much more so than we, and included them in the sacred.

In certain traditional cultures, daily life was lived with a feeling of connection to this larger mind. Once in a while, people had to leave this flow in order to accomplish a task that demanded more rational consciousness. Special rituals were used, led by shamans or medicine men, to take in the danger of this concerted rational effort. This happened among the Hopi when a group traveled a long, dangerous journey to get salt. It happened among other tribes, too, when they traveled to dig turquoise. These efforts were undertaken for a short time for a specific purpose, and when they were over, rituals were needed to bring the people back into the flow, back into the daily life of their place. In our modern industrial growth society we do the opposite. We live most of our lives trying to accomplish the rational, one-pointed, concerted efforts. Modern people tend to ignore ritual, thinking that human beings have evolved beyond all that. This is just another trap of the rational mind.

J W: Has there been some biological or physiological change over the last ten thousand years that might account for the difference in our relation to this mind at large?

D L: We and our ancestors are the same people. A study from Stanford called "The Changing Images of Man" states that our intellectual and spiritual capacity has remained at the same level for at least twelve thousand years. What may be needed, the report says, is a "blending of our cognitive and spiritual capacities with a new set of supporting tools and social technology." It has been suggested that nature rituals become a part of this social technology. Such rituals can produce a better understanding of our place within the greater whole of nature.

The feeling we're talking about—this feeling I get from powder skiing or mountain climbing—can be achieved through ritual. Ritual began with early humans in the sacred sharing of meat from the hunt, with the understanding that the animal gave itself to them. The stone knife was the ritual *thing*. When agriculture began, the food given by the earth was the central ritual object. In the Pawnee rite called the Hako, the ear of Mother Corn leads them through the land. In the most sacred of the ancient Greek mysteries, the Eleusinian mystery, the culminating moment of the rite was the display of an ear of wheat, cut and harvested and displayed in silence. The underlying meaning of this ritual can be understood by looking at the Greek word *Zoe*, which means not only the life of men and all living creatures but also what is eaten.

There are lots of different rituals, but I'm most concerned with the ones that enable humans to celebrate or invoke the sacred, in the largest sense. Real ritual puts everything together—the old things and the new things, nature and animals. Roy Rappaport says that "ritual is not simply an alternative way to express things, but . . . certain things can be expressed *only* in ritual." I like that.

J W: It seems like these experiences that we all know about but don't quite have words for—of bliss, of total alertness, of connectedness— are not just magical moments but a vital part of what it means to be human. So I wonder if getting back on track has something to do with getting back to these experiences?

D L: Yes. If we're going to rediscover a viable relationship with nature, it will not be through more ideas but through experiences where you know you are part of nature, with no questions asked. When you've had these experiences you know what you want and you can't be pushed around.

We can find our way to more of these experiences by following the wisdom of other cultures who know that their relationship to the natural world requires the whole of their being. What we call their ritual and ceremony is a sophisticated social and spiritual technology, refined through thousands of years of successful relationship to the natural world. We've forgotten so much in the last two hundred years that we hardly know where to begin. But it helps to begin remembering. In the first place, all traditional cultures—even our own long-gone Western European cultural ancestors—had seasonal festivals and rituals. The origin of most of our modern holidays dates back to these seasonal festivals. The four major ones are the winter and summer solstices, where the sun reverses its trends, and the spring and autumn equinoxes, where night and day are equal. The dates that fall midway between each of these are known as cross-quarter days. May 1 is a cross-quarter day, for example, which was celebrated in Europe with May poles, gathering flowers, and fertility rites. The fall cross-quarter day is Hallowe'en, the ancient Samhain of the Celts. In early February, midway between the winter solstice and spring equinox, we celebrate

Candlemas. Seasonal festivals revive the *topocosm,* a Greek word for "the world order of a particular place." This includes not only the human community but the total community—the plants, animals, and soil of the place. It also includes more than just the present living community. These festivals make use of myths, art, dance, and games, all of which serve to connect the conscious with the unconscious, the right and left hemispheres of the brain, and the human with the nonhuman.

The next step after the seasonal rites is to acknowledge the nonhuman coinhabitants of your place. Native cultures often had totem animals, which were animals who taught them something they needed to learn. As Freeman House says, totemism is a way of perceiving power through the recognition and respect for the vitality and interdependence of other species.

Salmon is a totem animal of the North Pacific rim, and, as House says, "Only Salmon, as a species, informs us humans, as a species, of the vastness and unity of the North Pacific Ocean and its rim." For at least twenty thousand years the native people from around the rim have ordered their daily lives according to the timing of the salmon population.

Several years ago I discovered that salmon was the totem animal of the Celts, too. It's not surprising. Salmon offers a perfect way to ritualize the link between planetary villages around the earth. Salmon teaches us, among other things, to reclaim our waterways so the fish can flourish. If we do this, we reclaim the soil, the plants, and the other species of the ecosystem. We restore them to aboriginal health, and thus ensure full health to our children as well.

j w: There are many events that are promoted in the name of ritual. How can we recognize which ones are authentic?

d l: First of all, human beings cannot function without ritual. In a good culture, the rituals serve to unite the group both within and without in their natural place. Ritual builds bridges continually between all these entities. In a confused culture, such as ours, rituals are consciously manipulated by those in power to control those under them.

These rituals are divisive. They are often manipulated by one person to draw attention to themselves. This is the type of ritual gurus use. No one is aware of what is going on, but they get control over the unconscious that way. Ritual is always wrong when it is promoting separation or vying for control.

Rappaport says, "Rituals mend ever again worlds forever breaking apart under the blows of usage and the slashing distinctions of language." If you talk for too long about anything, it becomes depressing. Those of us who know this must be willing to break off the talk gracefully by chanting, drumming, and so on, or ruthlessly walking off into the "great outside."

If you don't have true rituals that involve the entire brain/body/ senses and nature around you, then you have addiction. The greatest mind-numbing addiction in the U.S. today is watching television.

I want to say a word about this spacey new age idea that we all "become one," us and nature. No way. The Taoists say it best: "It's more a sensitive non-interference, a transparent resonance with things . . . we ourselves must enter an evocative resonance among things, by means of which we become ourselves."

J W: Is it appropriate to use rituals from other cultures or ancient times in our present cultural context?

D L: A tricky question; but yes, you can. When the Navajos, who were originally a nomadic tribe from the north (what is Canada today), came to the Southwest, they adapted the local Pueblo culture in an advantageous way. What they used helped them to relate to that land more easily and therefore it was good. And because they continued to live there, ceremoniously, the rituals became deeper and more healing and more their own. When the Spanish—and later, the North Americans—invaded the Southwest they kept the same Eurocentric, Christian rituals and ignored the ones that had grown out of the resident native cultures. The result of this is further alienation, from the native people and from the land itself. It's this kind of alienation that allowed for the destruction of these people and their land for the sake of newfound riches.

If rituals tie you closer to the land where you live, they are good, no matter where they come from. If they tie you to a far distant power structure, either as a good consumer, a faithful Christian, or an obedient citizen, they're bad.

J W: Will you give an example of an older ritual and how it has worked for you in a contemporary context?

D L: Ten years ago I began using the Pawnee Hako pattern for ritual journeys into nature because I felt it would help people begin to feel a real connection with the nonhuman beings of their own place. I had no idea then of the depth of commitment the ceremony opens up after practiced in the same place for a number of years.

The Pawnee *Hakkow,* which means "breathing mouth of wood," was actually a journey where they ritually greeted each of the other beings they encountered: trees, rivers, mountains, and rocks. Ethnologists now call such ceremonies Hako. There are many variations of this Hako and many similar practices among other native groups, including the Omaha *Wawan,* "to sing for someone" and the Lakota Sioux *Hankapi,* "the making of relations."

The two wooden staffs, or hako, are the most important ritual symbols of the journey. The Pawnee made them from ash wood, but we usually use a local wood like willow. One staff is painted blue to symbolize the sky and the other red, to symbolize life. Feathers are attached to both, along with red and white streamers to represent the sun and moon, day and night. In making these hako, remember to use only those things that are given. Don't kill a bird for its feathers, or cut down a tree for a staff. We often find just what we need to complete the hako during the journey itself.

Traditionally, the Pawnee leader carried an ear of Mother Corn. In our Hako, we use a local edible plant. We also carry gourd rattles, which represent the gift of food to humans and the breast of the mother. If we don't have enough gourds to go around, we use plastic vitamin bottles filled with dry split peas. These make a good sound and hold up well.

We usually start the journey with a ritual crossing, a zigzagging through thick trees, or leading people through a narrow place in the mountains or rocks. This gets everyone's attention quickly. People are encouraged to talk if they want, but not about abstract things such as politics or philosophy. And it is explained from the beginning that the sacred also includes laughter.

During the Hako journey we stop to acknowledge the beings and the places we encounter. We read poetry to the trees, touch the rocks, sing to the river, tell stories to the wind. I like to use both traditional and contemporary material for this. I should also say that there's an uneasiness when a group first gathers together for a ritual like this, especially if it's new to them. It feels strange and awkward. But once you take a gourd rattle in your hand, within moments your hesitations are displaced by a feeling of connection to the others in the group and the natural environment. Very soon it feels like the most natural thing in the world.

The goal of the journey is a place that is powerful but also peaceful. Many events can take place once you arrive there. We often have lunch, get some rest, and then build a small fire in the center of the space. We do this even when it's hot out because a fire provides a good focus. We might do some chanting here or use our rattles, or both. In sacred rituals many different techniques are used, including chanting, drumming, dancing, singing, and fasting. The physiological effect of these "ways" is complex, but essentially what happens is they help to supersaturate the left brain so that the right brain is able to fully function. This feeling is called tuning. Bonding develops out of this tuning, and bonding is the real basis of all society, both human and nonhuman.

When the rattles are set aside, one of the leaders introduces the "talking staff" ritual. As one of the hako staffs is passed around the circle, each person tells of his or her experiences during the journey or how they feel right now. Only the person holding the staff can speak.

We usually close a ritual with some chanting. Over the years I've discovered that when you chant you can be totally yourself and yet totally with all the others. This seems like a paradox because in our culture we believe that we are exclusively individual. Chuang Tsu says, "Becoming oneself need hardly imply coming into conflict with others. Self becoming . . . could well mean for each to become himself *to-*

gether." When a group has experienced a ritual event like the Hako, more things happen all at once than any one person can possibly comprehend.

J W: Can these rituals work in an urban context?

D L: There's hardly anything humans do anywhere that is *not* ritual. In Italy there's a town with a population of fifty-nine thousand called Siena. It has the lowest crime rate of any Western city of its size. Drug addiction, delinquency, and violence are virtually unknown there. Why? Because it's a tribal, ritualized city organized around clans with names like snail and turtle and an annual horse race called the Palio. These clans function as independent city-states, each with its own flag, boundaries, song, patron saint, and rituals. The ritualized city customs extend clear back to the worship of Diana, the Roman goddess of the moon. Writers such as Henry James, Ezra Pound, and Aldous Huxley sensed the energy of Siena and tried to write about it, but none of them could grasp the ritualized life behind it.

About a week before the day of the Palio, Siena workmen carry in yellow earth from the fields outside of town and spread it over the great central square, thus linking the city with its origins in the earth. During the year, sad people are cheered up by being reminded of this event. *"La terra in piazza,"* they are told, which means, "Soon there will be earth in the square."

The Palio, or horse race, serves two main purposes. In the intense rivalry surrounding the race, each clan rekindles its own sense of identity. The Palio also provides the Sienese with an outlet for their aggression and as such is a ritual war. The horse race grew out of games that actually mimic battles and were used to mark the ends of religious festivals.

The Palio is truly a religious event. On this one day of the year the clan's horse is brought into the church of its patron saint. In the act of blessing the horse, the clan itself is blessed. This horse race is the community's greatest rite. According to a local priest, Don Vittorio, "In the Palio, all the flames of Hell are transformed into the lights of Paradise."

J W: Can community rituals like the Palio function as a substitute for the more personal experiences we have in nature?

D L: One of the reasons I began doing rituals is to enable people who are unable or unwilling to endure the hardships out in nature to have a similar experience. I've found that we don't have to take people out into the wilderness but that they can do ritual in their own backyard and experience the real wilderness inside themselves. All they need is a tree or a flower, the sun or the moon. The one thing we always have on our side is that deep down we are still originally human. We can touch this with a minimum of ritual, almost anywhere.

Some people have the illusion that simply by taking humans out into the wilderness they will see the beauty and realize the importance of saving the environment. I think this is nonsense. If we want to build a sustainable culture it is not enough to "go back to the land." That's exactly where our pioneering ancestors lived and, as the painter Charles Russell said, "A pioneer is a man who comes to virgin country, traps off all the furs, kills off the wild meat, plows the roots up, and then moves on." If we are to truly reconnect to the land, we need to change our perception and approach more than we need to change our location. Heidegger says that "dwelling is not primarily inhabiting, but taking care of and creating that space in which something comes into its own and flourishes. It takes both time and ritual for real dwelling."

Ritual is a focused way we can both experience and express respect. And most important of all, during rituals we have the experience of neither opposing nature nor trying to be in communion with it. Instead, we have the experience of finding ourselves within nature, and that is the key to sustainable culture.

J W: How has your own practice of Tai Chi played a role in finding yourself within nature?

D L: I'm glad you brought that up. Tai Chi teaches Chinese organic philosophy—of relationship—through the body itself and thus dissolves all the dichotomies inherent in Eurocentric thinking. In Tai Chi there is no split between human and nature or between the body and the mind.

I didn't know about Tai Chi until after my husband and I left Alta. It sounds ridiculous, but when we left there in 1970, I was very worried about how I would live without powder skiing. I had never known anything else that made me feel that way.

The summer we left Alta, some friends came to visit us on the Olympic Peninsula in Washington. We had spent the previous sixteen summers there doing research on the Blue Glacier. We were all on Shi Shi beach one day and these friends started doing this strange thing. I was watching from a sea stack, and from that distance the motion looked like powder skiing. "What are you doing?" I asked. And they said, "It's our version of Tai Chi." Well, it looked to me like this might be a way to get some of that feeling again, so I found a teacher and learned. The next summer I was up on the Blue Glacier, a place that sits five thousand feet directly above the Pacific. I did Tai Chi up there and saw a mountain I'd never seen before. It was always there, but I had never seen it in all the sixteen summers of being there. That was the first time I realized there was another way of seeing. But also, the feeling I got while doing Tai Chi was like skiing powder snow! I learned and practiced a lot and then started teaching it. I found out early on that I could do twenty minutes of Tai Chi in the mountains and feel as good as I feel after several days of backpacking. I was very excited!

Tai Chi was developed in the Taoist Shaolin Monastery in the mountains of China. Each of its 108 forms are used specifically to loosen up the pelvic area or the *sacrum,* which is the bony plate that gets its name from the same Latin root as the word *sacred.* The pelvic area—or "sacred middle"—is the center of the functions of sex, pre-natal life, birth, assimilation of food, and deep emotions.

Several years ago I was doing Tai Chi on the top of Golden Horn, a thirteen-thousand-foot peak in Colorado. Just after finishing, I felt a haunting sadness. It was similar to the feeling that welled up when my rolfer, Tom Wing, was completing my final session. There's a move the rolfer does that is impossible to describe but is designed to realign the central body core. When Tom finished doing this to me, he waited a few seconds and then asked how I felt. I tried to explain my sense of loss. He recognized the feeling from his own rolfing sessions and thought that it might be the body itself remembering its original animal-being.

I've felt this sadness after doing Tai Chi several times since then, and I'm still not sure what it is. It's not a crying thing, but more like a feeling of loss. The more I experience it, the more I think it comes from the memory of our original human nature. You see, when you do Tai Chi, you enter a real wilderness within that joins with the wilderness without. There's no ego, only awareness and a kind of bonding quality. It's infinitely satisfying and wholly what you need. You only know that you've reached that level when you come out of it, when you become conscious of it. At that point you know you were there and that you're not there anymore. That's what real wilderness is. You can't control it, you can't push it around, and you can't make it happen. It happens when it's right. We only get a chance to feel this once in a while, and that's the sorrow—the longing to experience our original nature.

J W: In your book, *Sacred Land, Sacred Sex,* you discuss the Taoist perspective of following the pattern, not the law, of nature. Explain how this is different from our Western view and what we can learn from it.

D L: Unlike the Western model of civilization, which is a linear cause-and-effect model, the Chinese have a more systemic view. They see ultimate reality as relationship, not as substance. Taoism doesn't consider that the order of nature comes from rules or laws but from the spontaneous cooperation of all beings brought about by following the pattern of their own natures.

In Ancient China, *Li,* or pattern, came from the way fields were laid out for cultivation. *Li* was also used to describe patterns in jade or the fibers in muscles. Eventually the word came to be used to talk about the principle of organization in the universe. If things do not conform to their own *Li,* or their natural pattern, they lose their relational position in the whole and become something other than themselves. Maintaining this position is the underlying reason for the elaborate seasonal rituals practiced throughout Chinese history.

The best analogy I know to explain this is in skiing deep powder where there are no rules or laws to follow. In three feet of snow there is no base, no solidity anywhere; instead, there is a continual interaction between the human being, gravity, and snow. If you try to force a turn, you inevitably fall. In Taoist thinking that's called *Wu Wei,* which is not "doing nothing" but "refraining from activity contrary to nature."

When you start seeing the world as patterns instead of laws, everything opens up. Vision itself changes. We have been told that seeing depends on the eye, which is connected to the brain, which does all the work. Well, vision is more than that; it's a whole perceptual system. One sees with the eyes in a turning head, on a moving body, supported by the earth which is turning around the sun. It's all a moving system based on patterns and relationships. The Renaissance perception taught us that the object farthest away is the smallest. How do you know if it's something far away or just small? You don't, unless you are moving and can see the planes shift. "Observation involves movement," as James Gibson points out in his book, *The Ecological Approach to Visual Perception.* What we really see, he says, is not depth but "one thing behind another." As you walk toward the mountains, the nearby hills rise up and cover the more distant ones. If you change your direction, the nearby hills sink and the mountains behind them rise up. If you walk to the right or left, the mountains slide in front of and behind one another; so do the rocks and trees. "The blue mountains are constantly walking," as the Japanese Zen Master Dogen wrote. There is a continuous interaction between you and the environment.

I've tried to teach this to people on land, but it's difficult. The best place was Canyonlands. While giving the seminar on the *Crusader,* I found that the slow movement of the boat through the islands and promontories was ideal for "seeing" in this way.

J W: I think people who practice a certain craft over a long period pick up an extraordinary skill for seeing subtle patterns and relationships. As a carpenter, I notice that my eye has been trained to see relationships, too. If a house is under construction near a large body of water and trees, for example, you can learn to use the surrounding landscape as a pattern for level and plumb. You can do this by standing back and watching relationships. If you're in good practice, you could build a house without a level or a square, or without a tape measure, for that matter. I know carpenters who are that attentive to relationships.

DL: In the winter of 1963 some friends and I were skiing on a steep run on the west slope of Alta. It was the last run of the day, and I was leading because I was the only one who had skied that route before. But my binding came off. I stopped to fix it as the others went on. As soon as I took off, the whole slope of snow slid on the crust beneath. It was so steep that I was thrown in the air immediately, turning over and over. I broke the top of a tree and landed eight hundred yards below, covered by the avalanche. I woke up the next morning in a full body cast.

All this happened because I wasn't paying attention. I should have remembered the sun was on the west slope. When you ski in a place long enough, you learn to pay attention to certain patterns and colors in the snow. We don't have words for it, but we have all learned to see these things. A wind slab, where wind has been piling snow on top of a slab of ice, has a certain shade of gray. When you try to ski that and you break the slab, the whole thing goes instantly. It's one of the worst avalanches. There are other patterns and colors in the snow that give you important information. It's funny how we have no words for it. Snow is just white in our language.

As a rock climber I have long known the importance of watching the cliff under different light to see where the cracks run down the slope and so on. This is second nature. Many facets of the cliff are obvious to a climber but completely hidden to other people. There are times the light reveals tiny holes you can't otherwise see. That's when you pick your route. I learned this early on from route finding. The other day I was noticing the waves reflecting on the ceiling of our boat. It was a beautiful pattern. That's what is known as ambient light. It's not directly from the sun but reflected. That's the kind of light that reveals patterns, that gives information, the same kind of light that reveals a route up a rock face. I was on the dock before we left, watching the water. I was so surprised because it was making Haida eyes all over the place. I've always liked Northwest Coast Indian art with its form lines and ovoid eyes but I never read or heard about where these shapes come from. Now I know.

J W: Some people say you can see these shapes in the flesh of halibut also.

D L: Why wouldn't you? They're all over the place! Here in Alaska I see them in the cliffs, in the geological stress lines, in the rocks. They're all natural patterns. And now all over the water. What's more is they're watching you. You're not just watching back but all these eyes are watching you!

J W: I can see how the life-centered perspective is both radical and all-encompassing. Have you ever encountered anything that doesn't fit?

D L: I used to think many things were disparate until I let go of the idea that I needed to give them meaning. When you practice this approach, you discover it is not you that gives meaning to life. As the Japanese Zen Master Dogen says, "That the self advances and confirms myriad things is called delusion. That myriad things advance and confirm the self is enlightenment." Once you understand this, there's really no reason to go on talking.

In Touch with the Wind

M ATTHEW FOX is a Catholic priest, the founder of the Institute
in Culture and Creation Spirituality in Oakland, California,
the editor-in-chief of *Creation Spirituality* magazine, and the author
of over fourteen books, including *The Coming of the Cosmic Christ*
(1988), *Creation Spirituality: Liberating Gifts for the Peoples of the Earth*
(1988), and *Sheer Joy: Conversations with Thomas Aquinas on Creation
Spirituality* (1992). In 1990 the readers of *Common Boundary* magazine selected Matthew Fox's *Original Blessing: A Primer in Creation
Spirituality* as "the most influential psychospiritual book of the
1980's."

Born in Madison, Wisconsin, in 1940, Matthew was one of seven
children. A bout with polio at the age of twelve left him in a hospital
for almost a year, isolated from friends and family who could speak to
him only through the windows of his enclosure. Although the doctors
were uncertain whether he would ever regain the use of his legs, Matthew was walking before the year was over. "It was a time of deep 'letting go,'" he says, "and I decided that if my legs were to return to me I
would not waste my life or my legs."

And he hasn't. He received his master's degrees in Philosophy and
Theology from the Aquinas Institute of Theology in 1967, the same
year he was ordained into the Dominican Order of the Catholic
Church. On the advice of Thomas Merton, Matthew went on to the

Institut Catholique de Paris, where he received his doctorate in Theology and the History of Spirituality in 1970. In Paris he met his mentor, M. D. Chenu, who introduced him to the creation-centered spiritual tradition. "By naming the creation tradition," Matthew writes, "Father Chenu was able to lay out for me how mysticism and prophecy go together."

In 1971 Matthew accepted a teaching position at Barat College, an all-women's college in Lake Forest, Illinois. Four years later he was asked to conduct a study of spirituality and religious education in the United States. In response to his findings, Matthew developed a new program that included feminist theory, mysticism, ecology, dance, art, and traditional spiritual studies. In 1977 Matthew established a program based on this model at Mundelein College in Chicago, naming it the Institute in Culture and Creation Spirituality. Six years later, he moved the Institute to Holy Names College in Oakland, California, where it now thrives.

In December of 1988 the Vatican accused Matthew Fox of being a "fervent feminist" who advocates the ordination of women, original blessing (as opposed to original sin), and sexual issues "not inspired by the magisterium." He was charged with calling God both Mother and Child as well as Father, with hiring a self-declared witch to teach at his Institute, and with refusing to condemn homosexuals. For this, the Vatican sentenced him to a year of public silence. In the spring of 1993, after refusing the command to return to a monastery in Chicago, Matthew received word that the Vatican had dismissed him from the Dominican Order of which he had been a member for thirty-three years.

～·～·～

JONATHAN WHITE: In the classic essay entitled "The Historical Roots of Our Ecological Crisis," the historian Lynn White says, "What people do about ecology depends on what they believe about who they are, about their relation to other people, and about their destiny. Every culture, whether it is overtly religious or not, is shaped primarily by its religion." White goes on to say that the Judeo-Christian

beliefs on which Western society is founded are the most anthropocentric in the world. In contrast to older traditions such as paganism or
animism, Christianity established a division between humankind and
nature, insisting that it is God's will that we exploit the rest of nature
for our proper ends. "Once the Church had effected man's monopoly
on spirit in this world," White says, "the old inhibitions to the exploi-
tation of nature crumbled." This kind of criticism seems to be coming
from many directions today. As a Catholic priest, how do you respond
to this?

MATTHEW FOX: I think it's all true of the dominant Western tradition of Christianity, as represented by the patriarchal and dualistic
fourth-century theologian Saint Augustine of Hippo. Augustine was
not interested in the cosmos, nature, or equality, but in the question of
personal guilt and salvation. He was a neo-Platonist who believed you
have to escape the body to find spirit. In fact, he defined spirit as "whatever is not matter," which is the basis of all dualistic thinking. Augustine's theology of original sin and redemption legitimized the lack of
mother love in the cosmos, chasing both nature and woman into the
shadows. "Man but not woman is made in the image and likeness of
God," he said. Inheriting (although misconstruing) the Greek concept
that man is the measure of all things, Augustine passed on an extremely human-centered and individualistic theology. The individu-
alism of Descartes, who said thirteen hundred years later, "I think,
therefore I am," is directly traceable to Augustine.

JW: Lynn White closes his essay by saying, "Since the roots of our
trouble are so largely religious, the remedy must also be essentially religious, whether we call it that or not."

MF: He's exactly right about that. My work is to show there is another
tradition within Christianity that has been purposely forgotten, often
condemned, or misconstrued. That tradition is "creation spirituality,"
which is not a human-centered path but a creation-centered one. It
celebrates the original blessing of creation, which includes all beings

and all things. It includes the galaxies and the stars, trees, wolves, microorganisms, rocks, mountains, and children. Everything. This is not just a human story or a human perspective. Creation spirituality welcomes the new cosmic story offered by science, which is a story of a universe a trillion galaxies large and fifteen billion years old. The human species is a newcomer in this creation story. In fact, without the evolution of a precise set of conditions over the eons, human life may never have appeared on Earth at all. This new creation story from science is as full of mystery and awe as anything "theological."

The idea of original sin was introduced by Saint Augustine. Ironically, it has never been clearly defined by the Church, and thus, we've lived with it like a skeleton in the closet for sixteen hundred years. It's my feeling that the sin behind all sin is dualism. It's our species' temptation to think in terms of either/or. You have to be saved or unsaved, choose between soul or body, spirit or matter. This kind of thinking doesn't work in the new cosmology. In Einstein's famous equation for relativity ($E = mc^2$), he was talking about the convertibility of matter and energy. It's nondualistic. The ecological movement is dealing with this same question: are we masters of nature or are we interdependent?

The patriarchal tradition that builds off of the idea of original sin not only cripples humanity but is also a symptom of our insidious anthropocentrism. Some scientists have suggested that if we think of the four-billion-year-old history of the earth as the Eiffel Tower, then the entire history of humankind can be represented in the last thin layer of paint at the top. When you consider how young we are as a species, it seems all the more ludicrous to limit our cosmology to our own history. What about all the wonderfully creative, exploding, spiraling, dancing, evolving life that happened before we arrived? On top of that, we call the whole thing original sin! To begin religious experience this way, instead of celebrating the blessing that the cosmos is, trivializes religion.

Theism, the belief in God, has a connotation of dualism because it implies there is a God "out there" and a person "in here." Jung said there are two ways to lose your soul, and one of them is to worship a God that is separate from the self. Creation spirituality breaks down this dualism through an understanding that we are in God and God is in us. As the thirteenth-century mystic Meister Eckhart said, "The eye with which I see God is the same eye with which God sees me." Without this kind of spirituality, there can be no authentic ecological consciousness, because there can be no true sense of the interdependence of all things.

JW: Where do you find support for this kind of tradition within Christianity?

MF: Creation spirituality is the oldest tradition in the Hebrew Bible. If you read the Yahwist author, or what is known as the J source, you find that it's all about a creation-centered theology. So are many of the scriptures in the wisdom literature of the Old Testament, such as the book of Job, the book of Proverbs, and the Psalms. The parables of Jesus are full of creation imagery, as is his preaching about the Kingdom of God. The "Song of Songs," the great book of wisdom literature from the Sofia Tradition in Israel, praises all creation and recognizes nature as a source of revelation of the Divine. As the theologian Dorothee Soelle points out, "In the 'Song of Songs,' nature, animals, men, and women partake of the joy, the abundance, the fullness of life in the garden." This imagery of the garden is, in fact, the ultimate teaching of the Bible. It includes the whole vineyard theme: "I am the vine and you are the branches," as Christ says in John's gospel. That's hardly anti-Earth. It's a realization that the Divine flows through everything. It also confirms the tradition of the Cosmic Christ, where Christ is in all things, not just in the historic person we call Jesus. When you look at the world this way, every being has something to reveal about the Divine.

Creation spirituality was alive and well in medieval Europe during the twelfth and thirteenth centuries. It was a period of spiritual renaissance that involved an awakening of scientists and mystics who saw nature as a source of divine revelation. This was the period that gave us the beautiful Chartres Cathedral, which is presided over by the Mother Goddess, and the mystical teachings of Hildegard of Bingen, Thomas Aquinas, Meister Eckhart, and Francis of Assisi. Julian of Norwich and Nicholas of Cusa, who lived in the next few centuries, were also mystics, but their voices are all but lost.

J W: As you mentioned earlier, many of these mystics were forgotten or condemned by the Church. Can you talk about how and why these people are important to creation spirituality?

M F: There's a lot of history here, and it's hard to know exactly where to begin. The early Celtic mystics from Ireland, Scotland, and Wales have been almost completely neglected. Many of them settled in the Rhineland area, and their influence can be seen in what we call the Rhineland Mystical Tradition, which begins with Hildegard of Bingen in the twelfth century. Hildegard was a scientist, musician, artist, and mystic. She composed a series of songs, "The Symphony of the Harmony of Heavenly Revelations," in which she expresses her deep mystical experiences of the Comic Christ. She believed that if you sing the words, their true meaning can evoke a mystical experience in the body. One of her paintings depicts the universe within the belly of divinity, which she calls a "Lady Named Love." She writes, "[T]here is no creature that does not have a radiance. Be it greenness or seed, blossom or beauty. It could not be creation without it. . . . It is God whom human beings know in every creature."

Francis of Assisi, who follows Hildegard in this tradition, lived in Northern Italy. He struggled for church reform and renewal by creating a life-style that would displace greed and the systems of feudalism and emerging capitalism. Unfortunately, we've sentimentalized him, putting him in a birdbath along with the birds he sang to. He was far more politically aware than most people know. His great poem, "The Canticle of the Sun," never mentions the historic Jesus. It's about the Cosmic Christ, about the divine image in everything: water, earth, sky, moon, flowers, and so forth. He also names both male and female aspects of the universe, an influence inherited from the Celtic tradition:

> All praise be yours, my Lord, through Sister Moon and Stars;
> In the heavens you have made them bright
> and precious and fair.

The fourteenth-century Dominican Meister Eckhart lived and preached in Strasbourg and Cologne, which are both located on the Rhine. Where Saint Augustine said, "The soul makes war with the body," Eckhart said, "The soul loves the body." Eckhart was a great nature mystic and nondualist. In one of my favorite passages he says,

> If I were alone in a desert
> and feeling afraid,
> I would want to have a child with me.
> For then my fear would disappear
> and I would be made strong. . . .

> But if I could not have a child with me
> I would like to have at least a living animal
> at my side to comfort me.

> Therefore,
> let those who bring about wonderful things
> in their big, dark books
> take an animal—perhaps a dog—
> to help them.

> The life within the animal
> will give them strength in turn.
> For equality
> gives strength in all things
> and at all times.

Thomas Aquinas, who is not usually recognized by scholars as a mystic, said, "A mistake about nature is a mistake about God." He developed a cosmology based on the science of Aristotle, whose work was just being translated in the West and was extremely controversial. As you can imagine, this got Aquinas in a lot of trouble, particularly with the fundamentalists of his day who thought science and theology had nothing in common.

We tend to believe that the teachings about interdependence of all beings through time and space is a new idea, but the mystics have had an intuition about this for centuries. Creation spirituality is not anti-science. It never has been. Hildegard of Bingen said, "All science comes from God."

There are others in the mystical tradition to whom we owe a great spiritual debt, like Mechtild of Magdeburg and Dante Alighieri. Unfortunately, the dominant tradition in Christianity never goes to these sources. Instead, it's always using the dualistic texts of Tomas a Kempis, the medieval author of *The Imitation of Christ,* for example. So, when people criticize Christianity or the Bible, they are only criticizing one tradition. Just a month ago I heard the Australian environmental activist John Seed say, "I used to go around blaming the Bible and Christianity for all the world's trouble, especially in the area of ecology. But when I learned about creation spirituality, I realized that I had to criticize only one tradition of Christianity, not the whole thing." It's true, you can't read any of the creation-centered mystics with an open mind and still say all Christianity is the cause of our dualistic problems. If you look at the stories of these people and at the response of the Church to their teachings, you can get a view of how radical their thinking was. Thomas Aquinas, for example, was condemned three times before he was canonized. Eckhart was condemned and is *still* on the condemnation list. Hildegard was forgotten for seven hundred years until we started translating her material fifteen years ago. Nicholas of Cusa was also forgotten. David Bohm, the great British physicist, says he owes more to Nicholas of Cusa than he does to Einstein! The point is, those who make too great a generalization about Christianity's role in our consciousness should learn more about the nuances within the different traditions.

J W: You are outspokenly critical of anthropocentrism, the bias toward interpreting everything in terms of the human. In *Creation Spir-*

ituality, you write that "the angel that rolls away the boulder of anthropocentrism is cosmology." Yet it seems that some of your discussion can be construed as having the same anthropocentric qualities you're trying to escape. For example, after describing the expansion of the original fireball that created the earth and the "chance" evolution of the conditions that made human life possible, you say that these were decisions made by the universe itself on our behalf. Are you saying that the universe chose us? If so, isn't that an anthropocentric notion? How do you interpret Hildegard of Bingen when she writes, "Humanity alone is called to assist God," or Saint Francis of Assisi when he says, "Mother Earth is a royal person"?

M F: To celebrate the divinity in all beings you do not have to put down humanity. Indeed, humanity seems to be the one species that doubts and denies its own right to be here, its own royal personhood. The opposite of cosmology is not human-bashing but saying that humanity is the center of the universe or the only image of God. Thomas Aquinas says, "The most excellent thing in the universe is not the human—it is the universe itself." We are all here to serve the universe.

Hildegard is celebrating how humans are the image and likeness of God, that our immense creativity is so godlike that we have to choose between "assisting God" or being demonic with our creativity by destroying all life systems on this planet. Other species fit in; humans have to choose to fit in and "assist God."

J W: Anthropologists suggest that the shift from animism to monotheism may have happened between five and ten thousand years ago, around the same time we shifted from hunter-gatherers to farmers. Human ecologist Paul Shepard believes that a sky-centered spirituality may have been a male response against the Mother Goddess associated with agriculture.

M F: If it's true that agriculture brought about a shift in the work and consciousness of people, then I'm sure there was some anxiety that went along with it. The work of hunting and gathering, which was largely done by men, gradually became less important than seeding, which was done by women. It's understandable, then, that men felt somewhat displaced. A lot of commentators on the rise of patriarchy, such as Otto Rank, say that the male problem is essentially an envy of the capacity to give birth, to become a mother. To compensate, men took over religion, making up severe rituals that were really designed to create birth pangs. It's an extremely rationalistic approach to birthing, and, in a very interesting fashion, it all seems to fit. Divinity is removed from the natural world and placed in the sky, where it is unreachable by the Earth Goddess and all she represents, including the women and men working in the fields.

The mystical tradition restores the image of God to the fields. Eckhart said, "Every creature is a word of God and a book about God." The idea that every creature has divine stories to tell is the basis of authentic Christian mysticism. And it's these stories that will give us the energy to change our ways and defend our kin. I don't believe these changes can be accomplished out of a sense of "stewardship." That's just more patriarchal duty, and feeling motivated out of a sense of duty or guilt or shame doesn't create big souls. I think the mystical approach is the way to go, where the divine image, or Cosmic Wisdom, is in every creature. *That's* why we defend creation, not because we are stewards left to do the dirty work for a god who is off in the sky someplace. When creatures are suffering at our hands, divinity is suffering. It's the archetypal crucifixion story told all over again. Christ is dying when whales die, or when rain forests die.

J W: In *The Coming of the Cosmic Christ,* you write about "the crucifixion story of our time," which includes the dying of the environment, as you just mentioned, creativity, youth, wisdom, and the Church itself. Would you explain what you mean by the dying Church?

M F: I think the forms in which we recognize Christianity today are just about out of energy. Take worship, for example. Once a week we force ourselves to go to church and listen to a sermon. We sit in neat rows, on pews that are screwed to the floor. Our bodies ache while we try not to fall asleep from boredom. Where is the joy, the celebration of creation? Where is mysticism? Where is nature? Many of these forms of worship were inherited from the sixteenth century and haven't changed at all since. That was the era that marked the end of the cosmology of creation mysticism and the beginning of our present mechanistic worldview. The splintering of the Christian church into competitive factions increased geometrically with this new mechanistic view. You can get a sense of what I'm talking about by comparing Saint Peter's Basilica, a sixteenth-century cathedral made of nothing but cement, cold marble, and exaggerated male statues, to the medieval Chartres Cathedral, which is dedicated to the Mother Goddess. At Chartres, and at other cathedrals built during that time, nature and cosmology are the center of everything. The goddess (Mary) sits on her throne (*cathedra*), which represents the center of the universe. The green man is also celebrated in each of these cosmic temples.

In *The Coming of the Cosmic Christ,* I described the Church as a giant, dying, patriarchal dinosaur. Unfortunately, it's resisting its own death. Its tail is whipping about, killing everything within range. Father Bede Griffen, an eighty-eight-year-old monk, said, "If Christianity can't recover its mystical tradition and teach it, it should just fold up and go out of business. It has nothing to offer." I agree, but the problem is that the Church is dying on top of its own treasure of mystics and prophets, of good news and wisdom stories. We have to stand clear of the lethal tail and at the same time convince the dinosaur to roll over so we can rescue its treasure for the next millennium of spiritual practice. It's not really a matter of blame but of understanding what we have to leave behind and where we have to go next.

J W: Your ideas are obviously not very popular within the Church. How do you deal with the resistance, and why do you choose to stay in a tradition where so much of your energy is usurped in fighting internal battles?

M F: It's no picnic. Thomas Kuhn says one sign of a paradigm shift is the amount of resistance you receive. In other words, if you're not getting a lot of resistance, you're probably not doing it right. That gives me some comfort. My focus, however, is not really to fight battles but to offer positive alternatives to conventional religious education. Ironically, fighting the battles helps this effort. For example, when the Vatican silences you, everyone wants to hear your voice. So you have to play that card, too. It's like the practice of aikido, where you yield in order to keep your enemies off balance. So there's this kind of dance going on. It's not what I would pick for myself, but it hasn't hurt the movement. In fact, it's made it more visible.

I've chosen to stay within my Western tradition for several reasons. First, I don't think we're going to change the West by going East. We can hold a mirror up to the East and learn something, but the fact is we carry our cultural and religious DNA within us. Jung warned that Westerners cannot "pirate wisdom from foreign shores as if our own culture was an error outlived." A more radical approach to cultural change is to create it within our own tradition. Jesus, Isaiah, Hildegard, Aquinas, Eckhart, and all these other people from the mystical traditions would have been environmental prophets today. The wisdom these people offer shouldn't be thrown out with everything else.

My question is, How do you bring about cultural change? I don't think you can do it by jumping to another culture, although I'm not condemning those who have. I derive great wisdom from people like Joanna Macy, who started out as a Calvinist and is now a Buddhist, or other spiritual warriors like John Seed and Gary Snyder, who are both Buddhists. Each of us needs to find our own spiritual practice, something that allows us to maintain our centeredness. Often this serves as a funnel for bringing Eastern or Native American wisdom into Western hearts. I encourage anyone who feels called that way. But, for myself, I think the way I can move a civilization is to work within its institutions, including education, politics, economics, art, and religion.

Although I work within the Christian tradition, I believe in deep ecumenism, which is the acceptance of wisdom in all traditions. In our program at the Institute in Culture and Creation Spirituality, we have African and Native American, Taoist, Jewish, Buddhist, Pagan, and Christian teachers. I think that's the future. We have to be open to wisdom wherever we find it. *Spirituality* means, literally, to breathe, to be alive, in touch with the wind. Spirituality is a life-filled path, a spirit-filled way of living. That's why all true paths are essentially one path—because there is only one spirit, one breath, one energy in the universe, and it belongs to none of us and to all of us.

Part of the education problem is that seminaries are not teaching anything about the mystical traditions. Do you think they're studying Meister Eckhart, Julian of Norwich, or Hildegard of Bingen in these facilities? No! The whole system is so left-brained and Cartesian that the professors don't even know the questions to ask. It's a scandal. At the Institute in Culture and Creation Spirituality, we're trying to create an alternative model of religious education that recovers the mystical teachings both inside and outside of the tradition.

It doesn't surprise me when I hear of Protestant and Catholic seminaries going down the tube. The energy is leaving those institutions because they're not responding to the desire in all of us for a new story. They are not nourishing our souls, they are not teaching people how to pray or how to lead others into mystical experiences. They can—and will, in the future—because they'll have to.

J W: In *The Coming of the Cosmic Christ,* you say that we can't hope to recover our balance with the rest of nature without awakening to an authentic mysticism. You've talked about the mystical tradition and some of the mystics themselves, but what exactly is mysticism, and why is it so necessary for us to awaken to it?

M F: There are many ways to look at mysticism. The word itself comes from the Greek *mystikos,* which has two meanings: "to shut one's senses" and "to enter the mysteries." The dominant Christian tradition of the West interprets the first of those meanings as the killing of the senses, linking mysticism with a distrust of the body and nature. It's easy to see how this interpretation leads to asceticism and the need for control over passion, ecstasy, sexuality, and so forth. One of the passages from *Directorium Asceticum: Guide to the Spiritual Life,* a book published early this century, describes a nun who was so holy that "she never allowed herself to look at or touch any part of her person, even such as decency does not require us to veil." In the same volume, you find that Bishop St. Hugh, "though compelled by his pastoral charge to deal with women . . . had never for forty years looked one in the face." Unfortunately, there are lots of other examples of this, which is why mysticism has such a pejorative connotation in the West.

The creation tradition interprets mysticism as the human psyche's capacity for aliveness, wakefulness, and rebirth. To "shut one's senses" is seen as a silencing or a slowing down. It's like unplugging the television or the radio and sitting in the quiet. The body or the senses are not denied but recognized as part of the divine gift, the original blessing. If we want to heal the body/soul split, then we need to let go of the idea that the body is "out there" and embrace its earthiness "in here." The anthropologist Laurens van der Post says that we should honor the wilderness and the natural person within ourselves. That is where the balance comes from. Our greed and aggression and corruption by power, he says, come from cheating that first person within ourselves out of his/her natural inheritance.

We put others down, whether it be other species or other people, because we haven't dealt with our own inner wilderness. We've put mystics in the closet, and we've put ourselves in there, too.

One of the ways we cheat ourselves is by not knowing what our real work is. Since the Industrial Revolution, we've been producing as much as possible, as fast as possible. Millions of Americans work in factories that are now beginning to shut down. The automobile manufacturers in the Midwest are a good example. Everyone mourns this, but I think it might be a blessing. We already have six hundred million cars in the world. That may be enough. The question is, What should we be producing in the 1990s and beyond? As Schumacher says, "Everywhere people ask what can I do? The answer is as simple as it is disconcerting: We can each of us work to put our inner house in order."

j w: Our conventional image of a journey inward is an encounter with the shadow—a dark, ugly, frightening being. It seems to require a willingness to let everything fall apart, which is antithetical to the emphasis in our culture on "keeping it together."

m f: That's right. Our patriarchal tradition keeps us looking out and up for enlightenment. We're afraid of what might be waiting for us below, in the dark, including an encounter with our own death. Why would we want to explore this area? Hildegard of Bingen says that the worst thing the devil can say to the human race is, "O, human, you do not even know who you are."

Creation spirituality shares the feminist tradition of honoring creativity and the birthing process. In fact, as we discussed a little earlier, women seem to know more about this journey into the dark than men because of the pain involved in childbirth. One view of "the dark night of the soul" is that it grew out of women's experience of bearing children. By entering into the death process, symbolically or otherwise, we go through our fear of death and give birth. This again is the honoring of creative process, which was apparently a part of every matriarchal society for thousands of years before the coming of patriarchy.

In creation spirituality, the theme of life, death, and resurrection is not just a story of the historic Jesus but a cosmic story. In the universe, stars are born and live for thousands of years before they die. In the process of death, the supernova may in fact provide the building blocks for new stars or planets. This theme of life, death, and rebirth is everywhere in nature. As we accept this, the fear of our own "dark night of the soul" dissipates. As a civilization, and particularly as men, we need to stop looking upward when we pray. The word *environment* comes from the word *environ,* which means "around." The Divine is not just up—or down, for that matter—but everywhere around.

j w: What are some of the ways we can practice this "praying around"?

m f: Well, thinking about God is no substitute for an experience of God. And the best way I know of experiencing God is through the body, which is why the body and senses are a blessing and a necessity for spirituality instead of an impediment to it.

Tai Chi, circle dances, massage, yoga, aikido, artwork are all good forms of prayer. Making love can be, also, because it can lead us into an awesome experience of cosmic awareness. All ritual and the observance of cultural and personal rites of passage are wonderful ways to pray together. We don't do enough of that, and what we do in the white West doesn't take us to the edges of things. Sweat lodges, for example, are a great way to face death together. As the combination of a return into the womb and a journey into death, sweat lodges can take us to our edges and offer renewal. We pray to the rocks, our elders, sing songs, and burn sage to invoke the wisdom of our ancestors. The first time I went into a sweat lodge was with some Native Americans in Minnesota. I was so hot and uncomfortable, I thought I was going to die. After about twenty minutes, I realized there was no way to escape and I had to surrender to the experience. At that moment, the real prayer began.

Robert Bly says that men learn only through ritual. The African spiritual teacher Malidoma Somé says, "Any civilization without rites of passage has a sick soul. You know our souls are sick in the West for three reasons: we have no elders, our youth are violent, and our adults are bewildered." Now, doesn't that name our civilization? Our youth are violent, to others and to themselves, because they're not invited into a larger world. They're invited into shopping malls and parking lots instead. And they're alone in these places, without guidance from elders and without self-respect. Addictions to alcohol, drugs, sex, television, and so forth are symptoms of a loss of self-love. Our culture gives us a license to drive at sixteen, legal adulthood and voting privileges at eighteen, and a card to drink alcohol at twenty-one. This is what our culture offers to feed the soul. And, even in these puny efforts, we tend to throw it all away. The great mysteries that are more deeply part of our nature, like sexuality, love relationships, suffering, birth, and death, are passed on from adults to children in sealed envelopes, if at all.

Art as meditation is the basic prayer form in the creation spirituality tradition. In a way, every creative process is a rite of passage. There's a dying or a letting go involved, and always a rebirth. It's a daring thing to stand up and say, "I made this." The price we pay for that experience of renewal is sometimes small and subtle, but at other times we feel like we may lose everything we are. Meister Eckhart says,

> Does your heart suffer?
> Do the hearts of those around you suffer?
> Then,
> you are not yet a mother.
> You are still on the way to giving birth. . . .

In another poem he assures us,

> The outward work
> will never be puny
> if the inward work
> is great.

Artists have been relegated to the spiritual and economic periphery of our culture. The new cosmology will bring them back into the center and allow us to follow their lead, along with the mystics, into the spiritual wilderness and beyond. Whether it's working in clay, paint, dance, or music, these forms all offer a way into spirituality.

J W: What about the connection between our personal spirituality and the rest of nature?

M F: Well, you know there's a connection because we're so deeply moved by our experiences in the natural world. I grew up among the lakes and hills and seasons of Wisconsin. I used to have dreams— visions, really—about the land. It's all still very much alive to me. In a way, I found God in nature, or God found me. It was always an experience of mystery, which is the same feeling I get when I go to Bodega Bay or Yosemite.

Americans are still deeply touched by the sacredness in nature. The beauty of a place like Yosemite awakens something in our gut and in our heart. We are awed, and we feel small in the face of it. It's a great mystery. When we experience grief, we can go to the woods, to the ocean, or to the mountains for spiritual guidance. If we give of ourselves there, we remember that we are not alone. As Rilke said,

> And if the earthly no longer knows your name,
> whisper to the silent earth: I'm flowing.
> To the flashing water say: I am.

When your suffering is so great that you no longer know who you are, you can say to the waters, "I am." The water can give you your "I amness" back. This all makes perfect sense, because we are literally interdependent with the soil, the waters, the sky, and other beings. When we go to the water, we are returning to our origins; we are remembering who we are. It's a palpable experience of scientific truth, and it's also an experience of the sacred. As the sixteenth-century Indian mystic Kabir says, "O seekers, remember, all distances are traversed by those who yearn to be near the source of their being." If you've ever had yearnings to be "near the source of your being," then you've had mystical yearnings. The origin of the word *religion*, in fact, is the Latin *religare*, which means "to bind again" or "to bind back."

Experiences of being near the source of our being can give us the passion to defend the natural world. Falling in love is another way because when we fall in love, a couple of things happen. First, our awareness of death is raised. It's ironic, but love makes you more sensitive to losing your beloved. That's why parents dash out and get life insurance after they have their first child. The other thing love does is give us energy. Lovers always have energy! And imagination! When you have energy and imagination, you come up with ways to defend your beloved.

I gave a talk at the Schumacher Lectures last year. Lester Brown, from the World Watch Institute, spoke just before me, and the last thing he said before sitting down was that the primary obstacle to the environmental revolution is inertia. It was a perfect lead-in for me, because inertia is a spiritual sin. The root of the word *inertia* is *acedia*. In spiritual terms, it's not having the energy to see things differently, to let go and to start over again. Where do we get that energy? Aquinas says zeal comes from an intense experience of the lovability of things—from an experience of beauty and awe. When your heart leaps with the beauty of other animals, clear water, and lush rain forests, you're going to have the energy to let go of old forms and live differently. That's where the connection is. In the last line of Rilke's beautiful poem "Archaic Torso of Apollo," he says, "You must change your life." That's the difference between inertia and beauty. Creation spirituality is all about goodness and beauty. If our spirituality starts from there, instead of an anthropocentric debate about sin and redemption, then we'll have the energy and imagination to protect what we love. Aquinas says, "The foremost meaning of salvation is to preserve things in the good." That's what *salvation* means. Now, isn't that a perfect line for the environmental revolution? Preserve things in the good, that's what it's all about.

There are many ways to approach the task of rediscovering the goodness and beauty of life. We've talked about the different kinds of prayer, about returning to "the source of our being," and about rituals such as the sweat lodge. Circle dances are another good way to remember the delight of being a child again. I was at a conference a year ago in Portland, Oregon, where we all did this. A young man came up to me afterward and said, "I've been an environmental zealot for eighteen years. I couldn't care less about religion, but what we did today in this circle dancing is much more radical than anything my group does in the field. If I can get my coworkers to do this, our entire approach would change." I met him several months later and asked how he was doing. "Fine," he said, "we're dancing together and finding all kinds of ways to celebrate. And our imaginations are flying! We're coming up with new and more creative ways to work with loggers and hunters and politicians."

J W: From the Gaian perspective, the earth itself is not threatened by what we call our eco-crisis. According to the geological record, the earth has survived over thirty catastrophes, each of them far more extreme than anything humans can do, including an all-out nuclear war. Lynn Margulis, James Lovelock, and other scientists agree, however, that if we push the biosphere to an extreme state, the earth may roll over on us and establish a new steady-state regime. The new regime would undoubtedly support life, but perhaps not human life. How do you respond to this perspective?

M F: We're an amazing species, and it would be a shame if we were eliminated because of another planetary catastrophe, although right now that seems like a distinct possibility. The poignancy of this story is that we may eliminate not only ourselves but all the other wonderful creatures that depend on the same ecosystems that we do. When we damage those systems, we're bringing harm to other life. Over the last six thousand years we've clearly demonstrated a potential for destruction, but as I was saying earlier, the awakening of love and creativity and imagination can give us the energy to turn our behavior around. The stories that these scientists give us can help, because they point out the logical conclusions of our current behavior.

J W: Are we saving the earth or are we saving ourselves?

M F: People *are* Earth. We are Earth on two legs. You have to save both at once. The earth may not need humans for its survival, but humans certainly need the earth. At bottom, we can't hope to save ourselves without saving the earth. Yet I don't think the hope of our own survival is enough to bring about the necessary changes. We're not that selfish, and we're not that alone. Without other life forms, the earth would be a lonely place. Our spirits would die. I don't think the earth really needs humans, but the fact is we can't save ourselves without saving the earth.

J W: In Wendell Berry's book *What Are People For?* he says that the idea of saving the earth is too abstract. "We are not smart enough or conscious enough or alert enough to work responsibly on a gigantic scale," he says. David Brower's response to this is, "That's the cause of our trouble. We've been concentrating on ourselves—contemplating our own navels—too long. It's this whole business of being so concerned about what happens to you that you forget what's happening to everything else. As a result . . . the life support system has degenerated."

M F: Again, I don't think it's either-or. It's both-and. Wendell Berry is saying that we have to act locally. The earth is not just something out there but the land we're standing on right now; it's the land we farm, the food we eat, the people we relate to, and the children we give birth to. That's all local Earth; that's all soul. I think Brower is reacting to the privatization of soul that has happened over the last few centuries. This privatization has taken the meaning out of the soul Wendell Berry talks about.

I think anyone who works on the community level—not just the human community, but the greater, all-inclusive community of nature and Earth—has to be grounded. Howard Thurman, the African American mystic, put it wonderfully when he said, "The more I relate to the universe everywhere, the more I must relate to something somewhere." If we're going to expand our consciousness, we need to deepen our roots. The new creation stories do just this—they ground us in the earth's billion-year-old history. They give our life perspective, and out of that grows a new cosmology. It's not about spacing out, it's about growing deeper roots. Wendell Berry is absolutely right about this. And so is David Brower. We have to do both.

J W: Do you have hope for the future?

M F: I'm glad you used the word *hope* and not *optimism,* because I don't have optimism. I do, however, have a little hope. Hope grows out of despair. I think the very despair of our times is a reason for hope, because maybe it can wake us up. Necessity moves the human species; it changes history. I think we are at a moment of necessity. Lester Brown says we have until 2010 to change our ways. That fact gives me hope.

I do a lot of work in Europe now, and I'm learning that in some ways they're ahead of us on the environmental front. The raising of the veil on Eastern Europe is revealing just how bad the ecological devastation is in Czechoslovakia, Poland, and the former East Germany. For Europe, this is local devastation. There's no place to run to, and it's waking them up. In the United States, we're still living the myth of the frontier. Once we use up something, we throw it out or move on. Well, in Europe, much more so than here, there is no more "out" and no more land to move on to. The necessity is more urgent and tangible there, which is giving them great energy for change. Our comparative complacency scares me a lot. Juan Ramón Jiménez's poem "Oceans" speaks eloquently to this:

> I have a feeling that my boat
> has struck, down there in the depths,
> against a great thing.
> > And nothing
> happens! Nothing . . . Silence . . . Waves . . .
> —Nothing happens? Or has everything happened,
> and are we standing now, quietly, in the new life?

Many of the twenty-three- to twenty-eight-year-olds who are enrolling at our institute see our situation very clearly. They're not in denial, like many older adults are. They hear the news and they get it. They know it's their life, their children, and their children's children who will suffer. Because of this awareness, they're seeing the necessity of integrating their lives with the ecological movement, whether it be working in politics, science, art, or religion. And they want a spirituality that serves them in those fields.

The environmental revolution can't happen without spirituality. I'm sure of that. It's not a left-wing, secular, ideological battle. It's something much deeper, and it involves all of us. I have some hope, but it's not going to be easy. We clutch our investments, not just what we own or the way we see the world, but all those less-than-conscious habits that we pass from one generation to the next. I often call those habits patriarchal, but it's much more than that. These habits are based on male domination and control, anthropocentrism, shame, denial, and fear. And it's not just an American problem or a Western problem or a Christian problem. It's a soul problem. That's exactly what Schumacher meant when he said the first work is putting our inner houses in order. It just can't be done without that. It's too important, too vast, and too beautiful a piece of work.

The Unreturning Arrow

IF YOU WANT a quick insight into the mind of human ecologist
Paul Shepard, just read one of his course descriptions from the cat-
alogue of Pitzer College. He calls one of his classes "Confrontations
and Encounters: Human Ecology in the Western World" and lists
over twenty discussion topics, such as "Eden Was No Garden—The
Primal Cosmology"; "Romantic Intuition, Organic Metaphor, Holistic Theology"; "Ecofeminism"; "Fathers, Mothers, Sons, and Paternal
Epiphany"; and "Ecology, the Subversive Science." And that's just the
syllabus.

Paul's work in environmental perception and human ecology
spans more than forty years. His recent studies emphasize the importance of animals in modern culture and their symbolic role in dreams,
developmental processes, and other psychological and religious contexts. "We owe much of what we are as humans," he says, "to those
others who help define us, give shape to our thoughts, and who have
been our companions for thousands of years."

Paul's first book, *Man in the Landscape: A Historic View of the Es-
thetics of Nature,* was published in 1967. He has published seven others
since then, including *The Tender Carnivore and the Sacred Game*
(1973), *Thinking Animals* (1978), *Nature and Madness* (1982), and *The
Sacred Paw* (1985, with Barry Sanders). His forthcoming book, *The
Others: Animals and Human Being,* will be published in 1994.

Paul was born in Kansas City, Missouri, in 1925. While still a young
boy, the family moved to the Missouri Ozarks, where Paul remembers

spending much of his free time alone, collecting butterflies and birds' eggs. After serving in World War II, he returned to the University of Missouri and graduated in 1949 with an A.B. in English and Wildlife Conservation. He went on to Yale University, receiving an M.S. in Conservation in 1952 and a Ph.D. in interdisciplinary studies in 1954. Since then, Paul has taught at Knox College in Illinois (1954–1964), Smith College in Massachusetts (1965–1970), and Dartmouth in New Hampshire (1971–1973), as well as fulfilled teaching fellowships in Australia, India, and New Zealand. He is now Avery Professor of Natural Philosophy and Human Ecology at Pitzer College and The Claremont Graduate School in California.

The following interview took place at Pitzer College. Paul was finishing up the fall term and preparing to leave for Wyoming, where he and his wife, Florence Krall, spend most of their free time these days.

～·～·～

JONATHAN WHITE: You describe yourself as a human ecologist. What does that mean?

PAUL SHEPARD: It means that I consider human history and culture as ecological factors. If I were studying the ecology of salamanders or prairies, I wouldn't have to deal with culture or written history. In the study of human ecology, however, I take as my primary data any evidence I can find—ideologies, religions, myths, histories of thought—that has to do with the way people interact with the environment. By *environment,* I mean not just our social environment but the larger environment, including the plants and animals around us.

J W: One of your first books, *Man in the Landscape,* explores the history of gardens and how they embody cultural ideas about the world. How did you get started on that project, and where did it lead you?

P S: I studied English and Wildlife Conservation at the University of Missouri, where we used Aldo Leopold's book, *Game Management,* as a text. The book was written in 1933 and is quite different than his later books and essays. I was discouraged by what I was learning about the application of ecology in game management. After graduating, I spent a year traveling and organizing local conservation clubs. During that winter I was in a serious accident, and while I was recovering in the hospital my mother sent me a clipping that described a new inter-disciplinary conservation program at Yale. To make a long story short, I ended up in that program, which was directed by conservationist Paul Sears and the evolutionary biologist G. Evelyn Hutchinson.

My master's thesis at Yale started out as a comparison of how land-scape painters saw nature and how I saw it as an ecologist. I traveled all over the Northeast and located the sites of perhaps 150 paintings done between 1820 and 1850. The project grew into a doctoral dissertation and, with the guidance of an interdisciplinary committee at the uni-versity, the thesis was eventually written on attitudes toward the American landscape during the first part of the nineteenth century. Up to that point, I had always been interested in gardens as a form of art and as a form that communicated something about how people saw their world. My thesis involved both landscape painting and the history of gardening. And, as you can probably guess, it didn't leave me as a particularly marketable graduate. I carried that manuscript around for thirteen years, rewriting it endlessly, until it was published under the title *Man in the Landscape* in 1967. It took another twenty years before people started to read it.

Just before *Man in the Landscape* was published, I was beginning to doubt whether landscape was an appropriate focal point for the study of human ecology. The way we use and relate to landscape is too closely influenced by trends and fashions. So in 1961 I began reading anthropology. It was an exciting time in that field, and also in paleon-tology and archaeology, because a lot of work on the past- and present-day hunter-gatherers was being done. These studies represented a re-turn to my training in biology and zoology, and I welcomed the chance to look for a new species model for understanding what human ecol-ogy might entail.

I started that new search by writing a book on hunting, *The Tender Carnivore and the Sacred Game,* which was a way of pulling together my own thoughts on that subject. *Thinking Animals* came next, which was an exploration of the role animals play in the thought processes of pre-civilized or non-civilized people. *Nature and Madness,* published in 1982, looked at the human developmental process as it relates to the natural world in a historical context. *The Sacred Paw,* which has a chapter written by Barry Sanders, was a look at the ecology of a specific animal, the bear. While I still have an interest in landscape, I am largely directed toward the model of hunter-gatherers as a context for the study of our own species' evolution.

J W: What are some of the characteristics of the hunter-gatherer lifestyle that attract you to it as a model?

P S: The relationship to nature that was shaped by the activity of hunting and gathering is only the beginning. The whole of personal existence, from birth to death, was also perceived differently. For the hunter-gatherer society, the life-cycle was ritualized, its metaphors inseparable from the everyday world in which they lived. Group size was small and ideal for human relationships, health was good in terms of diet, and ecological interaction was stable and nonpolluting. During the Pleistocene, humankind was in the humble position of being few in number, sensitive to the seasons, and comfortable as one species among many.

J W: How are these characteristics useful as a model for contemporary life?

P S: It's important to remember that we haven't evolved into beings separate from nature. Over the recent centuries, we've been led to believe that we are totally free from our biology, that we can do what we want, that we create our own environment, our own being, and that we are fundamentally different than other living forms. I think this is an immense error. The recent discoveries in genetics and molecular biology are confirming that modern humans are not separate from their biological past. Close to 99 percent of our DNA is precisely identical to the chimpanzee, and 30 percent is identical to the horse. What that says to me is that our primate ancestors are still a part of us, that in a strangely literal sense the chimpanzee and lizard are represented in our physical presence. Our heritage, then, is forever interfacing with our experience, our education, and our environment to make us what we are. The old question of whether we are determined by nature or culture is all out the window. The new answer is it's both! It's everything we do and everything we are.

Let me get back to your original question of how these Pleistocene characteristics can be useful today. It's common knowledge that the optimal group size for interacting and making decisions is twelve to twenty-five. Now, that's a Pleistocene characteristic, and you don't have to go back to being a hunter-gatherer to appreciate it. Academics have always known that a twelve-person adult class is an optimum size. Given the choice, the ideal learning situation is with a group of people who can sit around a modern-size table. Wherever my fellow teachers can do this, they do. That's why people pay a lot of money to go to small schools. I don't know much about corporate life, but I suspect the same principle is at work. Boards of directors are often close to this size. When you get more people, they tend to break off into cliques; when you have fewer people, the group suffers from lack of variety of personality and opinion, and so on. This optimum group size is not new, we've known about it for over two million years.

J W: It's not difficult to find examples of brutality, greed, and disrespect among hunter-gatherer peoples. Hunting by fire, driving large animals off cliffs, and etiquettes of retribution are just a few. How do you integrate that into your thinking?

P S: I deal with anthropologists who have examples like this all the time. I don't have all the answers to this question, but I will say that denying general characteristics simply by pointing out exceptions seems pointless. Just because some people are born with one leg or no legs doesn't mean that having two legs isn't a species characteristic. Anthropology has a history of emphasizing cultural differences rather than discovering commonalities.

Hunter-gatherers may not always live in perfect harmony with nature or each other, nor are they always happy, content, well-fed, free from disease, or profoundly philosophical. Like people everywhere, hunter-gatherers are in some sense incompetent. Do you remember the movie *Little Big Man?* I've always appreciated the scene where the chief lies down on the mountain to die. He gives an eloquent speech about joining the Great Spirit but gets only rain for his trouble.

J W: What other characteristics are part of our hunter-gatherer heritage?

P S: Well, I'm interested not only in social processes but also in the way in which humans relate to other creatures. The topic that carries the most emotional impact is the killing of animals for food. Our bodies and our psyches and our society are all organized around omnivory. Look at our teeth, the length of our gut, our whole metabolic system. To say that we're not omnivores or to choose to be herbivores is just another form of cultural arrogance, in which we think we can just decide to be whatever we want to be.

If we're going to harvest food, then we're going to kill living beings. Ultimately, this means we're going to be killing reasonably sized animals as a primary food source, or at least killing them to protect our gardens. These animals are most likely sentient—they think, feel, and suffer. Gary Snyder reminds us that we had better wake up to the fact that we are not only eaters but also the ones to be eaten. This relationship is an essential factor of organic existence. Diversity and kinship of life not only include the fact of death but require it.

The killing and eating of animals by hunter-gatherer groups is not seen as a victory over nature but as a part of the larger gift of life. The crucial aspect of the hunt is not the taking of a life but the expression of respect and affirmation for a giving world. Nor is the hunter alone considered responsible for the fatal stroke. The responsibility is groupwide, and the rites of purification, celebration, homage, and veneration that follow the hunt are participated in by all. This ties the killing of animals inextricably to the center of religious experience.

J W: In your essay "A Post-Modern Primitivism," you say everybody should have the experience of hunting. Do you still feel this way? Even if it is desirable, is it practical?

PS: It's a practical possibility if we realize that certain kinds of activities can transform our lives without having to be done repeatedly. Experiences such as hunting can be so intense that they address not only our conscious but also our unconscious life. We go through many initiatory experiences in our life—births, graduations, marriages, and so on. Causing death to an animal with whom we participate in the larger cosmological context can be one of those initiations. It's not just the killing that is valuable but all the skills you learn in preparing for the hunt. These skills, such as careful watching, tracking, and observing of animals and plants in the natural world, can be practiced over and over. They're good skills to have.

Participation in the hunt can be a kind of epiphany if we experience it once or twice, at an appropriate age, with the right kind of leadership, and with an abiding sense of respect and humility. If done this way, it may serve a valuable purpose without having to be an ongoing part of one's life. There must be ways to arrange for this without placing impossible demands on the natural world by our oversized population.

The effort to find practical ways of recovering these sensibilities is difficult at best. My friend Ivan Illich says of his own work, "I've spent my whole life trying to understand these problems, working on just what the question should be, and it's unfair to ask me to come up with all the solutions when clearly we're going to need whole cadres of specialists in a hundred different fields in order to get answers."

Like all human activity, hunting can run amok. We all know of the modern abuse of hunting and the secular trivialization of killing. The issue requires a lot of careful thinking, because the humane treatment of wild animals and the practice of hunting are not separable. We are easily seduced by our own empathy because of our fear and outrage at the indifferent destructiveness around us. However, kindness toward animals demands a true sense of kinship, which does not mean we should treat them like our babies. Instead, it means realizing the many connections and transformations—us into them, them into us, and them into each other from the beginning of time. To be *kindred* means to share consciously in the stream of life.

J W: Hunting also engages us in what you have called "the multitude out there, from human brothers and sisters to the distant stars, that are the "other." Throughout your work, and particularly in *Nature and Madness*, you claim that exposure to what is "other-than-us" is essential to normal human development. Will you explain what you mean by this?

P S: It's always a delight and a mystery to be reminded that the world is made up of a multitude of beings. These beings are in some ways like us and in some ways different. The assimilation of this likeness and difference plays an important role in our maturation process. For the infant, the shape of all otherness grows out of the maternal relationship and expands into the environment, which for most of human history was rich in natural smells, textures, and motion. The flicker of wild birds, the sound of wind and water, and the call of animals are all important elements of the infant world. These elements become internalized and incorporated in the growing sense of self.

The psychologist Erik Erikson and psychiatrist Harold Searles both suggest that we can look at human development as if it addressed itself to the central question, "Who am I?" If the question "Who am I?" is always before us, both consciously and unconsciously, then its corollary, "Who am I not?" must also play an important role. That is, to what extent am I not like you? As infants, this process begins with distinguishing one's mother from one's self. Soon after that, shadowy forms are made out within the family or community. Gradually, the child moves out into the larger world, where it continues to be fascinated by other beings. A child's interest in animals, for example, is much more than an arbitrary curiosity. To my understanding, this interest is a response to an interior calendar that tells the child something about addressing otherness in a larger-than-human context. At this stage in life, children are still engaged in a literal process, experiencing the sheer pleasure of discovering themselves as beings among other beings, learning names and sounds and behaviors. Children imitate animals all the time. They play at chasing and catching, hiding and seeking. They play at being an animal and then at not being an animal, or feeling like one kind of animal and then another. This is the enactment of the mystery of kinship, of likeness and difference. In the playful imitation of animals, children grow familiar with their inner zoology of fears, joys, and relationships. As the child matures into an adolescent, he or she does not graduate *from* this world, but *into* it, forever facing the questions of otherness that have to do with cosmology and religion.

The first twenty years of the human growth cycle are as unique as anything you'll find in biology. Anyone who thinks differently should spend a few hours with the forty-odd volumes of *The Psychoanalytic Study of the Child* or the issues of the *Journal of Child Development*. In the realm of nature, human development is a regular giraffe's neck of unlikely extension, vulnerability, and internal engineering. The nuances of this unlikely process have been worked out by thousands of generations of people before us. My own studies have led me to believe that this maturing process is more normal among hunter-gatherer groups than in our modern civilization and that the hunter-gatherer groups may again serve as a standard from which we have deviated. Furthermore, I would suggest that it was the hunter-gatherer way of life to which our development was fitted by natural selection. Normal development, then, may require cooperation, mentorship, and respect for a mysterious and beautiful world, a world where the clues to the meaning of life are embodied in natural things and experienced through ritual participation of individual stages and passages. Among the many good examples of present-day people who seem to give this kind of attention to childraising are the Manus of New Guinea, the Crow and Comanche of North America, the Aranda of Australia, and the !Kung San of Africa.

In our modern urban civilization we shortcut this maturing process by attempting to omit the eight to ten years of immersion in nonhuman nature. Consequently, maturity is always questionable because, although the individual may become precociously articulate and sensitive to human interplay, he or she doesn't have a grounding in nature. The grief and sense of loss that we often interpret as a failure in our personality is actually a feeling of emptiness where a beautiful and strange otherness should have been encountered.

J W: If we are not separate from our biological past—if, as you say, we are still Pleistocene beings—what accounts for the radical developments that have led us so far afield?

P S: History itself—that is, all the traditions and customs that carry the individual through the various stages of maturation—is the radical development that led us so far afield! We are Pleistocene beings living in an impoverished culture, one that no longer offers us the diversity that our genetic makeup expects in order to grow up in a healthy fashion.

The criticism I often hear of this perspective is that it's another form of biological determinism. There is tremendous opposition in our culture—both conscious and unconscious—to the notion that we are in some way constrained by our organs and our genes. Yet the idea of a built-in life-cycle has been known to biologists and appreciated by people who have children or who raise animals for a long time. It's people like Erikson who have taken this a step further and insisted that there are certain kinds of events that are appropriate to certain kinds of development. For example, it's not until the age of eleven or twelve that we begin to develop a capacity for symbolic or metaphorical thinking. Until that age, the world is experienced very literally. It's only after eleven that we start to get interested in puns and poetry and the meaning of words. It's inappropriate, then, to ask a ten-year-old to account for questions of religion or philosophy. I think a sense of this biological calendar has been surfacing in our consciousness for the last fifty years, and only now are we beginning to accept that our development follows a built-in calendar that prepares us, stage by stage, for certain life experiences.

Most of us fail to mature as gracefully as we might. The aggravation of our normal developmental process results in a kind of pathology that is still largely hidden from itself. Erich Fromm asks, "Can a society be sick?" In *The Sane Society* he says, "That millions of people share the same forms of mental pathology does not make these people sane." Consensual validation is no guarantee of mental health.

J w: In *Nature and Madness,* you suggest that our current crisis— both in terms of our psychology and our relationship to nature—has its roots in the shift from hunting and gathering to agricultural farming five to ten thousand years ago. Until recently, that has been considered an enormous step forward for humankind. What has led you to re-examine that shift?

P s: There were certainly people who began to question the general sentiment about the shift to agriculture some years ago. Ethnographers as far back as the nineteenth century were raising questions about it. In their work with present-day hunter-gatherers, they weren't finding evidence that these people were any less intelligent, artistic, complex, or inventive than anyone else. Contemporary students of anthropology and archaeology are challenging long-accepted notions about the shift, too. Nevertheless, the thinking on this issue has not changed much. By and large, historians still take for granted the assumption that the shift to agriculture was for the better.

My own ideas on this subject were strongly influenced by the work of N. J. Berrill, who wrote *Man's Emerging Mind* in 1955, by Loren Eiseley's work, and by Laurens van der Post's *Heart of a Hunter,* a study of the Kalahari people in Africa. I was probably influenced as a child by Ernest Thompson Seton's *Two Little Savages* and a little later by the whole romantic image of the American Indian that came out of the nineteenth century. I do think, however, that my arguments are not blind to the traps set for us by romanticizing indigenous peoples. It's misleading to supposed that a certain group of humans are personally better than other human beings. I don't think that's where I'm coming from.

If we accept ourselves as an integrated part of the ecological system, then we have to ask why that system has evolved to the point of crisis.

This way of thinking is quite different than the prevailing philosophy, religion, and history, which tell us that we are somehow unique and separate from nature. More and more scholars are re-examining this issue, and their findings reveal the biases that are built into religion and philosophy very early on. Part of my work in this area is to look at historical origins of Western concepts of what it means to be human, examining not only Christian and Jewish but also prebiblical assumptions that lead to these concepts. I think Descartes and Bacon and their mechanistic followers of the seventeenth century were only the final fruits of a way of thinking that was initiated during the shift to agriculture and a centralized political state five to ten thousand years ago.

J W: What are some of the reasons for the shift to agriculture?

P S: The reasons vary, of course. There are conjectures that propose a sudden advance in creativity or individual genius, but I don't think this is a very interesting way of looking at the question. First of all, I think we have to recognize that this shift did not take place all at once. For example, archaeological findings tell us that the first crops preceded the making of cities by about five thousand years. Very few prehistorians suppose that the earliest farmers and domesticators were conscious revolutionaries or even that changes were dramatic in a single lifetime. Most probably, the beginning of agriculture happened in one location—somewhere east of the Mediterranean Sea— and then spread out gradually from there. It may have happened in an area where certain wild plants and animals were disappearing, where climate was changing, or where the human populations were uniquely confined geographically. But why should this shift happen at that particular time and not fifty thousand years earlier? I don't think it's the result of a linear evolution of the human brain but a response to an unusual configuration of events. By the time of the Egyptian dynasties or the Mesopotamian civilizations, our perception of the world had changed dramatically from that of the Paleolithic past.

j w: In *The Food Crisis in Prehistory,* Mark Cohen writes that human populations may have been forced into agriculture due to the over-hunting of large mammal species. In fact, a common theory among anthropologists suggests that humans hunted many species to extinction during the late Pleistocene.

p s: I have a lot of problems with that theory. In general, I don't know of any ecological evidence of a large carnivore—or omnivore, for that matter—hunting another species to extinction. A possible exception to this might be found when you have populations confined on a small island. What happens when a large omnivore or carnivore begins to make some kind of dent in a prey species? Ecologists dealing with this question have found that the predator turns to alternate food sources. The energy and time that goes into hunting down the last remnants of a particular species aren't worth it. What we know about efficiency in food gathering and ecological systems, particularly at these upper ends of the food chain with less specialized, larger predators, tells us that they can shift to another food source quite readily.

My second objection is with the sheer mechanics of it. For example, I am asked to believe that hunters on foot, with bows and arrows, exterminated the North American horse during this time. Knowing a little bit about wild horses, I don't believe it's possible. Third, it's hard for me to imagine how any of the large extinct Pleistocene species could have become prey species for humans. I'm sure animals like dire wolves, giant condors, or the larger bears, such as the great members of the genus Arctodus, who stood seven feet at the shoulder, were very intimidating to hunter-gatherers. It's like expecting people with bows and arrows to exterminate animals they don't even eat! Were they actually hunting down large condors? I doubt it. You might argue that if you exterminate the things condors depend upon then you might have ramifications up the food chain. But from what we know about condors, they too are able to shift and eat other things. So I have a whole series of concerns about this issue, including the extermination of some Pleistocene species—certain birds for instance—for which there is no evidence of much contact at all.

I'm ready to acknowledge that there may have been members of a more primitive mammalian fauna—like giant sloths—who were highly vulnerable, and who apparently were killed in considerable numbers by human beings. In cases like this, humans may have played a role—along with other predators who ate giant sloths—in their mortality rates. I'm convinced that on some of the Polynesian islands or in New Zealand, humans did in fact play a major role in exterminating species like giant mollusks. There just isn't good evidence to support this kind of pressure on a continental basis.

JW: How did the shift to agricultural farming affect the lives of the people living then?

PS: When humans began cultivating plants, they moved from a world of perennials to a world of annuals. In fact, the ancestors of wheat and barley were perennial plants. *Annuals* are the pioneering plants—or the invaders—of environments that are in some way damaged or disturbed. They are the crudest and the most opportunistic. By reintroducing annuals, the rich and efficient structure of the climax environment was eliminated and replaced with a pioneer environment, which by its nature is less productive and far more fragile and unstable. Among hunter-gatherers, wild foods are harvested from a wide range of areas. When one area fails to produce its usual yield of berries, for example, another place will. Or, at worst, the gatherer doesn't eat berries that year but finds another food to replace them. In this system, the pressure on one area to yield a certain volume of food is not great. With the advent of farming and sedentary lifeways, all this changed. Unlike hunter-gatherers, the farmer must rely on a particular piece of land planted with one or two crops. Consequently, the farmer's fate is far more vulnerable to the vicissitudes of weather, crop diseases, and predation by wild creatures. Each year the farmer wonders, "Will the seeds come up? Will they be gobbled up by insects? Will a disease hit them? Will they be washed away in a flood?" With agriculture it is likely to be boom or bust, and in the bad years nature seems to withhold that to which the farmer, after all his labor, feels he has a right. The mysterious and uncertain growth-cycle of annual plants binds the farmer in uncertainty to the great seasonal round of life in a way that humans had never been bound before. The domestication of animals had effects that went far beyond economic implications. Changes brought about by capturing and breeding animals resulted in plumper, more rounded features, docility and submissiveness, reduced mobility and hardiness, and the simplification of behaviors, such as courtship. In short, the effect was infantilization. This new relationship to the natural world leads to the necessity for control. If the farmer can destroy his competitors, be they beetles, birds, deer, or anything else, he will be inclined to do so. Wild things become adversaries; they either take up space, sunlight, or water that the farmer needs for the crops or they directly invade the crops, eating or infecting them with diseases. As soon as people began to kill wolves to protect sheep or squash grasshoppers to protect crops, they were into an oppositional mode with the natural world. In such a mode, wild things become enemies of the tame. The wild "other" is no longer seen as the context but instead the opponent of "my" domain. Impulses, fears, and dreams—the realm of the unconscious—are no longer represented by the community of wild things with which the hunter-gatherer worked out a meaningful relationship.

I don't see evidence of this need for control among hunter-gatherers, probably because they feel there is enough to go around. The whole idea of the "limited good," which is the fundamental principle of modern economics, arises out of agriculture. My advantage becomes your disadvantage. That's one of the ways in which a kind of oppositional mode gets established, just by the dynamics of the economy itself. And you can see what I'm coming around to here, which could easily be labeled *economic determinism*. I object to this label because I would say that nothing is absolutely deterministic. Everything depends on interaction, action, and response. But the idea that we can understand and explain certain aspects of hunter-gatherers as an economy, or agriculture as an economy, or herding as an economy, regardless of geography, race, or period of history, appeals to me more and more.

J W: Will you talk more about how the shift to agricultural farming changed the human relationship to "the great round of life"? Was it this change that initiated the shift from animism to anthropomorphic gods?

P S: Yes, it is. The great round of life is a familiar metaphor for both agriculture and preagriculture peoples. As agriculture develops, however, the experience of this great round changes. Where annual events were experienced with relative leisure in hunter-gatherer groups, the farmer now experiences these events directly in the daily labor of preparing the soil, planting seeds, weeding, and harvesting. This agricultural process becomes a new model for life, more and more tied to human work schedules and obligations. And, as farmers take more personal responsibility for their food production and general well-being, it becomes less appropriate to ascribe the principal sacred power to animals, as hunter-gatherer groups usually do.

The worldview of the early farmers centers on the mystery of the earth's fecundity. The seed is analogous to semen, the earth to the womb, sowing and cultivation to impregnation, and the rain and sun to paternity. It's not surprising that some anthropologists regard farming culture as marking the birth of self-consciousness. It's during this period of agricultural development that we also find archaeological evidence of a shift from the animal as epiphany to that of the human figure. This transition suggests that sacred power was being exercised by a being who had human objectives in mind, at least to the extent that a sacred animal did not. And, because of the association of the female with the reproductive earth, the first sculpted human figures were probably female.

Joseph Campbell sees sacrifice as the central rite of agriculture's idea that the grain crop is the soul's metaphor. Sacrifice—the offering of fruit or grain, or the ritual slaughter of an animal or person—is a means of participating in the great round. But in agricultural farming, participation becomes manipulation. The game changes from chance to strategy, from reading one's state of grace in terms of the hunt to bartering for it, from finding to making, from a sacrament received to a negotiator with anthropocentric deities. Whether the goddess is called Inanna, Ishtar, Athena, Artemis, or any other name doesn't matter. She is represented as priestess in the temples, the temple itself being an image of the womb of the mother.

The metaphor of the Great Goddess enables emotions and bonds of kinship, compassion, and responsibility to be felt not only within the human group but to be directed to the earth itself, helping the group to survive the experience of the ecological double-bind: the fertile earth that sometimes fails to produce.

J W: You emphasize the development of agricultural farming, but wasn't there a parallel development of seminomadic people who took to the desert to herd sheep and goats?

P S: Yes. These two developments—agricultural farming and agricultural herding—are very different from each other. The agricultural farming consciousness is epitomized by the Mother Goddess and the principles of the feminine as associated with the earth. Agricultural herding consciousness, on the other hand, is not as concerned with the mysteries of the earth but more with the ability to control resources, including animals and their grazing lands. Instead of the emphasis on the goddess, the agricultural herders emphasized the male god. So not only do you have the separation of agricultural herders, you also have the growing conflict between the male god and the female god, and the gradual defeat of the feminine. In pastoral thinking, the figure of the goddess becomes the sacred prostitute, and the snake, which is sacred to the goddess, becomes an emblem of evil. Our present-day patriarchal societies are far more closely associated with these ancient agricultural herders than with early agricultural farmers.

Most hunter-gatherer groups do not show such a high degree of genderized opposition, conflict, and competition in the sense that we have come to know it. It's true that there are hunter-gatherer groups today in which there is considerable authority of males over females, but that doesn't hold true everywhere, particularly in North America. As long as people represent sacred power in a diversity of animals, it doesn't lead to conflict between the genders. But once they begin to anthropomorphize their deities, that sexual dominance is echoed all through society, in art, in economics, politics, family dynamics, and so on.

J W: You seem to be suggesting that the relationship between men and women partly determines how people use the environment.

P S: Judging from our primate background, males and females have always done different things as participants in society as a whole. It would not surprise me to learn that they therefore see the world differently.

Anatomical studies show differences in the male and female brain. Our bodies are different. I see no reason to suppose that our psychologies or even styles of intelligence might not also be different. What an anthropologist calls sexual politics in hunter-gatherer groups always has a certain humor to it because it's not very important. Since one sex does not dominate the other in these societies, decisions tend to be made in councils where opinions are heard regardless of which sex is voicing them. The Mistassini Cree of Quebec are among the many good examples of this kind of society.

In every society there's a "division of labor," although I don't think the phrase is a very apt one. It's just a division of what people do. In most hunter-gatherer societies, there are lots of other divisions made within the society such as age groups, memberships, and clans. People are also divided by their own choices and by their skills and experiences.

Once you escalate this polarization of gender roles into a power base, you begin conflict on a new scale and it really goes bad and mean because the males tend to dominate. It's not simply a matter of the assumption of power but of the location of the ultimate source of creative power. In the feminine model, it tended to be more earth-centered and in the masculine model, it tended to be more sky-centered and otherworldly. The predominant myth of a deity who is both male in his thinking and distant from the earth aggravates our sense of loss. This is not just because plants and animals are no longer sacred but because sacredness is concentrated in a single being who is removed from everything else. This process puts tremendous burden on what you might call our Pleistocene selves.

What we're doing now is trying to recover from this mastery of the patriarchal over the feminine. But it's a mistake to argue that we should try to recover the neolithic goddess culture. I don't think we're looking for that kind of identity or representation of our connectedness. I think the plant and animal world is a much better icon for the mysteries that hold the world together.

JW: The emergence of a new myth of a male and distant god also marks the beginning of the myth of history, doesn't it? In your essay, "A Post-Modern Primitivism," you describe history as the new anti-mythological myth. What do you mean by that?

PS: As a point of departure, I'm using the definition of myth from Herbert Schneidau's book, *Sacred Discontent*. Contrary to the common interpretation of anthropologists, Schneidau says that myth is identical to the kind of religion I spoke of as earth-centered. It's one that sees natural things as embodiments or incarnations of sacredness and that sees the feminine as the epitome of the basic events and structures of the earth. For Schneidau, myth is not just an explanatory story of a special kind, or even a consciousness that is associated with the religion of the earth, but also a different way of sensing time and space. Dorothy Lee described the Trobriand Islanders as living in a "nonlinear codification of reality," a space that is not defined by lines, where change is not a becoming but a new "areness." Walter Ong calls it "an event world, signified by sound, a world composed of interiors rather than surfaces, where events are embedded instead of reading like the lines of a book." Schneidau would say this mythological consciousness provides a different context for viewing the world, a view that contrasts with our familiar historical view. He describes a historical view as a conceptual view, one that I propose had its origins in the early agricultural herding consciousness. I would agree with Levi-Strauss, who was thinking along these lines long before me, that history is actually just another story. In an anthropological sense, history is just a different set of myths.

One version of the historical myth describes a world created by an outsider who reached in and made it, first with the word and then with the hand. By its own definition, this story is a declaration of independence from the deep past and its peoples, living and dead. According to the "maker" or "potter" myth, the world was created out of nonliving, nonsentient substance instead of its own inner creation or self-organizing process. The real lesson here is that history is no guide, because it admits of no roots beyond agriculture.

J W: When you say history's past is radically different from the one shaping human evolution, are you proposing that human evolution is shaped by myth?

P S: Evolution is a myth, too! It's important to understand that I'm not using the word *myth* to mean illusion or misunderstanding or falsity. *Myth* is a coherent narrative intended to explain something or to describe events that took place at an important time. And, as Joseph Campbell so ably said, myth is also a narrative of events that takes place inside each of us. This narrative has stages that are represented as figures in an inner story, just as though it had taken place outside. In this way, myth has a double function: first, it describes events that have to do with our own psyches, our own fears—what psychologists call our psychic structures; secondly, it describes the world at large and how it came into being, where the power is and what the power is doing.

J W: Are you saying historical thinking might be keeping us from having a different experience of time itself?

P S: My own path has led me to understand that history, which is an idea of the nature of time, is not a given. It's a creation, a body of ideas. History isn't something that simply tells us a record of events, it's a way of understanding time itself. Historical time is irreversible, an unreturning arrow. But most people, for most of human existence, have not believed this. They believed that time moved in curved pathways and arcs and circles, and if it didn't literally reverse itself, the patterns that structure the world were not considered to have an absolute beginning and ending.

I think one of the most pervasive misconceptions today is the insistence that you can't go back. I'm faced with people every day who say, "Well, that's all very nice. The Pleistocene may have been great, but it's all a lost paradise and you can't go back."

There are at least three mosaic structures that come into play when we think about this question of going back. One is our genetic makeup, a mosaic of information and component parts. Another is our ecosystem, a natural system composed of various plants and animals. A third mosaic is culture, which is made up of things we believe, things we do, images we have, and stories we tell. In every one of these mosaic structures you can take out parts. To reconnect to a hunter-gatherer culture, you don't have to become a Pleistocene hunter-gatherer in the literal sense. You can take out parts and inject them into your own culture. There are a lot of people who object to that notion, but we do it all the time! Look at the way we incorporate the Japanese tea ceremony or Zen practice, or the way in which styles in pottery or technology move between cultures. Nature does it in ecosystems, too. A starling from Europe fits easily into American ecosystems. The genetic reassembly of an individual from separate parts of two parents is another good example. Mutations are the substitution of a new part for an old. My point is that you can do this culturally, too. If you can identify the desirable characteristics of what it meant to be a Pleistocene person, the probability is that most of them could be adapted to the modern world. Once you did that, it would begin to reshape the way you see the world from the inside out. Instead of arguing that we have to toss out Christianity or machines or technology, we could begin in small ways to reinstitute elements of our Pleistocene heritage that fit more closely to the beings we truly are.

J W: If our current myth is history, and the tools we use to look at the world are essentially historical, how is it possible to conceive of anything outside that context? Isn't it a bit like Heisenberg's Uncertainty Principle, that the act of observing changes what is observed?

P S: My friend, the theologian John Cobb, says that "one of the characteristics of historical culture is a quality of self-scrutiny, self-doubt, dissection, and analysis. We are forever asking who we are, what we're doing, and what our purposes are. We inherited this behavior from the Hebrews." I think he's right. This business of self-scrutiny and the capacity to criticize one's own culture is developed in the Western mind to a more intense degree than in any other time or culture. If you had to name one characteristic of Western culture, it might be that. So, John says, "But look, Paul, in your criticism of modern society, you're exercising precisely the same characteristics of the historical culture which you speak out against. And you do all this in order to tell me that you want to be a Pleistocene person!" Well, that's hard to answer. But nonetheless, I see no reason why we can't come closer to what we are by conscious intent and by our own self-criticism than otherwise. It seems fair enough. I'm willing to accept that my generation may not recover that confident atonement with nature without analyzing it. I don't think I can do that. But if I choose to incorporate appropriate ways of living, my descendents might recover some of that feeling.

J W: You say that depth psychology has led us to understand that going back is going into ourselves, into what, from the civilized historic view, is the "heart of darkness." It sounds like a scary proposition.

P S: I think psychoanalysis is trying to approach that which is hidden from consciousness and at the heart of the human soul. The reason it's scary is that the historical consciousness places so much value on its own form of cognition. The fear of instinct or of behaviors that don't seem prompted by logic is deeply embedded in our modern society. The reason I use the phrase *heart of darkness* is precisely for that reason. Conrad's novel by that name is not only a geographic adventure but an adventure into our deepest past, which is still inside all of us. It was dark because of Conrad's fear of what is native to us. I don't think this journey is intrinsically scary, but we're so accustomed to being in control of our consciousness and our intellect that the idea of allowing another process to take place is unthinkable.

Freud imagined that a destructive and aggressive beast lived in the unconscious. Our conventional image of the journey inward is an encounter with an ugly, frightening being. The animal image in our unconscious is something we wish to destroy or transcend, and that is partly why there is such an emphasis on emerging toward the light rather than going into the dark.

J W: What would entice us to undertake such a journey?

P S: Two things would entice us. One is, I don't think we are happy in our present situation. Our unconscious informs us of that all the time. The other thing is simply an intellectual conviction that there are matters of great value in our heritage that we are suppressing. Our spontaneity and sense of connectedness to nonhuman life—which itself is positive and not fearful—should make us feel at home or in place on earth. The problem may be more difficult to understand than to solve. I'm convinced that a journey beneath the veneer of civilization would not reveal the barbarian but the human in us who knows the rightness of birth in gentle surroundings, the necessity of a rich nonhuman environment, and the expressive art of receiving food as a spiritual gift rather than as a product. That human knows how to play at being an animal, the importance of clan membership, and the profound claims and liberation of daily ritual. There is a secret person undamaged in each of us, aware of the validity of these experiences, and sensitive to their right moments in our lives.

Inochi, Life Integrity

JUDGING FROM the books and essays of Peter Matthiessen, it would seem that there is no place on Earth on which he has not at least set foot. In 1956, at age twenty-nine, he loaded his Ford with books, a sleeping bag, and a shotgun and set off to visit every wildlife refuge in the United States. The resulting book, *Wildlife in America,* was published in 1959, the same year he left for the South American wilderness to write *The Cloud Forest* (1961), and later, *At Play in the Fields of the Lord* (1965). *Under the Mountain Wall,* a chronicle of two seasons in New Guinea, was published two years later, followed closely by expeditions to the Bering Sea (*Oomingmak,* 1967), under the oceans off South Africa, Madagascar, and Australia in search of the Great White Shark (*Blue Meridian,* 1971) and on a turtle boat in the Caribbean Sea (*Far Tortuga,* 1975). He has returned to Africa more than a few times, mostly on overland safaris in search of wild places and wild people (*The Tree Where Man Was Born,* 1972, and *Sand Rivers,* 1981), but also aloft in a single-engine Cessna to survey forest elephants in the Congo Basin (*African Silences,* 1991). *The Snow Leopard,* for which he won the National Book Award in 1979, chronicles a trek across the Himalayas, combined with an inner journey guided by his study of Zen Buddhism. This is a man who claims he isn't brave: "I can nerve myself up to quite a lot," he says, "but I'm always delighted when it's over."

Peter has written over fifteen other books, including his most recent, *Killing Mister Watson* (1992). His controversial *In the Spirit of Crazy Horse* (1983) reconstructs the events surrounding a 1975 shootout on the Pine Ridge Reservation in South Dakota. Two FBI agents and a young Indian were killed in the battle, and American Indian Movement leader Leonard Peltier was later convicted for the agents' deaths. Upon publication of the book in 1983, two lawsuits totaling forty-nine million dollars were filed against Peter and Viking Press, initiating one of the longest and most bitterly fought libel suits in U.S. history. The last of these suits was dismissed in 1991. Unavailable since its original publication, *In the Spirit of Crazy Horse* was re-released in 1991.

Peter Matthiessen was born in New York City in 1927. He spent most of his childhood in rural New York State and Connecticut, where he developed an interest in and respect for the natural world. "It began as a passion for snakes," he says, "and then rapidly spread to marine life, mammals, and birds." After service in the Navy, Peter attended Yale University, spending his junior year at the Sorbonne in Paris. He returned to Paris in 1951 and cofounded the *Paris Review,* of which he is still an editor. In 1953 Peter settled on Long Island with his first wife, earning his living by commercial fishing and running a charter boat. "I don't think I could have done my writing without the fishing," Peter says, "because I needed something physical, something nonintellectual." He has made his living solely as a writer since 1959.

Peter still lives on the east end of Long Island. When at home, he writes seven days a week in a converted children's playhouse crowded with artifacts from his journeys, sketches of birds, rocks, books, and a United Farm Workers' flag. Across the property sits a zendo that he and some friends built from a former stable. Given Dharma transmission as a *sensei* (teacher) in 1989, Peter dons Buddhist robes and leads a meditation service in the zendo every morning at seven. Not far from the zendo are the former horse pastures where you'll often find him playing touch football on autumn Sundays.

⌐·⌐·⌐

JONATHAN WHITE: It seems that you get far more involved in your books, particularly those concerned with environmental or social causes, than your role as a writer might normally entail. Since the publication of *In the Spirit of Crazy Horse* in 1983, for example, you've dedicated tremendous time and energy to the Leonard Peltier case, even while you were fighting your own legal battles over the book. Will you tell the story of how you got interested in that case?

PETER MATTHIESSEN: In a sense, the case found me. I first heard about Leonard Peltier when I was working on a book called *Indian Country*. In 1979, while investigating the construction of a fuel terminal on Indian land in California, I took part in a sweat lodge ceremony led by Archie Fire Lame Deer, a Lakota medicine man. While we walked in the hills above Point Conception, Archie spoke about Leonard Peltier, describing him as a "true leader" whom the FBI was out to get. He told me Leonard had been transferred from the federal penitentiary in Marion, Illinois, where they feared he would be assassinated, to the Lompoc Correction Institute in California. Just a few weeks later, while I was in the Black Hills in North Dakota, Peltier escaped from Lompoc. One of the young Indians who had been indicted with Peltier, and with whom I had become friends, offered to take me down to the site of the shoot-out at Oglala, on the Pine Ridge Reservation, and show me just what had taken place. The more I learned of the case, the more convinced I was that Peltier had been framed. They really had nothing on him. At first, I thought it would be a long magazine piece, but the story and its implications grew more complex and shocking the farther I got into it.

JW: Why have you stayed involved in the case for all these years?

PM: Cesar Chavez, about whom I wrote in 1970 (*Sal Si Puedes*), taught me an important lesson. He said, "You can't encourage people to strike or protest and then go away if their protests aren't successful. Once they've stuck their necks out, their livelihoods are on the line, and you ought to see them through." I feel that way about Peltier. I'm not going to write the book and walk away. I talk to him once or twice a week. I'm part of his team, and I'll be involved until he's a free man. It's true, I could have written three novels in the time I've worked on

In the Spirit of Crazy Horse, the case, the lawsuits, the depositions, and so forth. But it's worth it. I've learned a lot, and I've met some wonderful people to whom I feel very close.

J W: I once heard you explain how important it is to have specific goals in taking on projects like *In the Spirit of Crazy Horse,* but that you would have burned out long ago if you imagined you were going to effect permanent change. Will you talk more about that?

P M: It's in our nature to serve, and I think we need to find a way to do that even if there's a feeling of ultimate futility about it. Anything we do on behalf of others is worth it, for our own fulfillment as well as the small changes our efforts can create. But if you're bent on solving large problems or changing human nature, I think you're doomed to worse than just burnout or disappointment. My goal in writing *In the Spirit of Crazy Horse,* for example, was to get justice for Leonard Peltier. The broader issue of the book, for which Peltier's case is emblematic, is three centuries of injustice to Indian people. If I believed I was going to undo all that injustice, I would not only burn out, I'd be a very dangerous person. That kind of idealism doesn't take into account the realities of human nature. How often does the news on television or in the newspapers change? It's essentially the same story repeated over and over again. The Bosnians and the Serbs have been fighting for hundreds of years, and human nature hasn't changed in forty thousand years. On the other hand, we can't disregard human misery, and we must help where we can. Our greatest enemy, it seems to me, is fundamentalism, a rigid mentality on the rise everywhere in the world. In this country, we have Pat Robertson, Pat Buchanan, Jesse Helms, and so forth, who are not necessarily fundamentalists, but their thinking or nonthinking is the same. Wherever you find it, whether in America or Iran or Bosnia, this mentality is very dangerous.

J W: Does your approach to writing change when you're not trying to advance a cause?

PM: From an artistic point of view, it's a mistake to impose so-called meaning on your work. It either has it or it doesn't. A good book originates spontaneously, in much the same way that a hen lays an egg. In a hen, the egg starts in the ovaries in a long series of eggs and makes its way down the fallopian tube. It starts very small, and when it reaches a certain size and weight, it's ready to be laid. That's the way a book happens, at least in my case. Something attaches itself to your imagination, and that's the seed, and it starts to grow. It grows and grows until you can't contain it anymore; you simply have to write it out of your system. Some people would argue, "That's easy for him to say, he's published." Okay, but if I had never published a single word, I'd still be a writer, whether other people thought so or not. You can't be dominated by how your work is received, because in writing for someone else, you're not being true to yourself or your reader.

JW: I can see how *The Snow Leopard* or *Killing Mister Watson* would represent this kind of organic process, but doesn't the process change when one of your goals is to advance a cause, as in *Men's Lives* or *In the Spirit of Crazy Horse?*

PM: It's uncommon for a book to be artistically sound and also have an agenda. Occasionally it happens, as in Rachel Carson's *Silent Spring,* but it's rare. There's a choice you have to make. *Men's Lives,* for example, is flawed from a literary point of view because of the statistics, legal information, and other data I had to include. That stuff spoils the harmonious flow of the book. The same is true of *In the Spirit of Crazy Horse.* But, again, that was a choice I made when I took on those projects.

JW: You've traveled and written about people and cultures from all over the world. I'm sure there are times when your reception has not been entirely hospitable, particularly as a white North American writer. Do you ever feel that your presence is an imposition?

PM: As a writer, you often feel like a terrible intruder because you're there to take something from the culture and sell it when you get home. That makes me very uncomfortable, so I try to give something back. As Albert Camus said when he won the Nobel Prize, the concerns of writers in the twentieth century must go beyond their art. Part of one's duty is to speak for those who cannot speak for themselves.

As a white person, whether you're a writer or not, it's often difficult to go into an Indian reservation, or any situation in which Indians are involved, because generally you're not liked very much. Most traditional people, as well as those involved in the American Indian Movement, are pretty cool toward outsiders. These people, who are generally courteous and gentle, will not immediately acknowledge you. You have to establish your good will. For instance, if you enter a house, even in the company of an Indian who is liked, he or she may be offered coffee but not you. I've had that happen, and it's disconcerting. People don't talk to you, they hardly look at you, and you have to go along with that. Maybe someone cracks a joke and you laugh, and if the laugh is genuine, well, perhaps the next remark will at least include you. The next thing you know there's coffee at your place, and then some soup or something else may come your way.

We're very nervous in our society about being liked, and we're uneasy if we're not immediately on a first-name basis with the people around us. Indians don't feel that way. Generally, they feel no urgency to like you or be liked by you. If the chemistry is right, the friendship develops naturally. It's not imposed from outside.

JW: A recurring theme among writers, particularly nature writers, is the value of living in one place for a long time. Gretel Ehrlich says, "When you walk out the door, you already know *so* much because of what the place has taught you. And the scene gets deeper each day. When you have that experience of intimacy with one place, you can apply it in any direction." Gary Snyder is outspoken about the value of staying in one place. Your approach is different in that you travel and write about places all over the world. In doing so, do you miss getting to know one place intimately?

P M: I don't see any conflict between what I'm doing and what Gretel and Gary and others say about staying in one place. I know exactly what they're talking about, and I agree. First of all, I've lived here in Suffolk County, New York, since I was two weeks old, and in this house for well over thirty years. I know every shrub, bird, and reptile here. I certainly could know it better, but I know it well. It's a funny county because it extends offshore through the islands, along the coast of Connecticut, almost as far as Rhode Island. In my mind the heart of the county is really out in the salt water, where I have fished all my life. *Men's Lives* is partly about my feeling for this place, and it's in that book that I say, "This is where I come from." No matter where I travel, I'm not at home anywhere else in the same sense that I'm at home on the coast of Suffolk County.

If you have the instinct to know your location well and be a part of it, you'll use that instinct wherever you go. If you notice the plants, animals, and other features of the landscape on your own land, you'll notice those things anywhere. It's part of what you do in order to feel at home wherever you go.

The great Zen Buddhist teacher Eihei Dogen said, "Why leave behind the seat that exists in your own home and go off aimlessly to the dusty realms of other lands? Do not be afraid of the true dragon." The dragon is the buddha nature, the essence of existence, which is everywhere. You don't have to go anywhere to find it, it's right here, right now. Once you have that sense of life, it doesn't matter where you are. You're always home.

J W: We're attracted to certain landscapes for different reasons—textures, smells, wetness or dryness, the kind of wildlife that lives there, and so forth. Beyond our own preferences, is there some less tangible quality in a landscape that either invites us in or holds us out?

P M: Indian people say there are certain landscapes that you should not enter. It's as if the land itself is telling you to stay out. I've found this to be true in my own experience. If you force your way into these places, it can be dangerous. You can feel it. It's like pushing back a very powerful spring. I've been in Indian power places where this is true to an extraordinary degree, and very scary. In other landscapes you feel immediately at home, whether it's just for a day, or for an hour, or even less. If someone asked you about the difference, you might not be able to define it, but something feels natural about being there, you are at home.

When you're camping or trekking, certain places feel right for resting or spending the night, and other places don't. It's not simply a matter of finding a level spot out of the wind or close to a stream. There are other intuitions that make a place feel right. What is it that our instincts pick up? It might not be the same for every person, but I'll bet it's the same for nine out of ten who are accustomed to being in the wilderness. This sense is developed to an extraordinary degree among some native people.

Survival in the city, on the other hand, depends on tuning in to a different set of clues. A city dweller uses his or her instincts to screen what would otherwise be an overload of loud, random signals. In consequence, receptivity to the more subtle messages of the natural world is dulled. Perhaps that's why some people complain that there's nothing going on outside the city. Well, it's like studying a tide pool. You have to stay and watch for a while before you see how alive this habitat is.

J W: Will you describe some of the experiences you've had in which, as you say, "It's as if the land itself is telling you to stay out"?

P M: Probably the most gripping one was a summer night in the Siskiyou Mountains in Northern California. I was with a man who was interested in the Sasquatch, and we were traveling in a region where lots of sightings had been reported. On one particularly clear, warm evening we were descending from a high, steep ridge down a logging road into Bluff Creek, which is where the first persuasive footage of a Sasquatch had been taken. With an hour or two of sunlight left, we wanted to get some water from the creek before heading back up onto the ridge to set up camp. As our VW bug wound its way down the mountain I began to get this weird feeling, as if we were compressing a huge spring, and at any moment the accumulated power would hurl us out of the canyon. I didn't say anything to my friend, because it seemed crazy to have such a feeling on a beautiful, still evening. But a few seconds later this growl came out of him, and when I turned, he was white as a sheet. "I don't know what's wrong, but we're getting out of here!" he said. He had felt it too, and he was terrified. By the time we got to the top of the ridge, the whole mountain was ringing and strange and weird. We built fire after fire, didn't sleep all night. Something was happening, something was imminent, but to this day I don't know what it was.

I had another experience like this in the Siskiyou, although it was years later and in a completely different circumstance. I was with a couple of Indian friends who wanted to show me this power place known as Doctor Rock. Again, it was a beautiful, clear, summer day. We hiked up through Blue Creek, where we could see Doctor Rock most of the way, but for some reason, we couldn't get there. There was always a cliff or a deep ravine in the way. We ended up on a high ridge, absolutely exhausted and a little scared, yet not even a half-mile from the place. It was as if we were being driven off by unknown powers.

j w: We've been talking about landscapes, but doesn't this experience apply to encounters with animals in the wild also? Although they can drive us off or invite us closer in less subtle ways than a landscape, there are still extraordinary moments when we find ourselves closer to an animal than we—or the animal—are used to.

p m: I had a wonderful experience in Africa with a female rhino and her calf. We came around a high bush, trekking cross-country, and there they were, right in front of us, scarcely twelve feet away. Behind us, the porters dropped their loads and ran, and I don't blame them. There was no way that animal wasn't going to charge. I stood there for a moment, terrified, my temples burning like there was lightning inside. But then, inexplicably, I calmed right down. I had a feeling of complete peace with that animal and I knew she wasn't going to charge or hurt me in any way. I was treed by a rhino once, so I knew how very different this encounter was.

I had another unusual encounter once when I was burying my wife's urn in a stony field. It was snowing, and when I paused—it was hard work—a chickadee came and perched on the handle of my pick. It stayed close by while I continued to dig, this gentle little bird. I felt like Saint Francis.

J W: You said earlier that native people seem to have an unusual ability to pick up messages from the land. Do you think this is something we can learn from them?

P M: Most traditional people don't feel the separation or estrangement from nature that we feel in Western culture. Their respect for the earth comes from a genuine feeling of being part of it. The land is who they *are,* that's the way they express it, and every part of it is precious. If a traditional Indian picks up a stone, for example, he doesn't toss it away mindlessly when he is finished, but returns it to the niche in the earth where he found it. It's not a sentimental or self-conscious thing but a gesture of respect, very like a Zen way of relating to land and life. My first Zen teacher, Soen-roshi, always made a little bow of gratitude to the world around him, and I learned that from him. It's a wonderful habit. Even if I'm leaving some neutral or lifeless place, like a motel room, it feels right to thank the room for its hospitality. In Zen practice, one bows to the buddha principle, the imminence of awakening, within oneself. I love that idea. A bow is a wonderful way to appreciate this moment, pay respectful attention to the world around you.

Dogen Zengi chastises a young monk for drawing too much water from the stream, then tossing what isn't to be used onto the bank. Because stream water, like everything else, has *inochi,* or "life integrity," it should be treated respectfully. Unused water should be returned to the stream with gratitude and with as little waste as possible.

In most indigenous cultures I know about, old people and children have an honored place, just like stream water or a stone. They have life integrity, *inochi.* The Dani of New Guinea, whom I lived with for a few months in 1961, show tremendous patience with their elders, and, like the North American Indians, they include their children in everything they do. No matter what's going on, the kids are right in the middle of it, running around, spilling food, making lots of noise. It's a nuisance at times, but in the end the children are less frustrated and a lot better behaved.

Many forms of behavior and ritual in indigenous cultures show the sense of connection the people feel with the world around them. We can learn something from this, but as Westerners I'm not sure we can fully experience it. The sense of being part of the land, instead of an observer or an "environmentalist," is probably what some of us are seeking, but I wonder if we will ever find it. The Indian's love of the earth has nothing to do with environmentalism. We can't consciously adopt Indian attitudes toward nature because traditional people don't *have* any attitudes toward nature. They *are* nature. Wilderness is a false concept to them. They have no word for it.

j w: It's awkward to talk about a "relationship with nature," because the statement itself implies that nature is something different or separate from us. James Hillman says that having an attitude at all, whether it be as caretaker or conqueror, keeps us separate and forever doing something *to* or *for* or *with* nature. The roots of sustainable culture, as Dolores LaChapelle suggests, are in experiences where we are neither opposing nature nor trying to be in communion with it, but rather finding ourselves within it.

p m: Yes, I think that's true. In Buddhism we teach that all self, all separation from the One, is illusion. There's a wonderful metaphor of a bottle of seawater floating in an ocean, and our ego is the glass bottle that separates our little bit of water from the whole. We're not different from the seawater in which we're floating, yet we assign our little bottle-selves a name, a social security number, a ZIP code. Every such idea or concept only fortifies the illusion of a separate existence.

This illusion of separation is not just between us and the rest of nature but also between us and the past and future. Our advanced science and technology leads us to believe that our brain has evolved beyond that of our ancestors. It isn't so. Scientists have known for a long time that the human brain has not advanced appreciably since the appearance of modern man, roughly forty thousand years ago. In New Guinea, the Dani people we lived with represented a "Stone Age" culture. All their tools—axes, adzes, spears, arrowheads, cooking ware, and so forth—were made of stone or wood. They had no metal. By modern Western standards, they were a "primitive" people, yet they showed many of the qualities we associate with "advanced" intelligence and culture. Among other things, they're an immensely humorous and subtle people. To judge from appearances, some of those children would be caught up in a few weeks if they were transplanted to a school in the States. They'd come out of the Stone Age and into modern times without serious problems.

J W: What about the prevalence of war and customs like chopping off little girls' fingers during mourning, or sending out raiding parties to kill anyone they encountered—men, women, or children?

P M: The Dani went to war about once a week, but their wars—or half-day battles, really—are nothing like ours. Unlike more advanced peoples, they're very easily satisfied when it comes to killing. If one warrior is killed, or often if someone is just badly wounded, the war is over. In fact, these events don't seem to be about killing at all but more like a ritualized contest in which the men can show off their bird of paradise plumes and the women can vent insults from the sideline. Really, the atmosphere is a lot like a football game. And one had the feeling that these so-called wars would be quite rare if the men didn't need an excuse to "guard the woman" and thereby get out of weeding or doing chores. The men built watchtowers and sentry posts where they sat around smoking tobacco, fixing their bird of paradise plumes, and watching the women work. Once in a while the women would protest, and in response the men would go over to the frontier and propose a war. The reply might be, "We can't come out to war today. We've got to harvest our sweet potatoes." "Oh, come on," the others would insist, "we'll give you the best part of the field, we'll only bring a hundred guys, you can have two hundred." It was all negotiated in advance, all but the death.

Raids on the enemy were infrequent, but if one group lost three or four people over a series of wars and the other side lost none, the first group might send out a raiding party to even things up. They also practiced mutilation, as you point out, but you'll find these so-called primitive customs practiced among people all over the world. Look at some of our own practices, such as circumcision.

J w: Our tendency to romanticize indigenous cultures doesn't seem to leave them much room to be real people.

P M: Romanticizing is patronizing, and a form of racism. We don't allow them to be simple human beings, to be great when they're great, and to be sons-of-bitches when they're sons-of-bitches. I think Western culture is so starved for spiritual identity that we exploit and ruin everything authentic that we find. We romanticize nature in the same way, and this intensifies the very sense of separation we're trying to dissolve.

Being an Indian is no guarantee of being a spiritual person. For example, although traditional people are usually very respectful toward the game they hunt, there are always exceptions. An Indian friend once told me a story of being out with another Indian who shot a deer, but the bullet only grazed its scalp. The deer fell, stunned, then staggered to its feet again. My friend said, "Well, finish it off." "You think I'm going to carry this son-of-a-bitch out of here?" the guy answered. He grabbed the deer by the antlers and marched it back to the car, and shot it there.

The only traditional people I've been with who seem to show disrespect for game are the Pygmies in the Ituri forests of Zaire. They're a raucous lot to begin with, naturally very funny and spontaneous, and wonderful woodsmen. But when they catch something, they throw it down and slit its throat without any respect whatsoever. They're very brutal, and it startled me to see that. The Pygmies in the mountains of

Zaire, which is farther south, seemed quite different. They were tracking gorillas when I was with them, and compared to the Ituri Pygmies,
these mountain hunters were remarkably gentle and quiet. Perhaps if
they were hunting and not tracking, or hunting something not dangerous to themselves, as these other Pygmies were, they would use
more brutal methods. I don't know. The perception of brutality or
disrespect could also be part of my own ignorance. Maybe for them it
was a celebration of some ritual. Who am I to say? But the Ituri hunters appeared more disrespectful toward game than most white men.
And that's saying something, because white people are generally disrespectful.

J W: You've witnessed a lot of killing out in the wild, and you write
about it beautifully in your books. In *The Tree Where Man Was Born*,
I was transfixed by the story of wild dogs hunting zebra in the Seren-
geti. What have those experiences taught you about predator-prey
relationships among other animals?

P M: I've always found it wonderful the way animals interact in situations in which one is being taken by another. And from what I've
seen, scientific theories of shock or whatever cannot entirely explain
their behavior. The story of the wild dogs and the zebra is a good example. In one case, it was a mare protecting her foal. She ran the dogs
off a few times, but they just circled back. They seemed to know she
wasn't serious. If she was, she could run them down and bite and kick
and stamp them to death in minutes. As a member of the horse tribe,
the zebra is very well armed. If you've ever watched horses fight or
tried to handle a mare that's just foaled, you know what I mean. We
had a mare give birth here once, and I'll tell you, that was a beast I
wouldn't want to go up against. I tried to get into the stall to see if
everything was okay, but she wasn't quite sure of my intentions and
wham! she came for me with her lips and ears back. I still remember
those teeth! So a mare is quite capable of doing damage, but in this instance with the wild dogs, she put up very little fight. Even the foal put
up only a token protest and then quit. He just stood there while one

dog hung by his muzzle to hold his head down and the other dogs eviscerated him. Perhaps in shock, he bowed his neck in a kind of offering. For the next few minutes, all you could hear was the wet sound of the dogs eating. It was a very unpleasant business, except that the foal seemed to be completely resigned to it. Meanwhile the mare, who was just twenty yards away, had already returned to grazing. Eighteen hours later, after the dogs had gone and the hyenas, vultures, jackals, eagles, ants, and beetles were all finished, nothing was left but a dark stain on the grass.

Anyway, my impression was that the mare's ears were not flattened back the way they are when animals are angry or frightened. When you see horses, dogs, or other animals fight amongst themselves, their ears are always back. But in this predator-prey situation, the ears were up and forward, even on the mare as she chased the dogs, or the foal as he was torn apart. It was as if they were performing a grim kind of dance. I've watched lions make a kill, and it's the same thing. They don't appear angry, their ears are shot forward all through the process. But when they fight another lion, their ears are flat to the head. I have to be careful here, because I don't like quasispiritual speculation in which everything turns to mush, but there seems to be a ritual acceptance of killing and being killed, of eating and being eaten. It's odd, but often the most interesting situations are also the most difficult to talk about. We have no vocabulary that suits the purpose.

j w: Have these experiences changed the way you look at your own death?

p m: Yes. They've given me more acceptance of the changes and passages we're all a part of. I can't say I enjoyed watching wild dog kills, but I was exhilarated by them. I wouldn't have missed them for anything. Isn't that strange? It's like Dostoyevsky's *The Idiot,* my favorite novel. It's truly a heartbreaking book, yet in the end one is not in the least depressed. In fact, because it attains a truth that's hard to grasp, it's very exciting. I hope the moment of my death will be an encounter with this kind of truth.

It's curious you should be asking about all this, because just last week I gave a Dharma talk about meditation and death here at our zendo. We all acknowledge the fact of death, but there is tremendous denial in our culture when it comes to confronting our own. There's a peculiar resistance, as if somehow each one of us was the exception. How terrified we are of death and dying! At one point, I could see my students' eyes glazing over, as if they were saying, "Of course, I know I'm going to die! But why are you making us look at it? Why be so morbid about it?" So I had them all turn and put their hands on the face of the person next to them. With the fingertips on the cheekbones and the thumb at the mouth corners, I had them pinch lightly, exposing the teeth and drawing the skin taut on the cheek bones. This exercise brings out the skull, the skeleton. There was a deadly pause, then startled moans. The skull isn't something that appears after death. It's right here now, and our death is, too. It's very important to perceive your death as part of your life, right now, not as something separate, in the future.

J W: Perhaps being sentimental about death is another form of separation.

P M: If taken too far, yes. If I find a bird dying on the beach, I'll twist its neck to put it out of its misery. I've been accused of being callous for that, but I think it's callous to let it suffer. Our values are so strange! In my hunting days, I knew a man who had a beautiful bird dog that fell into a spear pit. She was impaled in six or seven places. This guy refused to let the poor dog die. He took her to the veterinarian for operation after operation, at great cost. After eight or nine months, the dog was still alive, though she could scarcely walk. Think of the needless pain the poor creature suffered for this man's notions of "kindness" and "generosity."

J W: The Buddhist teacher Stephen Levine says that pity is a fearful, self-centered state with "a quality of considerable need about it." In *Healing into Life and Death,* he tells the story of a woman dying of cancer and how she noticed that there were two kinds of people who came to visit her in the hospital. The first kind could hardly sit down next to her, and when they did, they couldn't sit still. They would thumb through magazines or open a window if it was closed, or close it if it was open. The other kind of person could just come in and sit down quietly next to her. They had room for her pain because they had room for their own.

Our advanced technology, which is a remarkable achievement in its own right, seduces us into believing that we are in complete control, that we can make or break or fix anything. Nature has a way of reminding us that we are not in control, that we are not really on top, that we're going to feel pain, kill, and be killed, just like everything else. The psychologist James Hillman says that nature wants us to remember our death.

PM: We're taught that death is utter annihilation, utter loss: loss of the self, loss of the past, loss of the future. In a culture that lends itself to that kind of denial, who wouldn't be afraid? And who wouldn't want to avoid experiences that remind them of the unfathomable reality of their own death?

Anything unknown can be scary, but that doesn't mean we should dread it or keep it at a distance. Zen teachers treat death as a part of life; often they're still sitting up when they depart. I like that. Death shouldn't be a dark cloud that follows us around, shrouding our behavior and our attitudes toward life. I believe it's possible to be free of that. My ambition is to die the way ripe fruit lets go of a tree. Life is great, but that doesn't mean I want to go on with it forever. Of course, it's easy to talk now; I'm not on my death bed. When the time comes, I may be whining with the best of them.

On the Trail

A DESCENDANT OF Chief Seattle, Janet McCloud was born into the Bird Clan of the Tulalip Indian tribe in 1934. Shipped off to boarding school early, and failing every one of the six grades she attended, Janet entered her mid teens prepared to clean houses for a living. The struggle to protect native fishing rights in the Northwest that began in the late 1950s brought her in contact with traditional people. "I was shocked to learn we had a religion," she says. "We were ashamed to be Indians. To me, religious freedom meant you were free to be Catholic, Protestant, or Shaker."

Realizing the fishing rights issue was only part of a larger struggle for Indian rights throughout North America, Janet founded the Survival of the American Indian Association in 1964. In 1965 she began volunteering at McNeil Island State Prison, developing a cultural rehabilitation program for Indians that later served as a model for prisons throughout Washington state. In 1966, during a fishing protest on the Nisqually River, Janet was arrested for interfering with a police officer in the line of duty. She pleaded not guilty to the charges and, along with her sister-in-law Edith and activist Dick Gregory, stayed in prison on a hunger strike. In a *Turtle Island* interview, Janet says, "I didn't mind going to jail so much until Edith said, 'And we're not eating either.' I said, '*What??*' That was my first fast. We went six days without eating. And they'd bring lima beans with ham, fried potatoes, and everything I loved."

Janet McCloud's activism has never stalled. She was one of a forty-member team to develop an Indian legal redress system in the seventies, a member of the Native American Rights Fund, and the founder of the Northwest Indian Women's Circle, a grass-roots organization committed to assist Indian women in developing leadership skills based on traditional values. In 1985 she organized the Indigenous Women's Network, a coalition of women from the Americas and around the Pacific who are working to make a better future for their families and communities.

A mother of eight children and a grandmother of sixteen, Janet now lives in Yelm, Washington. When not traveling and giving talks on topics such as Native American education, comparative religions, environmental or women's issues, she is directing programs at Sapa Dawn Center, which she founded at her ten-acre home in 1989. At the Center, she teaches self-sufficiency through the practice of daily life-skills such as gardening, preserving food, beadwork, writing, and native rituals. The Center hosts a sweat lodge every Sunday, and once or twice a year dancers travel from all over the world to join in a ceremonial sun dance on the lower fields.

᙭·᙭·᙭

JONATHAN WHITE: Until a few years ago, you refused to give interviews because you were tired of "Indian wannabes." What do you mean by that?

JANET MCCLOUD: I'm talking about white people who want to be like Indians. They copy our ceremonies, our dress, and our way of life. They chant and dance and take a sweat lodge, and then expect to gain instant spirituality. Some of the things they do in a sweat lodge are so disrespectful that I don't want to mention them here. Charging money for any of these ceremonies is a desecration of the gifts of the Great Spirit.

We seldom take non-Indians into our ceremonies, and when we do it's only those we know or those who have worked with us before. The white people we work with are not pushy or disrespectful, and they

don't consider themselves part of some esoteric inner circle just because we've taken them in. They don't change their name to White
Eagle or Running Deer, or something equally ridiculous, and run
around announcing that they're an apprentice of so and so.

A few years ago, we heard a rumor that a Sioux sun dance was
going to be held in Germany. We couldn't believe it. Philip Deer from
Oklahoma and I went over to see what was going on. It was quite a
spectacle—teepees and tables filled with Indian paraphernalia for
sale. They were even charging admission for the sweat lodges. White
people often say that imitation is a form of flattery, but to us it isn't.
This kind of imitation is only a reminder of how much has been taken
from us. The last thing we have—and the last thing we have any hope
of keeping—is the rituals that connect us to the Creator. These are the
ways we find our sanity, our sobriety, and our spirituality. It's humili-
ating to watch these traditions desecrated by non-Indians. What's
worse, the perpetrators defend themselves by claiming they're the
heirs of our tradition, that we're of the "old age" that is dying off to
make room for a "new age."

J w: Why have you changed your mind about giving interviews?

J M: A few years ago, the Elders' Circle met in Haida Gwaii, or what
you call the Queen Charlotte Islands, which sit on the outer coast of
British Columbia. I wasn't at that meeting, but afterward the chiefs
and clan mothers told us we should open up our communications with
non-Indians. We were advised to speak about our spiritual traditions
and prophecies to the best of our ability. So I've been trying to speak
up ever since.

J w: You've been a member of the Elders' Circle since the mid sixties.
Will you talk more about how it got started and how it evolved?

J M: It wasn't called the Elders' Circle until the seventies, but I suppose the movement started in 1948 when the Hopi elders and medicine people met to compare the knowledge of their different kivas.

Until then, this knowledge was kept secret. They invited Pueblo people to join them, and later other tribes. Part of the purpose of the meeting was to tell the prophecy, which was first told by Massau'u the Creator. We don't have time to go into the Hopi prophecy here—and I am not a Hopi messenger. The prophecy takes days to tell, and many lifetimes to understand, but essentially it explains how we are living on the third planet in our third phase of life. It tells how we are the caretakers of life, how our choices affect the balance of nature to such an extent that our actions alone may bring prosperity or disaster to future generations. The previous worlds were destroyed by greed, pollution, and lack of understanding of nature. We will go into the next phase of life only if we can restore the spiritual balance that was part of our original life plan, as given to us by the Creator. The prophecy is a message for everyone, not just the Hopi or other Indians. *Hopi* means "peaceful people." Anyone who lives in peace with themselves, others, and nature is a Hopi.

In 1955 the Hopi circle of elders, which had expanded to include many of the Southwest tribes, traveled to the East Coast. They were following their instructions, which told them of a "house of mica"— which they interpreted as the United Nations—where world leaders would gather. But the United Nations wouldn't allow them to speak, so they traveled farther north to Onandaga, the capital of the Iroquois Nation. As it turns out, the Iroquois were remembering their own original instructions from the Creator to make a journey throughout Turtle Island, which is what you call North America. They wanted to find out who was still speaking native languages, singing ceremonial songs, and practicing traditional teachings. So the Hopi and the Iroquois joined up, along with the Seminoles from Florida, and in the early 1960s they began a journey called the Spiritual Unity Caravan.

J W: How did you get involved?

J M: In the early 1960s I was active in the struggle for indigenous fishing rights here in Washington state. The issue was getting a lot of media attention, and I think that's why the Spiritual Unity Caravan sent some people up this way. When they arrived, they were surprised to find so many of us. "We thought all the Indians were dead up here," they said. Well, I took to these people from the caravan like a duck to water. After a few days of meetings I decided to join them, and they became my teachers throughout the sixties and seventies.

Over the years, thousands of people tapped into the Spiritual Unity Caravan. Some people traveled with us in old beat-up cars just one or two reservations down the road, and others stayed on for longer. Some never traveled with us at all but welcomed us with food and lodging and heard our messages. In 1975 in Old Oraibi, Arizona, we ran out of everything—money, food, transportation, everything. In six years, the caravan had logged over 156,000 miles. One of the leaders, Mad Bear, explained how we had come full circle, accomplishing what we had set out to do. It was time for each of us to return to our own homes, he said, and continue the work there.

A few years later, a bunch of us met at the headwaters of the Missouri River in Montana. We decided it would be a good thing to bring the elders together at least once a year to discuss Indian prophecies and instructions. That was when we gave it the name Elders' Circle. A core of about thirty of us, all from different tribes, have been meeting ever since.

J W: How has the support you found in the Elders' Circle influenced your own work?

J M: The Elders' Circle gave me a chance to open up and connect with others who understood my problems. Although I was immediately attracted to the circle, I was very quiet and unsure at first. Like everyone else who is educated in Western society, I was taught that Indians are dirty, lazy, no-good savages. It's a paralyzing image, one that took a long time and a lot of work to shake. With the elders' guidance, I eventually learned to trust myself. And as I did that, I grew more hungry for the spiritual support and teachings of the Elders' Circle. In fact, I hated to come home after those gatherings. I felt so high when I was there, and so alone when I came home. I wanted the feeling to last.

When I pestered my teachers about this, they said, "You have to learn to bring those feelings into your own home, Janet." I didn't understand that at all. Not at first. But then, in small ways, I began to see how I could do this. We've had a sweat lodge on our property for twenty-five years, for instance, but we always had to wait for someone else to come and run it. A friend finally said, "Hey, you've got to learn to do this— for yourself and others." So I learned how to run a sweat lodge, and now I can pass that knowledge on right here in my backyard.

j w: Learning how to bring those feelings and skills into our own homes seems like our only hope of finding a reliable sense of peace. If we refuse to bring it home, isn't that the same as refusing to be a part of it?

j m: Exactly. Bringing these feelings home is a form of atonement, or at-one-ment, with our own nature, inside and outside. Because Western civilization is unwilling to give up its position of separation, it will always educate its children to believe that their spiritual and physical connection is provided by something outside of themselves. That's why people in this society are never truly satisfied. They think they're going to find what they need in a new relationship, a new car, or a new job. They think they're going to find a connectedness to nature by spending a weekend in the mountains. It's always something else, somewhere else. That's the motivation behind a wannabe. And whether it's wanting to be an Indian or a rich white person or a Trappist monk, it's all the same. The greed and impatience of Western society is a symptom of a deep spiritual poverty.

I don't mean to say that we can't find wisdom and guidance in other places or traditions. I've learned a lot from the Europeans I've met. But that shouldn't stand in the way of doing your own work. On one of my visits to Germany, I met some people who wanted me to perform a ceremony on their land. "Why are you looking at me?" I asked. "Look at this beautiful, spiritual land. It's just waiting for you to recognize it." There's no mystery to finding our atonement with nature; it's something we can all realize anytime, anywhere.

J W: Perhaps it's something we all know, but on some level isn't it convenient to think of ourselves as separate? How else could we manage our conscience while continuing to exploit the rest of nature?

J M: I think you're right. The purpose of education in this society is to perpetuate the military-industrial complex. If it pays off to teach children that they're separate from nature—and it does—then that's what they'll be taught. As a result, nature gets pushed farther and farther away, until it's a pretty painting, a playground, or a church you go to on Sundays. You can shut the door or turn the lights off whenever you want, and that's exactly why we don't see how our very life-style threatens to destroy it.

I meet young people from all over the earth who say, "I've got to get back to nature." To me, that sounds like insanity. *Everyone* is part of nature. Just look at the miracle of your own body. It's your first teacher. Look at your hands, your heart, your digestive system. They all work according to the laws of creation. In white society, you often say "know yourself." Well, part of coming home is doing just that, literally. It's not another mind trip; it's not traveling to India or Japan or the Himalayas in search of the most spiritual mountain to climb. It's knowing there's a mountain inside you, too.

J W: Is there a way to maintain this connection, even in a busy urban environment?

J M: Of course. Your heart is always beating and your breath is always moving in and out, isn't it? The laws of nature are with you wherever you are. It's marvelous when you see this—when you see that we live in symbiotic relationship to everything around us. Your body *is* nature. You have a river, a sun, and a moon inside, too. Everything that's out there is also in here.

Our body is connected to the mineral world through the skeleton. I always tell children that the bones and rocks we use in the sweat lodge are their grandmothers and grandfathers. "When you leave your body behind," I tell them, "your skeleton will become the min-

erals of the earth, and in the distant future, you may become the rocks
and bones of your children's sweat lodge." We're connected to the trees
and plants through our nervous system, and to the four-legged animal
world through eating and reproducing.

J w: Are there other experiences in the natural world that confirm
this connectedness?

J m: Yes, many. It would be more difficult to find experiences that
don't confirm this connectedness. I feel it when I pray, use the sweat
lodge, or participate in other ceremonies. I feel it when I'm trying to
protect the water quality of the river, when I'm fighting for fishing
rights, or attending community education meetings. And I feel it
when I look at my children and grandchildren.

Sometimes when I'm praying, an eagle will come and circle over
me. I can't say it's giving me a message, but its presence reminds me of
the connection we're talking about. These things happen all the time.
In 1968, while a group of us were protesting in Olympia, Washington,
we suddenly heard the strangest sound. We all stopped and someone
said, "Listen to the elk!" We could hear them and see an image of
them, right there on the capitol grounds! I'm the worst skeptic I know,
but I'm learning to talk about these experiences because they're not
just figments of our imagination. They're a lot more real than what
passes for reality in the movies or on television. People watch commercials or look at magazine pictures and they think that's reality.
They never look at the reality that's here, which is far more mysterious
and extraordinary.

Once in a while I have a dream vision. The first few times it happened, I was terrified. I didn't know what was going on. My elders said
there was no reason to be afraid, that these visions are a sign that I had
been selected to do a job. I should watch carefully, they said, because
within a few days I would be shown what to do. They were right, it
always happened that way. Now I love to get those visions. They fill me
with energy. I can't eat or sleep. For days I feel like a field of flowers.

I've tried to create that feeling on my own, by taking mushrooms or fasting or through other ritual, but it never works. I can burn tobacco and holler all night, but they don't seem to take any notice whatsoever. They come when I'm doing something else, like a gift from beyond us, though I wouldn't want to say from whom or what. But these experiences of connecting with that something beyond myself gives me hope. It makes life all the more beautiful.

J W: Earlier you mentioned the use of ceremony. There are many of them, I'm sure, but I'm struck by the story of honoring the first salmon. Would you be willing to describe that ceremony?

J M: If I'm going to tell that story, I need to give you a little background. One of the natural laws among our people is the need to find a true relationship with all other beings. Even though our legends are different and often contradictory in their details, they're all designed to help us learn how to live. In one creation story, all life was the same. There wasn't even a difference between day and night. The whole world was dark. Then Creator came along—Coyote or Raven, depending on where you are—and made changes. He kept talking about daylight, even though no one knew what it was. Finally he went to the spirit world and, through a lot of trickery, stole the sun and brought it back in a box. Everyone crowded around to see. "What's light, what's light?" they kept asking. "Be careful," warned Raven, "you have to get used to it a little at a time." But they kept pushing to get closer until the box fell out of Raven's hands. The sun flew out and so terrified the people that they ran in all directions. About a third of them jumped into the water and became the salmon and whales. Another third ran into the forest and became the birds and animals. The last third became the two-legged beings.

That's a very short version, but it explains why we say the salmon are like our brothers. They always remember their home and they always come back to us. Our people have a name and a welcoming song for each one as it swims into the river. The first one caught is brought into the longhouse as an honored guest. We sing a prayer song for it, which is a way to welcome this highest guest. The salmon is then cooked by the women and handed out in small pieces to all the people, along with a little drink of water. The skeleton is put back in the river, facing the direction it came from, and let go. Someone speaks to it: "Be sure to tell your tribe how well we treated you, how respectful we were, so that they will come and visit us again and again."

We had the same kind of relationship with salmon that the Plains Indians had with buffalo. We had strict codes of how to catch, cut, and prepare the salmon. In the midst of plenty, we never wasted. Even the bones were boiled and eaten or used for necklaces. Because we virtually lived by eating salmon, they used to say we were Salmon People walking on land.

The Indians who live over the mountains just east of us felt the same way about the roots they dug. Each spring they had a root ceremony where the elder women who had passed menopause would fast and sweat and pray for four days. Afterward, they would sing a special song as they gathered the first roots. These ceremonies are all a way of giving thanks and welcoming, and acknowledging that we eat living food.

J W: Perhaps one of the lessons we can learn from native people is how to use ritual in our daily lives. But what makes a ritual authentic?

J M: An authentic ritual is one that helps you develop your own humanity. It allows you to look at things differently. Anytime you see a ritual or a ceremony advertised, you can be sure it's not authentic. Spirituality isn't for sale. You can't buy it in a drugstore or find it in a book. It's just not there.

Not long ago, I was on a panel with a group of scientists at King Alfred University in England. I felt kind of crazy because I didn't understand a word they were saying. What the hell was I doing there? The place was packed with people, and I was supposed to lead a three-hour meditation about how to get back to nature. I asked one of the clan mothers, Dewasenta, what I should do. "I don't know, Janet," she said, "you're going to have to figure this one out for yourself." Well, it finally came to me, and when my turn came I made everyone go outside and form a circle. I told them to walk around the inside of the circle, one at a time, and introduce themselves. "Shake hands, say a little something, and then move on," I said. The circle was so big—about the size of a soccer field—that it took three hours for everyone to get around. Afterward, Sir Alfred Tennyson told me that it was the most amazing experience he had ever had at a conference. "I'm always talking to people from behind a podium," he said. "It's only the assertive ones that I meet face to face. It's not very satisfying to travel from conference to conference without a feeling of personal contact with the audience." I know that's true, because I've experienced it myself. But when you have these circles, everyone talks and everyone gets their time. Everyone is equal in the circle. There's no mystery to it, but people are touched because it's simple and authentic.

J W: Dolores LaChapelle says that ritual is always wrong when it promotes separation or is designed to get power over others. Has that been true in your experience?

J M: Yes. People who manipulate others for power, either in ritual or otherwise, are energy vampires. I meet a lot of them when I travel. They might have plenty of intellectual skill, which is a kind of power in itself, but spiritually they're very weak. These people want more than power over others, they want spiritual energy. And the law of spirit is the same as the law of water: it finds the lowest level. That's why any kind of ceremony led by a power seeker is going to leave you deflated.

Years ago I was invited to Millennium One Thousand at the Houston Astrodome in Texas. Maharishi Ji was there too, along with thousands of his followers. They were all young white kids, "preemies," they called them—short for "premature," I guess. These are the same kids that run around looking for gurus on Indian reservations. Anyway, they asked if I thought Maharishi Ji was God. "No, I don't," I answered. "Why not?" they asked. "There's only one answer I have for you," I said. "If this man is God, he doesn't need me to believe in him. If he isn't God, then he's looking for more power and energy than I can or want to give him."

J W: Earlier in our conversation, you referred to the stories that tell of a time when all life was the same. It was Raven, or Coyote, that created the different creatures. According to the Hopi prophecy, didn't the Creator also give each life form a distinctive way to worship, to speak, and to gather food? If that's true, how are humans unique?

J M: Yes, the Creator gave us all an individualized life plan. The difference between humans, or two-legged beings, and four-legged beings is that we have the power to consider who we are and why we're here. Animals don't do that. Most animals, and particularly predators, are more worried about where their next meal is going to come from. They can't store food in large quantities the way we do, so they have to be more opportunistic in their hunting and gathering. In a sense, their greediness is necessary for their survival. Humans are supposed to be different; we're supposed to share. That's one of the natural laws of being. Our spirituality is in our potential to give; that's why Indians have so many giveaways. That's what Mother Earth does, she gives.

Some of the other natural laws tell us to respect differences, be honest, know your weaknesses, and maintain a clean and healthy land. We need to learn these laws as children of the earth. We need to value our lives, to see them as gifts from the Creator—gifts that cannot last forever. The seasons of our life begin in the spring, when we are born, and progress through the summer, autumn, and winter, when the snow gets on our hair. We can't stop that motion, and we can't go back. We can only learn to value this cycle, which is the most important lesson of our humanity. Some people think they can move directly from the animal to the spiritual. I don't think that's possible. You aren't going to find spirituality until you find humanity.

J W: Will you talk more about the Indian giveaway, or *potlatch,* and the role it plays in your community?

J M: Giveaways are an important part of our economic system. Instead of gathering wealth for yourself and storing it in a bank somewhere, the Indian system encourages the gathering of wealth only in order to give it away. The one who gives everything away is the richest person in the community. I think this system originated when food was so plentiful—whether it was buffalo or seal or clams or salmon—that you could gather all you needed for the year in a matter of three or four months. The rest of the year was spent making baskets, carving canoes, or telling stories in the longhouse at night. There was no scarcity of resources and no need to worry whether you would receive what you needed. The giveaway was an event that drew people together, a way to create good energy and to affirm bonds of family, friendship, and community.

I organized my first giveaway about eighteen years ago, in celebration of receiving my name, Yet Si Blue, which means "a mother to all." I went up to Tulalip to ask my sponsor how many blankets I would have to give away. I was worried about it, because we were having a hard time financially, and some of these events can cost a lot of money. My sponsor laughed, "Janet, you're known all over the world. There's no way you're going to get away with a cheap little giveaway." Well, that bothered me, because at the time I was very materialistic. Why buy all these things I wanted for myself, only to give them away?

I started to gather things slowly, begrudgingly. At about the same time, my daughter announced her plans to get married. Her husband-to-be was an Iroquois, and we had to bring one of his leaders out and conduct a ceremony in the longhouse tradition. Afterward, the family of the groom arranged a large giveaway in our backyard. So we had two giveaways, back to back, first theirs and then mine.

I gave away a lot of different things—blankets, clothing, jewelry, appliances, and so forth. When it was over, I had almost nothing left, but I felt a freedom I had never felt before. In fact, I felt so good that I wanted to do it again, right away. I had to learn to slow down with that, too.

J W: Some accounts of the giveaway indicate that it was also used as a spectacle for displaying and confirming social status, particularly among the northern tribes of the Northwest Coast. Long speeches were given by the potlatch giver, explaining in detail what was owned—berry patches, salmon streams, stories, songs, and so forth. Possessions, and sometimes slaves, were publicly destroyed. In some cases, the gifts to the audience were considered payment for acknowledging the claims of ownership and social standing made by the gift-giver.

J M: Anything can be taken too far. That's what I was just saying about myself. I'm sure those things happened. In fact, I've read and heard about them myself, but that hasn't been my personal experience with the giveaway.

I'm not trying to convince anyone that Indians are all romantic, nature-loving people. We have a dark side, too. We've done a lot of things in the past that we're not proud of. But I think all of us are coming from a past that needs some improvement. Bringing our lives back into balance is going to take a lot of work, by a lot of people. Native Americans don't have the answer, but we can offer one piece of the puzzle.

J W: I imagine the tendency to romanticize native people is as difficult to deal with as any other kind of racism.

J M: We're not angels, we're human beings. Someone complained to me recently about getting ripped off by one of these so-called traditional Indians. "I don't know what you're crying to me about," I said, "we're all vulnerable to deception, no matter what form it comes in." When you put Indians on a pedestal, you're bound to be disappointed—and so are we.

I do feel badly when I have to walk behind someone who has left a mess on the trail. Do you know what I mean? When I hear about Indians ripping people off, for instance, I feel ashamed because it reflects on us all. When I ask them about this, they usually answer, "That's my private life, and it's none of your business." Well, that's true, but when you're a public figure, as some of these people are, you live in a goldfish bowl. Everything you say and do is seen. I found that out early in my own life, and wherever I go I'm conscious of it. I don't want to leave a dirty trail behind me.

J W: It seems that one of the challenges we're all facing today, on many levels, is walking on a messy trail. How do we make progress on the trail—perhaps even clean it up a little as we go—and yet avoid getting stuck in the messes?

J M: By not living in denial. Everyone says, "It isn't *my* fault what my grandparents did to the Indians." Or in Germany they say, "It isn't *my* fault what my grandparents did to the Jews and Poles."

When I was at a conference in Germany in the early eighties, we had a free day, and the young Germans we were with asked my daughter and me what we wanted to do. When I told them we wanted to go to Dachau, they couldn't believe it. "No, no, you don't want to go there. Why would you want to go there?" they asked. "Because we want to see," I said. Well, even before we got there, I felt this terrible sadness for the place. Once inside, the sadness turned to horror. I could almost smell the ovens and hear the people screaming in agony. The whole feeling went inside us. There were a lot of angry, earth-bound spirits around that place, so when we left we offered tobacco and took a long time to zigzag out. Spirits can only travel in straight lines, and we didn't want any of them to follow us home. I'm sure the other tourists thought we were crazy.

The problem with Dachau and other places like it is that they're closed off from the rest of life. We're doing the same thing to those places that we're doing to the rest of nature. We set them aside like we set wilderness aside. They're not part of us, and therefore they can't receive our prayers. That's the difference between a place like Dachau and Hiroshima or Nagasaki. The Japanese still live in those cities, and they pray for the spirits of the people who suffered there. They tell me the people of Israel are praying for the spirits of Dachau, but I'm not sure what good it does way over there.

The point I'm trying to make is that we inherit the past. Whether we like it or not, we walk the same trail. Just as the Christian doctrine teaches, "The sins of the father are visited on the sons." As Native Americans, we understand that, too. We try to make decisions by considering the effect they will have seven generations into the future. We can't go into the past and undo it, but we do have the freedom to make new choices.

Further Reading

I asked each of the people interviewed to recommend several books for further reading on the subject of their chapter. There are so many good books about nature and creativity that listing just a few is not easy. For additional suggestions and a list of books written by the authors themselves, please refer to the individual chapters.

TALKING ON THE WATER, *Jonathan White*

Watson, Lyall. *Gifts of Unknown Things*. Rochester, Vermont: Inner Traditions, 1991.

Rogers, Pattiann. *The Tattooed Lady in the Garden*. Connecticut: Wesleyan University Press, 1986.

Bleibtreu, John. *The Parable of the Beast*. New York: Macmillan, 1968.

Gladwin, Thomas. *East Is a Big Bird*. Massachusetts: Harvard University Press, 1970.

Martin, Calvin. *Keepers of the Game*. Berkeley: University of California Press, 1978.

A CALL FROM ONE KINGDOM TO ANOTHER, *Gretel Ehrlich*

Minor, Earl, trans. *Japanese Poetic Diaries*. Berkeley: University of California Press, 1969.

Calvino, Italo, trans. *Invisible Cities*. New York: Harcourt Brace Jovanovich, 1978.

Emerson, Ralph Waldo. *The Selected Writings of Ralph Waldo Emerson*. New York: Random House, 1940.

Hunt, Tim, ed. (Volumes I, II, and III). *The Collected Poetry of Robinson Jeffers*. Stanford: Stanford University Press, 1988.

Stevens, Wallace. *The Collected Poems of Wallace Stevens*. New York: Random House, 1923.

VOICES FROM THE SEA, *Roger Payne*

Darling, James, with photographs by Flip Nicklin. *With the Whales.* Wisconsin: NorthWord Press, 1990.

Leatherwood, Stephen and Randall Reeves, with paintings by Larry Foster. *The Sierra Club Handbook of Whales and Dolphins.* San Francisco: Sierra Club Books, 1983.

Corrigan, Patricia. *Where The Whales Are.* Connecticut: The Globe Pequot Press, 1991.

Slijper, Everhard. *Whales and Dolphins.* Ann Arbor: University of Michigan Press, 1976.

Gaskin, David. *The Ecology of Whales and Dolphins.* London: Heinemann Press, 1982.

THE ARCHDRUID HIMSELF, *David Brower*

McPhee, John. *Encounters with the Archdruid.* New York: Farrar, Straus and Giroux, 1971.

Leopold, Aldo. *A Sand County Almanac.* New York: Oxford University Press, 1949.

Carson, Rachel. *Silent Spring.* New York: Houghton Mifflin, 1987.

Mander, Jerry. *In the Absence of the Sacred.* San Francisco: Sierra Club Books, 1991.

LIVING BY GAIA, *Lynn Margulis*

Barlow, Connie, ed. *From Gaia to Selfish Genes: Selected Writings in the Life Sciences.* Cambridge: MIT Press, 1992.

Lovelock, James. *Healing Gaia: Practical Medicine for the Planet.* New York: Harmony Books, 1991.

Lovelock, James. *The Ages of Gaia: A Biography of Our Living Earth.* New York: W. W. Norton and Company, 1988.

Sagan, Dorion. *Biospheres: Reproducing Planet Earth.* New York: Bantam Books, 1992.

Gest, Howard. *The World of Microbes.* Madison: Science Tech Publishers, Inc., 1987.

Sonea, Sorin and M. A. Panisset. *A New Bacteriology.* Boston: Jones and Bartlett, 1983.

LIFE-WAYS OF THE HUNTER, *Richard Nelson*

Devall, Bill and George Sessions. *Deep Ecology: Living as if Nature Mattered.* Salt Lake City: Peregrine Smith, 1985.

Berry, Wendell. *The Unsettling of America.* San Francisco: Sierra Club Books, 1977.

Luckert, Karl. *The Navajo Hunter Tradition.* Tucson: University of Arizona Press, 1975.

Snyder, Gary. *The Practice of the Wild.* San Francisco: North Point Press, 1990.

Tedlock, Dennis and Barbara Tedlock. *Teaching from the American Earth.* New York: Liveright, 1975.

COMING BACK FROM THE SILENCE, *Ursula Le Guin*

Allen, Paula. *The Sacred Hoop.* New York: Beacon Press, 1992.

Ramsey, Jarold. *Coyote Was Going There.* Seattle: University of Washington Press, 1977.

Hymes, Dell. *In Vain I Tried to Tell You.* Philadelphia: University of Pennsylvania Press, 1981.

Tedlock, Dennis. *The Spoken Word and the Work of Interpretation.* Philadelphia: University of Pennsylvania Press, 1983.

Neihardt, John. *Black Elk Speaks.* Lincoln: University of Nebraska Press, 1961.

ANIMAL PRESENCE, *James Hillman*

Moore, Thomas. *Care of the Soul.* New York: HarperCollins, 1992.

Bly, Robert, ed. *News of the Universe.* San Francisco: Sierra Club Books, 1980.

Campbell, Joseph. *The Way of the Animal Powers.* San Francisco: HarperCollins, 1988.

Meade, Michael. *Men and the Water of Life.* San Francisco: Harper, 1993.

HANGING OUT WITH RAVEN, *Gary Snyder*

Jochelson, Waldemar, collector, and Bergsland and Dirk, ed. *Aleut Tales and Narratives.* Fairbanks: University of Alaska Languages Center, 1990.

Price, Grenfell, ed. *The Explorations of Captain James Cook 1768–1779.* New York: Dover, 1971.

Dauenhauer, Nora and Richard Dauenhauer. *Haa Shuka, Our Ancestors.* Seattle: University of Washington, 1987.

Andruss, Van and Judith Plant, ed. *Home! A Bioregional Reader.* Santa Cruz: New Society, 1990.

Stegner, Wallace. *The American West as Living Space.* Ann Arbor: University of Michigan Press, 1987.

MOUNTAINS CONSTANTLY WALKING, *Dolores LaChapelle*

Bateson, Gregory. *Mind and Nature.* New York: Bantam, 1988.

Rothenberg, Jerome and Diane Rothenberg. *Symposium of the Whole.* Berkeley: University of California Press, 1983.

Wu, Kuang-ming. *Chuang Tzu: World Philosopher at Play.* Atlanta: Scholars Press, 1989.

Rappaport, Roy. *Ecology, Meaning and Religion.* Berkeley: North Atlantic Books, 1988.

Oelschlaeger, Max. *The Wilderness Condition.* San Francisco: Sierra Club Books, 1992.

IN TOUCH WITH THE WIND, *Matthew Fox*

Swimme, Brian and Thomas Berry. *The Universe Story.* San Francisco: HarperCollins, 1992.

Soelle, Dorothee. *To Work Is to Love.* Philadelphia: Fortress, 1984.

Schumacher, E. F. *Small Is Beautiful.* London: Abacus, 1973.

Sheldrake, Rupert. *Rebirth of Nature.* New York: Bantam, 1991.

Rank, Otto. *Art and Artists.* New York: Agathon Press, 1975.

Heschel, Abraham Joshua. *I Asked for Wonder.* New York: Crossroad, 1987.

THE UNRETURNING ARROW, *Paul Shepard*

Cobb, Edith. *The Ecology of Imagination in Childhood.* New York: Columbia University Press, 1977.

Eaton, Boyd, Marjorie Shostak, and Melvin Konner. *The Paleolithic Prescription.* New York: Harper, 1988.

Martin, Calvin. *In the Spirit of the Earth.* Baltimore: Johns Hopkins, 1992.

Meeker, Michael. *The Pastoral Son and the Spirit of Patriarchy.* Madison: University of Wisconsin, 1989.

Schneidau, Herbert. *Sacred Discontent.* Baton Rouge: Louisiana State University, 1976.

INOCHI, LIFE INTEGRITY, *Peter Matthiessen*

Suzuki, Shunryu. *Zen Mind, Beginner's Mind.* New York: Weatherhill, 1970.

Arsenev, Vladimir. *Dersu The Trapper.* New York: Dutton, 1941.

Tinbergen, Nikolas. *The Herring Gull's World.* London: Collins, 1953.

Lame Deer, John (Fire), and Richard Erdoes. *Lame Deer: Seeker of Visions.* New York: Simon and Schuster, 1972.

Beston, Henry. *The Outermost House.* New York: Doubleday and Company, 1928.

ON THE TRAIL, *Janet McCloud*

Hammerschlag, Carl. *The Dancing Healers.* New York: HarperCollins, 1988.

Hammerschlag, Carl. *The Theft of the Spirit.* New York: Simon and Schuster, 1993.

Wall, Steve and Harvey Arden. *Wisdomkeepers.* Oregon: Beyond Words, 1990.

Hyde, Lewis. *The Gift.* New York: Random House, 1983.

About the Contributors

GRETEL EHRLICH is not only an accomplished and respected writer of fiction and nonfiction prose, she also has extensive experience in theater, dance, and film. Her essays have appeared in *The New York Times, Harper's,* and *The Atlantic Monthly.* She is the author of *The Solace of Open Spaces, Heart Mountain,* and *Drinking Dry Clouds.* She received a Guggenheim fellowship to write her 1991 book, *Islands, Universe, Home.* Born in 1946, Ehrlich currently lives near her place of birth in Santa Barbara, California.

DR. ROGER PAYNE has been involved in extensive whale studies since 1965. With a long list of awards and honorary memberships, including a MacArthur Fellowship, he is the director and founder of The Whale and Dolphin Conservation Society, based in Massachusetts. A particular interest in underwater acoustics led him and a colleague to the discovery that humpback whales sing, a discovery that has profoundly affected scientific thinking and public awareness of whales ever since. Payne was born in New York City in 1935, and now lives in London, England.

A member of The Sierra Club since 1933, DAVID BROWER served as its first executive director for thirty-five years. He started more than thirty different organizations, among them The Friends of the Earth (with sister organizations in thirty-eight countries), The League of Conservation Voters, and Earth Island Institute. He has been awarded nine honorary degrees and nominated twice for the Nobel Peace Prize. David Brower was born in Berkeley, California in 1912, and now lives in the foothills east of San Francisco.

Dr. Lynn Margulis is a prominent biologist, writer, and co-originator of the Gaia hypothesis (with James Lovelock). She is widely known for her studies of the microcosm, especially the biological Kingdom Protoctista, which includes an estimated 250,000 algae, seaweeds, amoebas, and other little-known life forms. She has written over 140 scientific articles and fifty reviews. Among her eight books are: *Symbiosis in Cell Evolution, Microcosmos,* and *The Garden of Microbial Delights.* Margulis was born in Chicago in 1938. She has raised four children and now teaches at the University of Massachusetts at Amherst.

Dr. Richard Nelson is a writer and cultural anthropologist who has spent the last twenty-seven years studying native Alaskan peoples and their relationship to nature. He is known for his books of ethnography, such as *Hunters of the Northern Ice* and *Make Prayers to the Raven,* as well as his recent book, *The Island Within,* which is a more personal exploration of his relationship with nature and home. *The Island Within* received the John Burroughs Award for Nature Writing in 1991. Born in Madison, Wisconsin in 1941, Nelson now makes his home in southeast Alaska.

With over three million books in print, Ursula Le Guin is one of the most widely read writers in North America. She has published over twelve science fiction novels, three books of poems, six books for children, and four books of short story collections. For these and other works, she has received numerous awards, including the Boston Globe-Horn Book Award for *A Wizard of Earthsea;* the Hugo and Nebula awards for *The Left Hand of Darkness;* the National Book Award for *The Farthest Shore;* and the Kafka Book Award for *Always Coming Home.* Born in 1929 in Berkeley, California, Le Guin now lives in Portland, Oregon.

Dr. James Hillman is perhaps the most widely known Jungian analyst in the world today. His books include *Suicide of the Soul, The Feeling Function, The Dream and the Underworld, A Blue Fire,* and, with Michael Ventura, *We've Had a Hundred Years of Psychotherapy, and the World's Get-*

ting Worse. His major post-Jungian work, *Revisioning Psychology,* was nominated for a Pulitzer Prize in 1975. Born in 1926 in Atlantic City, New Jersey, Hillman now lives and works in rural Connecticut.

Born in San Francisco in 1930 and raised in the Northwest, GARY SNYDER is widely known for his books of poetry and essays that focus on the relationship of humankind to the natural world. His books of poetry include *Riprap and Cold Mountain Poems, Axe Handles, Left Out in the Rain, No Nature,* and *Turtle Island,* for which he won the Pulitzer Prize in 1975. His collections of essays include *The Real Work* and *The Practice of the Wild.* Snyder now lives with his family in the foothills of the Sierra Nevada.

DOLORES LACHAPELLE was born in Kentucky in 1926 and raised in Denver, Colorado. She teaches Tai Chi, writes, climbs, skis, directs the Way of Mountain Learning Center at her home in Silverton, Colorado, and lectures throughout the United States and Canada. Her books include *Earth Festivals, Earth Wisdom,* and *Sacred Land, Sacred Sex: Rapture of the Deep.* LaChapelle's essays appear in *Deep Ecology: Living as if Nature Mattered,* by Bill Devall and George Sessions and *The Wilderness Condition,* by Max Oelschlaeger.

MATTHEW FOX is the founder of the Institute in Culture and Creation Spirituality in Oakland, California, the editor-in-chief of *Creation Spirituality* magazine, and the author of over fourteen books, including *The Coming of the Cosmic Christ, Creation Spirituality: Liberating Gifts for the Peoples of the Earth,* and *Sheer Joy: Conversations with Thomas Aquinas on Creation Spirituality.* In 1990 the readers of *Common Boundary* magazine selected Matthew Fox's *Original Blessing* as "the most influential psychospiritual book of the 1980's." Born in 1940 in Madison, Wisconsin, Fox now lives in Oakland, California.

DR. PAUL SHEPARD's work in environmental perception and human ecology spans more than forty years. He has taught at Smith College and Dartmouth, and fulfilled teaching fellowships in India, Australia, and New Zealand. His books include *Man in the Landscape, The Tender Carnivore and the Sacred Game, Thinking Animals,* and *Nature and Madness.* Born in

1925 in Kansas City, Missouri, Shepard is now Avery Professor of Natural Philosophy and Human Ecology at Pitzer College and the Claremont Graduate School in California.

PETER MATTHIESSEN is one of the most important wilderness writers of the twentieth century. He has published over twenty-five books of fiction and nonfiction, including *At Play in the Fields of the Lord, Wildlife in America, Far Tortuga, The Tree Where Man Was Born,* and *African Silences.* Among his numerous literary honors is the Christopher Book Award for *Sal Si Puedes,* the National Book Award for *The Snow Leopard,* and the John Burroughs Medal and African Wildlife Leadership Foundation Award for *Sand Rivers.* Born in New York City in 1927, Matthiessen now lives on Long Island.

A descendent of Chief Seattle, JANET MCCLOUD was born in 1934 into the Bird Clan of the Tulalip Indian tribe of northern Washington. A feminist, environmental activist, and mother of eight, she travels throughout the world giving talks on Indian rights, education, world peace, and comparative religions. She is a member of the Native American Rights Fund, and the founder of the Northwest Indian Women's Circle. In 1989, she founded the Sapa Dawn Center, an organization dedicated to teaching self-sufficiency skills to Native Americans, at her ten-acre home in Yelm, Washington.

Jonathan White is a writer, sailor, educator, and marine conservationist. He is the author of *Tides: The Science and Spirit of the Ocean* (Trinity University Press), and his essays have appeared in the *Christian Science Monitor, The Sun, Sierra,* the *Whole Earth Review,* the *Surfer's Journal,* and *Fine Homebuilding.* The former president of the Resource Institute, a Seattle-based nonprofit focusing on the culture and traditions of the Northwest, he lives on Orcas Island, Washington, with his wife and son.